UN ADMINISTRATION

OF ECONOMIC AND SOCIAL PROGRAMS

NUMBER THREE

*Columbia University Studies
in International Organization*

EDITORS

Leland M. Goodrich and William T. R. Fox

U N Administration

of Economic

and Social Programs

Edited by GERARD J. MANGONE

CONTRIBUTORS

Leland M. Goodrich

Robert Gregg

Gerard J. Mangone

Theodor Meron

Walter R. Sharp

Columbia University Press

New York and London   1966

COLUMBIA UNIVERSITY STUDIES
IN INTERNATIONAL ORGANIZATION

This series of monographs was initiated to provide for the publication under University auspices of studies in the field of international organization undertaken and carried out, in whole or in part, by members of the Columbia Faculties or with the assistance of funds made available under research programs of the University. Work in this field has been substantially assisted by grants from the Rockefeller and Ford Foundations.

The series is not intended to provide a systematic coverage of the field of international organization nor is it anticipated that volumes will appear with any set regularity. The value of the contribution which the monograph makes to knowledge and understanding of the role of international organization and its functioning in the world in which we live will be the dominant consideration in determining inclusion.

The series is published under the joint editorship of Leland M. Goodrich and William T. R. Fox, with Andrew W. Cordier and Louis Henkin, acting in an advisory capacity.

FOREWORD

This book on *UN Administration of Economic and Social Programs*, planned and edited by Dean Gerard J. Mangone of the Maxwell School of Citizenship and Public Affairs of Syracuse University, provides an enlightening and authoritative, up-to-date account of the innumerable developments and problems in the administration of the United Nations and its related agencies. All of the scholars contributing to the volume are authorities in their respective fields and present the story with discriminating understanding.

Staff members in international organizations function anonymously and, therefore, quietly. As a result, the public understanding of the role of administration in relation to the effectiveness of policy-making organs is almost always minimal. It is, therefore, a service to the cause of placing the elements that influence international affairs in proper proportion to present the administrative arm of international effort with the fullness characterizing this book. The mass media and a large share of research focus primary attention upon activities relating to the political crises before the United Nations. Some 90 percent of the staff of the United Nations and the agencies, as well as 90 percent of the resources, relate to the extensive and constructive economic and social programs which are being quietly pursued the year round among more than 100 nations.

All of the chapters reflect administrative response to changing needs and generally to enlarging programs. They reflect, also, emphasis upon processes of coordination as well as the strong forces that militate against their full and satisfactory effectiveness.

In reviewing the developments at the United Nations Secretariat since 1945, Professor Leland Goodrich stresses the importance of a truly international civil service free from government pressures. He describes as well the forces that have operated to weaken that role. If the Secretary-General is to carry out his numerous and important duties, he must have a supporting staff, each member of which is loyal to him and responsible to his instructions, and his alone. The provisions of Article 100 and 101 of the Charter are very explicit on this issue, both with respect to the single-minded devotion of staff members to the interests of the Organization alone, as well as the restraint to be exercised by Members in avoiding instructions or efforts at influencing members of the staff. This independence, impartiality, and objectivity of staff members, combined with competence, are sources of strength to the Organization and are indispensable to the fulfillment of the Secretary-General's obligations. Staff members having a divided loyalty in the performance of their duties are less than dependable when called upon by the Secretary-General to perform specific tasks. A truly international civil servant owing no loyalty in the performance of duties except to the Organization is one of its major elements of strength and derogation from such standards must be adamantly opposed if the Organization is to play its proper role.

The obligation to provide wide geographical distribution within the staff has sometimes been interpreted to mean that nationals of varying ideologies and systems inescapably reflect those ideologies and systems in the performance of duties, thus giving this provision of the Charter overriding significance in relation to competence and integrity. This is a misreading of the Charter. Each member of the staff should possess the competence corresponding to his duties and that independence, objectivity, and impartiality required by the Charter regardless of his nationality origin.

The last four chapters of the book, focusing respectively on the Advisory Committee on Administrative and Budgetary Questions of the General Assembly, the specialized agencies, the resident representatives in the field of technical assistance, and the Regional Economic Commissions, are major case studies in the processes and problems of coordination. While the Advisory Committee exercises a major influence in the administrative and budgetary coordination of the United Nations itself, it has never been able to exercise an effective influence on the budgetary trends of the specialized agencies. The Administrative Committee on Coordination, consisting of the Directors-General, and chaired by the Secretary-General, has at times played a greater role, particularly in ironing out program overlappings and policy confusion, although it, too, has had little influence on the budgetary levels of the specialized agencies. There are those, indeed the majority, who justify program enlargement with consequent budgetary increases as a logical response to increasing world needs. There are others who regard such expansion as being badly planned and ill conceived. Assuming more rational planning, more effective coordination would produce better results for the money expended. The real difficulty seems to rest on the lack of coordinated policies within the governments of Member countries. Each agency has its own legislative conference which is the final authority in the approval of programs and budgets. Its membership is made up of plenipotentiary representatives from Member countries who come from the particular department or profession represented by the agency, representatives who often do not coordinate the policies with the foreign office or any other overriding authority. Opponents of such coordination argue that the personnel of the average foreign office would often fail to have a proper knowledge or appreciation of needs in the field of education, health, labor, agriculture, and other major interests represented by the specialized agencies.

The effectiveness of the coordinating role of the resident representatives in recipient countries has only been achieved by demonstrating its value both to the recipient country and to the agencies offering aid. The Resident Representative has generally had to earn his right to a respected level of influence in planning and coordinating programs of technical assistance. To the degree that the advice of a Resident Representative is sought by the government in planning technical assistance programs and establishing priorities, his task of coordinating the program of the technical assistance experts provided by the agencies is facilitated. Many steps have been taken over the years by the Expanded Programme of Technical Assistance and the Special Fund to strengthen the hands of the resident representatives, and the union of these two operations into the United Nations Development Programme should further strengthen their role.

The last chapter of the book analyzes the decentralization of economic operations and policies reflected in the increased responsibilities of the regional economic commissions. The pros and cons of the wisdom of such a course continue to be debated, perhaps leading to the proper conclusion that neither extreme centralization nor extreme decentralization would represent the proper course.

ANDREW W. CORDIER

Dean
School of International Affairs
Columbia University

PREFACE

The eyes of the world constantly flicker upon the brazen headlines of world conflict, and too often the United Nations system, designed to maintain international peace and security, is viewed solely through the highly publicized work of the Security Council and the General Assembly. Yet some of the most creative work in fashioning a cooperative community of states, which are endeavoring to raise the economic and social standards of their citizens, lies in the day-to-day administration of the United Nations organization and its family of agencies.

Hardly a subject for front-page news and rarely a topic of popular discussion, the administration of international agencies reflects many of the currents of contemporary world discontent and some of the finest hopes for constructing rational international government that will preserve the diversity and independence of states while ensuring peaceful collaboration to develop the magnificent potential of the people of all nations. Every improvement of the international secretariat by better recruitment, selection, training, and personal incentive enhances the performance of the UN in meeting its complex, world-wide responsibilities. Improvements must also be made in the organization of the General Assembly and the Economic and Social Council to focus upon the myriad needs of the underdeveloped world, and to bring the collective judgment of the UN to bear wisely upon program administration. Finally, the UN, with its far-flung economic and social activities on all continents, must be equipped with an efficient field organization, sound methods of distributing resources and evaluating results, and sure skills in centralizing or decentralizing its administration.

These are some of the subjects discussed in this book. Bolstered by facts and figures, the patient unraveling of administrative problems in the UN with respect to economic and social programs will hopefully provide a few keys to understanding the sprawling, complicated, overlapping, dynamic, never-ending UN system, which goes far beyond the stark statements of peace-keeping activities.

Administration and policy are always intertwined. In the UN system where decisions must be collegial, often based upon diverse and conflicting motivations, administration can often turn the key to the achievement of goals. In law, justice largely depends upon procedure rather than the generalized ambitions of legislation; in an international political organization, like the UN, the most lucid pages of progress toward peace and prosperity may be written by unsung officials making modest interpretations of a great and noble Charter.

The research for this book was originally presented by the authors to the First Maxwell Institute on the United Nations held at Albedor Lodge in the Adirondack Mountains of New York in the summer of 1964. Discussions by scholars from eleven universities and the commentaries of another dozen United Nations officials led to constructive revisions of a complete manuscript in 1965 and final editing. The number of people to whom we are indebted—in the UN at New York and Geneva, in the U.S. State Department Bureau of International Organization Affairs, in the country and regional UN offices in Africa, Asia, Latin America, and Europe, and in the specialized agencies—would run to several pages. In large measure it is their book as well as ours, for they generously shared with us their first-hand experience and wise observations on the problems of United Nations economic and social administration.

We are personally grateful to Andrew Cordier, Dean of the School of International Affairs at Columbia University, who so kindly assisted in the publication of this book; to Bettie Robinson who typed and retyped the entire manuscript, and to Sandra Lewis Linney who served as a devoted research associate.

GERARD J. MANGONE

Syracuse, New York
March 1966

CONTENTS

TABLES

CHARTS

ABBREVIATIONS FOR

UNITED NATIONS ORGANS AND THE

SPECIALIZED AGENCIES

ACABQ   Advisory Committee on Administrative and Budgetary Questions—body of twelve experts elected by the Fifth Committee of the General Assembly to advise the Committee and the Assembly

ACC   Administrative Committee on Coordination—consists of the Secretary-General as chairman and the executive heads of the specialized agencies and the IAEA

BTAO   Bureau of Technical Assistance Operations—office in the Department of Economic and Social Affairs offering substantive support for all technical assistance projects executed by the UN

CCAQ   Consultative Committee on Administrative Questions—an inter-secretariat committee consisting of the heads of the administrative departments of the UN, the specialized agencies, IAEA, and GATT

ECA   Economic Commission for Africa—regional commission of thirty-three African members and ten associate members, including African countries and European countries with interests in Africa

ECAFE   Economic Commission for Asia and the Far East—regional commission of eighteen Asian members and Australia, France, the Netherlands, New Zealand, the USSR, the United Kingdom, and the United States, plus two associate members, Brunei and Hong Kong

ECE   Economic Commission for Europe—regional commission of twenty-nine Western and Eastern European members, plus the United States and a consultant, Switzerland

ECLA   Economic Commission for Latin America—regional commission of twenty-one Latin American members, the United States, Canada, France, the United Kingdom, and the Netherlands, plus an Associate Member, British Guiana

ECOSOC   Economic and Social Council—one of the five major organs of the UN consisting of eighteen member states (until 1965) elected by the General Assembly for three-year staggered terms (membership increased to twenty-seven beginning 1966)

EPTA   Expanded Programme of Technical Assistance—technical assistance program financed from voluntary contributions of member states and executed by the UN and the specialized agencies

FAO   Food and Agriculture Organization—specialized agency of the UN

GATT   General Agreement on Tariffs and Trade—establishes and administers code for orderly conduct of international trade on a multilateral most-favored-nation basis

GA   General Assembly (used only in footnotes)

IAEA   International Atomic Energy Agency—autonomous intergovernmental organization under the aegis of the UN

IBRD   International Bank for Reconstruction and Development (World Bank)

ICAO   International Civil Aviation Organization—specialized agency of the UN

ICSAB   International Civil Service Advisory Board—subsidiary body of eleven expert advisers to the ACC

IDA   International Development Association—an affiliate of IBRD

IFC   International Finance Corporation—an affiliate of IBRD

ILO   International Labour Organisation—specialized agency of the UN

IMCO   Intergovernmental Maritime Consultative Organization—specialized agency of the UN

IMF   International Monetary Fund—specialized agency of the UN

ITU   International Telecommunications Union—specialized agency of the UN

OPEX   Operational, Executive, and Administrative Personnel Programme —a technical assistance program within the regular UN program of technical assistance

TAA   Technical Assistance Administration—the former name of the administrative office for all technical assistance programs executed by the UN (in 1958 name changed to the BTAO)

TAB   Technical Assistance Board—interagency board until 1966 composed of thirty member states (eighteen members of ECOSOC and twelve additional members elected for staggered two-year terms from among members of the UN and/or the specialized agencies) responsible for basic EPTA policy decisions

TAC   Technical Assistance Committee—until 1966 the governing body of EPTA composed of all the member states of ECOSOC and twelve other states elected by ECOSOC

TARS   Technical Assistance Recruitment Services—office that undertakes the recruitment of experts needed to conduct technical assistance projects of the UN

UNCTAD United Nations Conference on Trade and Development—an institution of the General Assembly, for three year review and discussion of trade policies for development with fifty-five member Trade and Development Board to carry on activities between conferences

UNDP United Nations Development Programme—comprising since 1966 the Special Fund and EPTA under a single Governing Council of thirty-seven members elected by ECOSOC

UNESCO United Nations Educational, Scientific, and Cultural Organization—specialized agency of the UN

UNHCR United Nations High Commissioner for Refugees—individual elected for a two-year period by the General Assembly on the nomination of the Secretary-General

UNICEF United Nations Children's Fund—governed by a thirty-nation executive board whose work is reviewed by the General Assembly and ECOSOC, the Executive Director being appointed by the UN Secretary-General

UNTA United Nations Technical Assistance—the United Nations as a participating organization of EPTA

UPU Universal Postal Union—specialized agency of the UN

WFP World Food Programme—special UN assistance program aimed at distributing surplus food to needy nations for technical assistance projects

WHO World Health Organization—specialized agency of the UN

WMO World Meteorological Organization—specialized agency of the UN

BIBLIOGRAPHIC NOTE

ON UNITED NATIONS DOCUMENTS

For those unfamiliar with United Nations documentation, the following information may serve as a guide to the principal document symbols:

A/ refers to documents of the General Assembly. A/C documents are those of six of its Main Committees, e.g., A/C.1/909 is a document of the First Committee, A/C.2/L.790, a document of the Second Committee, the "L" denoting limited circulation. The symbol for documents of the seventh Main Committee of the Assembly, the Special Political Committee, is A/SPC/. A/AC documents are those of *ad hoc* bodies of the Assembly, e.g., A/AC.105/21 is a document of the Assembly's Committee on the Peaceful Uses of Outer Space.

E/ refers to documents of the Economic and Social Council. E/TAC/ indicates documents of the Council's Technical Assistance Committee. E/AC/ and E/C/ documents are those of the other Committees of the Council, e.g., E/AC.6/320 is a document of the Economic Committee, and E/C.2/638, a document of the Council Committee on Non-Governmental Organizations. E/CN/ documents are those of the Commissions of the Council, each of which also has its own number.

U.N.P. designates United Nations publications.

UN ADMINISTRATION

OF ECONOMIC AND SOCIAL PROGRAMS

By Leland M. Goodrich

THE SECRETARIAT OF
THE UNITED NATIONS

The sound administration of United Nations economic and social programs, amounting to over $300 million in 1965, requires a secretariat that is both competent and dedicated to the principles of an independent international service. Of the approximately 23,000 men and women employed throughout the UN system, including the Organization in New York and Geneva as well as the UN specialized agencies, some 20,500 are engaged in the programming, implementation, operation, and administration of economic and social activities. In these activities the role of the UN Secretariat is of central importance.

The Secretariat is one of the six principal organs of the UN. Borrowing from the terminology of national government, it may be characterized as the administrative organ of the UN, and the Secretary-General, at its head, has certain responsibilities that are analogous to those of a chief executive. While the authors of the UN Charter accorded to the Secretariat a more important place in the structure and work of the UN than had been given to the Secretariat of the League of Nations, it received less sustained public attention than did the other principal organs during the first years of the UN's existence. With the expansion of UN political, economic, and social activities and the assumption of the duties of Secretary-General by Dag Hammarskjöld in 1953, the Secretariat played an increasingly important role in the work of the UN.

The important and influential position of the Secretariat in the Organization derives from a number of sources. In the first place, the Secretariat, with the Secretary-General at its head, represents, more than any other organ, the basic commitments, the unity, and the continuity of the Organization. While other organs are only intermittently in session and, except for the International Court of Justice, are composed of representatives of member states, the Secretary-General and his staff are officials with primary loyalty to the UN, always on the job and pledged to devoting all their time and energies to advancing the purposes of the Organization. Second, the increasing demands placed upon the UN in dealing with political, economic, and social problems have been so numerous and complex as to make it necessary for the General Assembly and the Security, Trusteeship, and Economic and Social councils to delegate more responsibility for detailed implementation of their resolutions. This has been especially true both in peace-keeping operations and in programs of economic and social development where the need to cooperate with the UN specialized agencies has arisen. Finally, the Secretariat owes its important role in large measure to the expertness that it represents and the skill that it has demonstrated in the performance of tasks assigned to it. These qualities in no small degree have been due to the fact that in its initial establishment and subsequent operation it has reflected the concept of an international civil service independent of the control of national governments while recruited and administered in accordance with standards of efficiency, competence, and integrity.

The application of this concept to an international organization, composed of sovereign states with divergent interests and ideologies, that has been called upon increasingly to deal with situations in which the decisions taken by the political organs may cover basic disagreements rather than express clear consensus, presents problems of a unique and serious nature.

To a large extent these are problems of adaptation which arise from the necessity that the Secretariat faces, like any living organ, of adjusting to changing and unforeseen circumstances. Such problems include (1) the adaptation of the structure and organization to the changing demands upon it; (2) the harmonization of the increased political role of the Secretariat in a heterogeneous organization with the concept of an independent international service; (3) the combination of standards of "independence, efficiency, and integrity" in the recruitment and employment of the staff with "wide geographical distribution"; (4) the maintenance of the principle of career service, implying promotion on merit and security of tenure, with the introduction of personnel from outside the organization on fixed term appointments; and (5) the adjustment of the principle of international loyalty to the requirements of national security.

The Secretariat and the United Nations Charter

The Covenant of the League of Nations did not make an explicit choice between two types of international secretariats: either (1) an international service composed of persons chosen on the basis of merit and owing exclusive loyalty to the organization, or (2) an intergovernmental service composed of officials seconded by their respective governments for periods of time to perform secretariat functions. The Covenant simply provided for the establishment of a "permanent Secretariat," comprising a "Secretary-General and such secretaries and staffs as may be required," named the first Secretary-General, empowered him to appoint "the secretaries and the staff of the Secretariat" "with the approval of the Council," and directed him to act as "Secretary-General, at all meetings of the Assembly and of the Council." It was the first Secretary-General, Sir Eric Drummond, who decided that the Secretariat should be organized as an independent international service. His decision was accepted by the Council and the Assembly and was supported by the committees that subsequently were appointed to review the work of the Secretariat.[1]

The Secretariat as it developed under Sir Eric Drummond and his successors performed functions that were largely technical in character, involving little participation in decisions on policy and program. This was in line with Sir Eric's conception of his own position as an administrative official without political responsibilities, a view which he took over from the British civil service and which was completely acceptable to the governments and their representatives with whom he dealt in the work of the League. Furthermore, the League of Nations that Sir Eric and his staff were called upon to serve was under the dominant influence of states that had experience in their own national governments with this conception of a permanent service largely insulated from political controversy.

Though the principles of an independent international service as developed and put into operation by the first Secretary-General met with general acceptance during the League period, Sir Eric himself soon had to make some concessions to the concept of an intergovernmental service, for he found it expedient to take into account the factor of nationality in making appointments, particularly to the higher positions of responsibility in the Secretariat. Furthermore, the establishment of totalitarian regimes in certain member states, notably Italy and Germany, resulted in the nationals of these states in the Secretariat coming increasingly under the influence of their governments and greatly reduced the possibility of recruiting staff from these countries who would meet the requirements of an independent international service. Notwithstanding these political difficulties the reputation of the League Secretariat as an independent international service remained high down to 1939, when World

[1] See Egon F. Ranshofer-Wertheimer, *The International Secretariat* (Washington, D.C., Carnegie Endowment for International Peace, 1945), especially Part I.

War II intervened, and the demonstration of the validity and practicability of the concept was clearly one of the major achievements of the League of Nations and those devoted people who applied the idea in Geneva.

When it came to writing the Charter of a new international organization that would perform the functions of the League of Nations after World War II, there was wide agreement on the importance of the role of the Secretariat and that it should be organized and function as an independent international service closely following the League model. In the course of the discussions within the United States Department of State, at the Dumbarton Oaks Conference, and finally at San Francisco in 1945, only two issues about the Secretariat received prolonged attention with alternative solutions being considered. One was the extent and nature of the political role of the Secretary-General himself and the other was the related question of the method of selection of his principal assistants.

The San Francisco Conference decided that the Secretary-General should be given greater and more explicit political responsibilities than his predecessor in the League had been given by the Covenant or had assumed in practice. Different views have been expressed as to the origin of this conception of the Secretary-General's larger role. Dag Hammarskjöld, in his Oxford University lecture of 30 May 1961, suggested that the analogy to the American president was a factor.[2] There is also the possibility that the development of the role of the Director General of ILO by Albert Thomas influenced the decision. In any case, the idea embodied in Article 99 of the UN Charter, first proposed and agreed to at Dumbarton Oaks, appears to have been intended to remedy what was thought to be a defect of the League system that permitted only a member state to bring an alleged threat to the peace to the attention of the Coun-

[2] Wilder Foote, ed. *Dag Hammarskjöld: Servant of Peace* (New York, Harper and Row, 1962), pp. 335–36.

cil.[3] The San Francisco Conference also decided, despite the strong efforts by the Soviet Union to introduce national government influence and control over the Secretariat, that the Secretary-General alone would be responsible for the selection of his staff, including his principal advisers.

In the specific provisions of the Charter and by the recommendations of the Preparatory Commission regarding the initial establishment and operation of the Secretariat, the UN Secretariat was conceived as an independent international service like the Secretariat of the League, notwithstanding any changes in the responsibilities of the Secretary-General himself. The Commission stressed in its report the importance of the role of the Secretariat in realizing the objectives of the Charter and emphasized the necessity of its being "truly international in character." [4] It recognized, however, the possibility of conflict between the requirement that "the paramount consideration in the employment of the staff and in the determination of the conditions of service . . . is the necessity of securing the highest standards of efficiency, competence and integrity" and the provision that "due regard is also to be paid to the importance of recruiting the staff on as wide a geographical basis as possible." It observed that one of its major preoccupations had been "how best to ensure the fulfillment of these two principles—which, as experience has shown, can in large measure be reconciled." [5]

In its specific recommendations regarding the organization of the Secretariat, selection of personnel, and conditions of employment, the Commission stressed the need of proper classification and salary grading, adequate promotional opportunities, high standards of qualification, the methods of selection suited to

[3] Ruth B. Russell, *A History of the United Nations Charter* (Washington, D.C., Brookings Institution, 1958), pp. 431–32.
[4] *Report of the Preparatory Commission*, PC/20, 23 December 1945, p. 85, para. 2.
[5] *Ibid.*

obtaining properly qualified personnel, terms of appointment permitting "the bulk of the staff" to "make their career in the Secretariat,"[6] adequate salaries, and security. The Commission recognized that not all positions in the Secretariat should be filled on a permanent basis and listed a number of considerations that would justify departing from the principles of permanent appointments and filling higher positions through internal promotions. But the emphasis of the Commission's recommendations and of the Draft Provisional Staff Regulations was to make the Secretariat a career service, composed of qualified personnel, serving exclusively the Organization, subject to the authority of the Secretary-General and solely responsible to him.

The Commission recognized that the Secretary-General might have "an important role to play as a mediator and as an informal adviser of member governments" and would "undoubtedly be called upon from time to time, in the exercise of his administrative functions, to take decisions which may be justly called political." It also realized that under Article 99 he had been "given a quite special right which goes beyond any power previously accorded to the head of an international organization." Nevertheless, it did not appear to find in these considerations any reason for departing from the League model of an independent international service. In fact, the whole tone and substance of the Commission's recommendations suggests that the increased responsibilities of the Secretary-General and his staff provided added reasons for adhering to high standards of independence, integrity, and competence. Furthermore, it is significant that, while the Commission recommended that most of the commissions of ECOSOC under Article 68 should contain a majority of "responsible highly-qualified governmental representatives,"[7] it specifically stated that the Secretariat could not

[6] *Ibid.*, p. 92.
[7] *Ibid.*, p. 39, para. 37.

be composed, "even in part, of national representatives responsible to governments." [8]

The Development of the Secretariat since 1945

The UN Charter provisions for the Secretariat were prepared and adopted, and the preliminary plans for the establishment and operation of the Secretariat were drawn up when particular international political conditions existed with certain expectations about the future. Significant changes in the international system have since occurred influencing the development of the Secretariat.

In the early but critical period in the life of the UN following World War II, the pattern of international relations was unclear. Although the war had ended in a military victory for the anti-Axis coalition, a result achieved long before the Preparatory Commission completed its labor, the terms of the peace settlement and the relations between the victor nations were still obscure. In the actual construction of the new system of collective security, however, cooperation among the victors seemed essential to the effectiveness of an international organization to maintain peace, although in the immediate postwar situation good reasons existed to doubt that this position could be maintained.

During the actual drafting of the UN Charter provisions regarding the Secretariat, however, and in the preparation of initial arrangements for its establishment and operation, there is little evidence that the decisions taken were greatly influenced by any concern over the future of international power relations. The experts in the Department of State who had prepared the United States tentative proposals were very much under the influence of the League experience, even though the United States had never joined that organization, and the Administration in Washington was unalterably opposed to any attempt to revive

[8] *Ibid.*, p. 85, para. 3.

the League. Furthermore, at San Francisco, it was the representatives of those states that had been active in the League of Nations who took the most active interest in assuring the independent and international character of the Secretariat. They believed that an independent international secretariat was not only essential to achieving the purposes of the UN, but also, from a more narrow point of view, important as a means of protecting the smaller nations against the undue influence of the major powers, especially the United States and the Soviet Union. The role of the Secretariat under conditions of tension between the great powers was not seriously considered.

Another element in the political climate of 1945 was the assumption of a continuing dominance of Western power and Western ideas. Although Western Europe had been devastated, the United States and Great Britain were among the major victors, and the original members of the UN were predominantly states with a Western cultural tradition. The emergence of a Communist bloc and an increase in the number of Asian and African members made the UN initially a less homogeneous organization than the League had been, but it was still possible, in view of the leadership roles of the United States and the British Commonwealth countries and the active participation of West European and Latin American states, to regard the new organization, like its predecessor, as the embodiment of Western political ideas and institutional arrangements.

Finally, while the authors of the UN Charter deliberately made the Secretariat a more important organ than it had been in the League of Nations, and more particularly gave the Secretary-General responsibilities not possessed, or at least not exercised, by his League predecessor, they were not apparently aware of the magnitude or detailed character of this change. In its *Report,* the Preparatory Commission spoke of the "special right" of the Secretary-General under Article 99 to bring to the attention of the Security Council any matter which in his opinion may threaten the maintenance of international peace and security but the Commission frankly stated that it was "impossible to foresee" how the article would be applied.

While the Charter expressly provides that the Secretary-General shall perform such functions as are entrusted to him by other organs, there is no evidence of awareness of the extent to which this process would be carried and particularly the extent to which the Secretary-General would be asked to assume executive responsibilities in connection with field operations, whether in connection with keeping the peace or carrying out economic and social programs. From the few comments of the Preparatory Commission, the inference can fairly be drawn that the administrative and executive functions of the Secretary-General and his staff were regarded as of an essentially technical nature, though the Commission did recognize that the Secretary-General "undoubtedly may be called upon from time to time, in the exercise of his administrative duties, to take decisions which may be justly called political." [9]

Since 1945 important changes have occurred in the political environment in which the UN operates, in the membership of the Organization, and in the demands that are being made upon the Secretary-General and his staff. These have inevitably required considerable rethinking regarding the basic concepts of the UN Charter and an adaptation of established principles and methods to new conditions.

Among the more significant of these changes have been, first, the "cold war" between the Communist and non-Communist members of the alliance that succeeded the uneasy and limited cooperation of the 1941–45 war period. This has influenced the Secretariat in a number of ways. The inability of the Security Council to make decisions because of the veto and the assumption of increased responsibility by the General Assembly in the peace and security field have encouraged the development of

[9] *Report of the Preparatory Commission*, pp. 86–87.

the executive role of the Secretary-General, often under directives of a very general nature. Furthermore, as the Secretariat
has gained in importance, the cold war struggle has been introduced into it in the form of competition for posts, particularly
those appointments of great political importance. Even more
consequential has been the revival of the two opposing concepts
of the nature of the international secretariat—an intergovernmental service and an independent international civil service.

A second important development has been the change in the
membership of the Organization, and this has produced a shift
in the center of voting power and influence in the General
Assembly from the more economically and politically advanced
Western nations to the newly independent countries of Asia
and Africa. The result has been a much more heterogeneous
organization than originally existed and a weakening of the
influence of the developed countries that have strongly supported the concept and principles of an independent international civil service modeled on their own national administrative
services. Although most of the new Asian and African countries have recently been under colonial administrations based
on these principles, they have not yet developed to the point
where they are fully prepared to accept or implement such
advanced and sophisticated ideas. The struggle for power and
influence is viewed by them in much more direct and crude
terms. Another aspect of this development is that these nations
are making new and different demands upon the Organization,
including assistance in their economic and social development,
action in support of human rights, and help in getting rid of
colonialism—demands that involve the Secretariat quite differently from the administrative support and services originally
envisaged.

Finally, related to the altered political atmosphere and the
demands resulting from changes of influence within the Organization, the operational responsibilities of the UN have been

greatly increased over what was envisaged at the time the
Charter was written. The contrast between the UN and the
League in this respect has become so great as to justify the
conclusion that the UN has become an entirely different type
of organization. This has added greatly to the responsibilities
of the Secretary-General and his staff, a development favored
in no small degree by the willingness of successive Secretaries-
General not only to accept such responsibilities but in fact to
seek them.

The Structure of the Secretariat

The Preparatory Commission, in preparing its recommendations for the administrative organization of the Secretariat, accepted the principle of a unified Secretariat. The provisions of
the Charter, by requiring that appropriate staff be permanently
assigned to the organs of the UN, could have been interpreted
as giving support to the principle that the Secretariat should be
built primarily around organs. A second alternative would have
allowed the Secretariat to be organized around its major work
processes or functions. The Commission sought to combine the
possible advantages of these two approaches by proposing an
organization under which "every organ . . . has at its disposal
the services of the whole of the Secretariat, and each Department of the Secretariat serves all the organs as required" subject to the one exception that special units of the Department
of Security Council Affairs serve the Security Council only.[10]
The Commission also recommended that the Secretariat be
organized into eight departments: (1) Security Council Affairs;
(2) Economic Affairs; (3) Social Affairs; (4) Trusteeship and
Information from Non-Self-Governing Territories; (5) Public
Information; (6) Legal Department; (7) Conference and General Services; and, (8) Administrative and Financial Services.

This form of organization remained substantially in effect

---

[10] *Report of the Preparatory Commission*, pp. 87–88.

until 1954 when a reorganization was carried out along lines recommended by the new Secretary-General, Dag Hammarskjöld.[11] This reorganization sought to achieve a more streamlined structure and greater flexibility in the use of personnel. It provided for (1) making the Legal Department and the bureaus of Personnel and of Finance in the Department of Administrative and Financial Services into offices under the immediate and personal direction of the Secretary-General; (2) combining the departments of Economic and of Social Affairs; (3) separating the Department of Conference and General Services into two offices; (4) combining the two top echelons—Assistant Secretaries and Directors—into one—Under Secretaries, with essentially administrative responsibilities; and (5) having two Under Secretaries without portfolio to serve the Secretary-General on special questions.

The reorganization carried out under Dag Hammarskjöld has been maintained without any important change down to the present. It provides a unified and efficient administrative instrument to support the central activities of the Organization. However, for the special programs in the economic and social fields that are financed by voluntary contributions from a varying number of states, some of which are not members of the UN, and that involve cooperation with the specialized agencies, it has sometimes been found expedient to organize special staffs with special relations to the regular staff of the Secretariat. For example, UNICEF, though a subsidiary organ of the General Assembly, has a staff of its own "provided to the [Executive] Board by the Secretary-General."[12] Under the resolution that established EPTA, the Secretariat of TAB was appointed by the Executive Chairman, who in turn was appointed by the Secretary-General. That Secretariat included members seconded from the UN Secretariat and the staffs of the specialized agen-

[11] A/2554, 12 November 1953.
[12] GA Resolution 57 (I), 11 December 1946.

cies, as well as personnel recruited and appointed directly by the Executive Chairman.[13] The staff of UNHCR has been appointed by the High Commissioner, who in turn has been elected by the General Assembly.[14] In the case of the Special Fund, which was established by resolution of the General Assembly,[15] the Managing Director, who was appointed by the Secretary-General subject to General Assembly approval, in turn appointed his staff with conditions of service equal to those of other UN officials, except that tenure related only to the Fund. UNRWA also has had its separate staff.

The special requirements of programs financed on a voluntary basis and involving varying groups of states and agencies, therefore, have led to a departure from the concept of a unified Secretariat and caused the establishment of a number of staffs separate from the regular Secretariat but generally subject to the Staff Rules and Regulations of the UN. The organization of the Secretariat (as it was early in 1965) is shown in Chart I.

The Preparatory Commission in its *Report* also called attention to the need of a system of classification of posts and of salary-grading within the Secretariat. While it did not think it feasible to propose such a system, it urged upon the Secretary-General the urgency of the undertaking. At the request of the General Assembly and with the assistance of an Advisory Group of Experts, the Secretary-General prepared and put into effect a classification system that established nineteen grades with a number of salary steps within each grade. This system proved to be too inflexible and detailed; while possibly suited to the requirements of a national civil service, it was found to be unsuited to the needs of an international service. As a result, on the basis of the report of an expert committee in 1949,[16] a

[13] ECOSOC Resolution 222 (IX), 15 August 1949, as amended by Resolution 433 (XIV), 22 July 1952.
[14] GA Resolution 428 (V), 14 December 1950.
[15] GA Resolution 1240 (XIII), 14 October 1958.
[16] A/C.5/331, 31 October 1949.

THE UNITED NATIONS SECRETARIAT

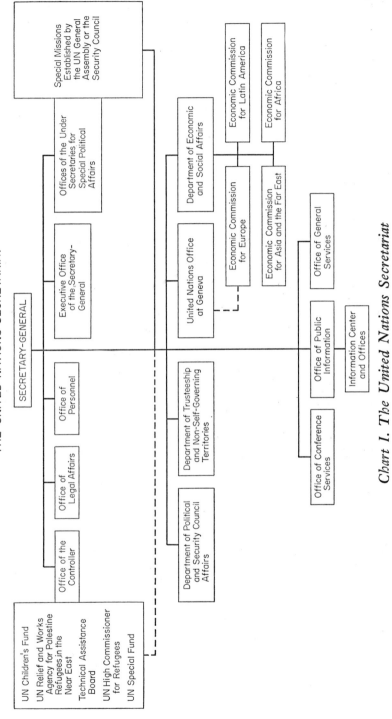

Chart 1. The United Nations Secretariat
(As of early 1965)

change was made to a simpler system more like that employed by the League Secretariat. That system is outlined in Table I which gives the categories, steps, and salary ranges of the UN Secretariat.

TABLE I

CATEGORIES, STEPS, AND SALARY RANGES OF THE
UNITED NATIONS SECRETARIAT

Category and Level	No. in 1965	Steps	Salary Range (Gross) (in U.S. dollars)
I. Under Secretary	19	1	27,000
Director (D-2)	41	1–3	20,500–22,300
Principal Officer (D-1)	98	1–7	16,300–20,500
II. Professional			
Senior Officer (P-5)	266	1–10	14,000–18,000
First Officer (P-4)	532	1–11	11,400–15,200
Second Officer (P-3)	686	1–12	9,300–12,800
Associate Officer (P-2)	424	1–10	7,500– 9,900
Assistant Officer (P-1)		1–9	5,750– 7,750
III. General Service			
Principal Level (G-5)*	234	1–10	6,650– 9,960
Other Levels (G-1-4)	2167	1–9 or 10	3,790– 7,750

SOURCE: The table is a composite one based on tables in Staff Rules (Doc. ST/SGB/ Staff Rules/1), pp. 68 and 71, and *Budget Estimates for the Fiscal Year 1966 and Information Annexes*, pp. 23, 86–87. It does not take account of increases authorized by the General Assembly in 1965.
* G-5 is highest at Headquarters; Geneva has G-6 and G-7 as promotional levels.

The Increased Political Role of the Secretariat

The problem of harmonizing the increased political role of the Secretary-General and his staff with the concept of an impartial independent international service has received considerable attention from scholars and public officials, particularly since the Soviet Union's attack on the Secretary-General in 1960 over the conduct of the UN Congo operation and the proposal by the USSR to substitute a "troika" arrangement for the single head of the Secretariat.[17]

[17] For a particularly incisive treatment, see Jean Siotis, *Essai sur le Secrétariat International* (Geneva, Librairie Droz, 1963). The matter was also discussed at length by Dag Hammarskjöld in his Oxford University address of 30 May 1961.

The problem arises from the fact that the concept of an impartial and independent international service was first developed and applied under conditions that in certain important respects are no longer the same. The League of Nations was a relatively homogeneous organization dominated by Western states with many common interests. Furthermore, its Secretariat was limited to work mainly of a technical nature and not involved directly in policy making nor expected to assume political responsibilities. The Secretary-General and his staff could therefore regard themselves as occupying positions comparable to members of the British or French permanent administrative services, who are not expected to assume political responsibilities. In the UN, however, a new element has been introduced, for the Secretary-General has both assumed and received from the political organs executive responsibilities involving the exercise of considerable discretion and the choice of alternative courses of action. The Secretary-General and his principal assistants have thus taken on something of the character of a chief executive officer with department heads who must accept some political responsibility for their acts and cannot entirely depend upon the protection accorded to members of a permanent administrative service presumably insulated from party conflict.

In his Oxford University address, Dag Hammarskjöld faced this problem and argued that, although the Secretary-General and his principal assistants may become involved in activities where they must "take stands of a politically controversial nature," they do this, however, on an international basis and without departing from the basic concept of neutrality.[18] His argument was that in those situations where the Secretary-General is confronted with mandates of a highly controversial character, expressing the bare minimum of agreement attainable in the political organs, as was the case in the Congo operation in 1960–61, and where he is required to choose between alternative

[18] Foote, *Dag Hammarskjöld*, p. 337.

courses of action, it is still possible for him to maintain the impartiality and objectivity of an international civil servant. This he can do by looking beyond the terms of the resolution to the provisions of the Charter, to the principles of international law, and to the precedents of the UN. He can gain further guidance by consulting the representatives of governments, especially those more directly involved. The responsibilities of final decision admittedly still remain with the Secretary-General, and, in the exercise of this discretion, the ultimate guarantee of impartiality is to be found in his integrity as an international official, his capacity to check his sympathies, and his resolution to act solely in accord with the aims and principles of the UN.

Such a line of reasoning will not satisfy those who believe that man is incapable of being neutral, that the thoughts and actions of every individual are determined by his particular social and economic environment, and that, therefore, an American or a Russian or a Swede will in his acts as an international official necessarily reflect the interests and attitudes of his country and his class. Even for those who accept the validity of the concept of the impartial international official, there is still some difficulty. Where the international official chooses, or is required, to take political decisions on his own responsibility and to act under conditions where he finds his only guidance in the purposes and principles of the UN Charter, the precedents of the Organization, and such counsel and advice as he chooses to solicit from governments, does he not assume a political responsibility to member governments? Can he properly seek to shield himself against criticism and political attack on the ground that he is acting as an international official outside the arena of political conflict? Is his position not more comparable to that of a minister or political under-secretary than to that of a permanent official?

Considerations such as these suggest that, if the Secretary-General wishes to maintain intact the concept of an international civil service, which is protected against political influence and accepted as exclusively concerned with serving the interests of the Organization, he must show restraint in the exercise of his political powers under the UN Charter. He must recognize that he does not have powers comparable to the President of the United States and that even though he is the principal administrative officer of the UN, his possibilities of effectively exercising the authority that he has under the UN Charter are largely determined by the measure of support that he is able to obtain from member states, and particularly from the major powers. Whereas he may be able to achieve his purposes by playing one group against another, this is a dangerous game with possible serious consequences both for himself and his staff, for once the Secretariat is recognized as an important center of influence and power, member states are bound to be increasingly concerned with the nationality, political views, and attitudes of Secretariat officials, especially those who occupy senior posts.

The Demand for Wide Geographical Distribution

The problem of harmonizing the requirements of "independence, efficiency, and integrity," with the criterion of wide geographical distribution in an international secretariat goes back to the League of Nations. The UN Charter provisions simply reflected the practice of the League Secretariat. The Preparatory Commission, observing in its *Report* that the two principles could be largely reconciled, by inference recognized the difficulties involved.[19]

When the UN Secretariat was first organized in 1945 and 1946, a condition of serious geographic imbalance was created by the fact that Secretary-General Trygve Lie was compelled to provide a large staff without delay and nationals of the United States, Canada, Great Britain, and countries of Western Europe were most readily available. At its second session the UN Gen-

[19] *Report of the Preparatory Commission*, p. 85, para. 7.

eral Assembly requested the Secretary-General to take steps to improve "the present geographical distribution of the staff." [20] The Assembly did not claim that the principle of wide geographical distribution should prevail over that of "independence, efficiency and integrity" but rather asserted that the two principles were not in conflict and that "in view of its international character and in order to avoid undue predominance of national practices, the policies and administrative methods of the Secretariat should reflect, and profit to the highest degree from, assets of the various cultures and the technical competence of all Member nations."

In reporting to the General Assembly in its third session, the Secretary-General defined his concept of wide geographical distribution as not requiring that nationals of a particular nation should have a specified number of posts at a particular grade or grades or that they should receive in salaries a particular percentage of total outlays, but rather providing that "the Secretariat is enriched by the experience and culture which each Member nation can furnish." [21] He emphasized that any rigid formula would restrict in an impractical manner the flexibility essential to good and efficient administration, but he proposed to make financial contribution the basic criterion for the number of nationals from each member state in the Secretariat, with a permissible range of 25 percent upward and downward. The deviation upward, however, would not apply to member states contributing more than 10 percent of the UN budget. Operating under this flexible formula, therefore, and aided by the relative stability of membership until 1955, the Secretary-General was able to achieve a generally acceptable distribution of posts.

The admission of a large number of new members in 1955 caused new demands for adjustments in the geographical distribution of posts in the Secretariat. In 1960 the influx of new

---

[20] GA Resolution 153 (II), 15 November 1947.
[21] A/652, especially Annex I, 2 September 1948.

African states and the importance of the Secretariat's role in the Congo led to wider and more intense dissatisfaction with the distribution of posts. The Soviet Union suddenly realized the importance of the Secretariat in connection with the UN Congo operation. Up until this time the USSR had evidenced no particular interest in having its nationals in the Secretariat, except for its constantly pressed claim to the top post in the Department of Political and Security Council Affairs. At the same time the equitable geographical distribution of the Secretariat became a matter of concern to the large number of African states suddenly admitted to the UN which were insistent on full participation in the work of the Organization and which found the Trygve Lie formula based exclusively on financial contribution unsatisfactory. In the 1960 General Assembly, therefore, complaints against the formula were raised not only by "under represented" states but also by states demanding a basic revision of the Lie formula.

In the discussions that took place in the Committee of Experts to Review the Activities and Organization of the Secretariat and in the Fifth Committee of the General Assembly, the representative of the USSR argued that wide geographical distribution and adequate representation of "varying political tendencies and social systems" were essential features of an international secretariat. He urged that these principles should also be applied more widely to other international staffs, such as those serving UNICEF, TAB, and the Special Fund, that had not been subject in the past to the application of the Trygve Lie formula, and he proposed that officials serve under "temporary contracts" to insure that they truly represent these tendencies and systems.[22] The last proposal in effect repudiated the idea of an independent international service in favor of an intergovernmental service. Representatives of other countries, especially of Asian and African countries, without repudiating the idea of an independ-

[22] A/4776, 14 June 1961, Appendix 1.

ent international service, argued that a wide geographical distribution was of primary importance for the Secretariat to perform its functions effectively, that any formula should take into account population and the principle of the equality of states as well as financial contributions, and that the present unbalanced situation should be quickly remedied. Finally, representatives of other members, particularly the Western states, while recognizing that adjustments should be made in order to secure wider geographic distribution, insisted that this be done in an orderly fashion and that primary consideration must be given to securing the highest standards of efficiency, competence, and integrity.

The final outcome of the debate was the adoption by the General Assembly of a resolution[23] reaffirming its earlier position that the principle of equitable geographical distribution does not conflict with the "paramount considerations of employment of staff, namely, the necessity of securing the highest standards of efficiency, competence and integrity," and recommending that the Secretary-General be guided in his efforts to achieve a more equitable geographical distribution by the following principles and factors:

(a) Due regard shall be paid in recruitment of all staff to securing as wide a geographical distribution as possible.

(b) In the Secretariat proper, an equitable geographical distribution should take account of the fact of membership, of members' contributions, and of their populations as outlined in the Secretary-General's report (A/5270), particularly paragraph 69(ii) thereof. No member state should be considered "overrepresented" if it has no more than five of its nationals on the staff by virtue of its membership.

(c) The relative importance of posts at different levels.

(d) The need for a more balanced regional composition of the staff at levels of D-1 and above.

[23] GA Resolution 1852 (XVII), 19 December 1962.

(e) Career appointments should take particular account of the need to reduce "under-representation."

In his report to the eighteenth General Assembly on geographical distribution, Secretary-General Thant explained how he proposed to express the "desirable ranges" of posts in arithmetical terms, taking account of the factors mentioned in the General Assembly's resolution. He expressly stated, however, that "these figures are not intended to be a substitute for the discretion and good sense of the chief administrative officer of the Organization." [24] In calculating the new desirable ranges of posts, the Secretary-General, on the assumption of a Secretariat of 1,500 members, first set aside 100 posts as a population reserve to be allocated regionally. Second, with 111 UN members (in 1963), he established a range of 111 to 555 posts for the membership factor. Finally, the balance of posts available for distribution according to the financial contribution factor fell within a complementary range of 1,289 to 845. [25]

Table II gives for selected countries the number of nationals in the Secretariat and a comparison of the desirable ranges under the Trygve Lie and the Thant formulas. Moreover, if one combines the ranges of the member states in a region and takes the midpoint of the combined desirable range, a comparison of the Trygve Lie and the Thant formulas will show that the proportion of posts allocated to Africa has been increased from 4.5 to 9.1 percent; to Asia and the Far East from 13.5 to 16.3 percent; to Latin America from 5.8 to 8.1 percent; and to the Middle East from 1.9 to 3.6 percent. On the other hand, the allocation to Eastern Europe has been reduced from 19.8 to 17.5 percent; to Western Europe, from 23.1 to 19.6 percent; and to North America and the Caribbean, from 31.4 to 25.8 percent. A major consequence of the new Thant formula has been to increase minimum ranges from 1–3 to 2–5.

[24] A/C.5/987, 11 October 1963, para. 6.
[25] For resulting ranges for members and by regions, see A/C.5/987, 11 October 1963.

TABLE II

COMPARISON OF NUMBER OF NATIONALS IN THE SECRETARIAT
AND DESIRABLE RANGES OF SELECTED COUNTRIES
UNDER TWO FORMULAS

Country	No. of Staff (excluding G-5) 31 August 1964*	Under Trygve Lie Formula (including G-5 at Headquarters)	Under Thant Formula (excluding G-5)*
Argentina	19	12–20	13–12
Australia	16	19–31	21–18
Belgium	18	14–23	16–15
Brazil	18	11–18	13–13
Canada	39	33–55	42–22
China	48	53–88	56–40
France	77	68–113	79–56
India	61	26–43	25–21
Indonesia	13	5–8	6–8
Italy	27	24–40	34–26
Japan	28	23–29	37–28
Netherlands	20	11–18	15–14
Norway	11	5–9	7–9
Poland	24	14–24	20–17
Sweden	16	15–24	17–16
USSR	74	144–192	192–130
United Arab Republic	21	3–6	4–7
United Kingdom	114	82–137	93–66
United States	276	343–457	410–273

* From *Report of the Secretary-General*, A/5841, 23 December 1964, Table 2.

To achieve wider geographical distribution under both the Trygve Lie formula and the Thant formula in 1963, preference in new appointments was given to "under-represented" states, especially those in Eastern Europe and Africa. For instance, during the period 1 September 1962 to 31 August 1963, of 176 appointments to posts subject to geographical distribution, 28 went to nationals of African members and 32 to Eastern European nationals while only 27 went to nationals of Western Europe (including six from non-self-governing territories) and 14 to nationals from the North American and Caribbean areas. In the North American area the United States has been substantially under-represented since G-5 at Headquarters was dropped from the categories subject to geographical distribution. Because of the large number of American nationals on the international staff and the desire to avoid stressing the nationality factor, the State Department has been reluctant to press a claim for better "representation."

Although the principle of wide geographical distribution can undoubtedly be reconciled with the requirement of competence, efficiency, and integrity under favorable conditions of reasonable stability of membership and general acceptance of the primary need of high personal qualifications, this becomes less easy if the basic concepts of an independent international service are challenged and if there is an unwillingness on the part of member states to allow time for existing imbalances to be remedied by procedures appropriate to the requirements of such a service. In this connection, the opinion of ICSAB in its 1950 report is pertinent. Commenting on the balancing of competence and geography, the Board said: "If, from whatever reason, the balance of geographical distribution is poor, it must be recognized that the process of correcting this state of affairs must be gradual if the efficiency of the organization is not to be seriously damaged." [26]

Certain attitudes of member states and some practices followed by the Secretariat under political pressure have undoubtedly resulted in a lowering of general competence and efficiency. The insistence of some members, notably the USSR, that appointments be made for fixed terms to achieve wide geographical distribution more quickly has resulted in greatly expanding the proportion of fixed-term appointments in the Secretariat, a trend that could have serious consequences. The appointment of nationals of the developing countries, moreover, in preference to better qualified persons from developed countries, means not only that less qualified persons have been chosen but also that the developing countries have been deprived of trained personnel needed at home. The appointment of persons from outside the

---

[26] ICSAB, *Report on Recruitment Methods and Standards for United Nations and the Specialized Agencies*, COORD/Civil Service/2/Rev. 1, p. 8.

Secretariat to higher posts, usually for fixed terms—what the "under-represented" countries usually want—limits promotional opportunities and weakens morale. Once reasonable geographical distribution has been achieved, the flexibility of the Thant formula permits a return to primary emphasis on "efficiency, competence, and integrity" as the Charter requires.

The principle of wide geographical distribution has not been applied uniformly or obtained similar results throughout the Secretariat. Formally, with its defined ranges of posts and the requirement of reports from the Secretary-General, the principle applies only to appointments of more than six months' duration to posts in the regular establishment at the professional level and above that are provided for in the regular budget. Even within these categories, posts with special language requirements are excluded. Moreover, while the General Assembly has requested that the Secretary-General review periodically the geographical distribution of the staffs of TAB, the Special Fund, and UNICEF, it has not demanded that these positions be included in the categories to which the 1963 formula on the range of posts applies. Furthermore, consultants appointed by the Secretary-General, technical assistance experts, and personnel specially appointed to UN missions have not been included. Thus there has been a wide range of posts at the professional or equivalent and higher levels that could be and have been filled without deference to any arithmetic formula of geographical distribution, although the General Assembly has requested that "due regard be paid to the principle of wide geographical distribution in the appointment of all staff."

Fixed Term versus Permanent Appointments

According to UN Staff Rules and Regulations, appointments of staff members may be temporary, permanent, or regular.[27] Temporary appointments are of three kinds: (1) probationary

[27] Rules 104.12 and 104.13.

appointments, normally for two years, of persons recruited for career service; (2) fixed-term appointments, having an expiration date specified in the letter of appointment, granted for a period not exceeding five years; and (3) indefinite appointments granted normally to persons specifically recruited for mission service or any agency or office specially designated by the Secretary-General. Permanent appointments are granted to persons who have demonstrated their suitability as international civil servants "and have shown that they meet the high standards of efficiency, competence, and integrity established in the Charter." Regular appointments are for indefinite periods and may last until retirement. They are usually granted to staff members in the General Service and Manual Worker categories.

As a result of demands for the quick achievement of an equitable geographical distribution and the USSR's challenge to the whole concept of an independent career service, the problem of harmonizing the basic principles of a career service and its opportunities for promotion within the service with the legitimate use of fixed-term appointments from outside to meet particular needs has become increasingly complex.

The Preparatory Commission came out strongly for a career service. It gave three special reasons in support of its view: (1) that otherwise many of the best candidates from all countries would be kept away; (2) that members detached temporarily from national administrations could not be expected to subordinate the special interests of their countries to the international interests; and (3) that only through a career service would the advantages of experience and sound administrative traditions be established. The Commission recognized, however, that it was "neither possible nor desirable" to recruit all personnel on a permanent basis and admitted the following categories as exceptions: (1) "Assistant Secretaries General, Directors and such other principal officers as the Secretary-General may determine"; (2) specialists in technical fields, as well as persons with special political qualifications; (3) "temporary appointments from geographical regions inadequately represented in the Secretariat if suitable candidates from that region are not readily available for permanent appointment"; and (4) appointments from national services "so that personal contacts between the Secretariat and national administrations may be strengthened and a body of national officials with international experience created." The Commission did not express an opinion as to the percentage of officials who might fall within these categories, but it did state that "the bulk of the staff should consist of persons who will make their career in the Secretariat." [28]

The question of the proportion of fixed-term appointments that was justifiable and the conditions under which fixed-term appointments might be made was not raised until after the influx of new members in 1955 when an increase in the proportion of fixed-term appointments came to be viewed by many delegations as a means of achieving a better geographical distribution. On 31 August 1957, out of a total of 1,113 internationally recruited staff members in the Director and Principal Officer (D) and Professional (P) categories, 153, or 13.8 percent, had fixed-term appointments. The Salary Review Committee, established by the General Assembly in December, 1955, felt that the proportion might be as high as 20 percent,[29] and the General Assembly recommended that such a proportion be achieved as a means of getting better geographical distribution. With the Communist states and the new African members of the UN joining in the demand for quick action to get a wider geographical distribution in the Secretariat and with many of these same countries unwilling to cooperate in making their nationals available except on fixed-term appointments, from 1960 onward the pressure to increase the proportion of fixed-term appointments mounted. The Committee of Experts on the Activities and Or-

[28] *Report of the Preparatory Commission,* pp. 92–93.
[29] GA *Official Records,* 11th Session, Agenda Item 51, A/3209, November 1956, p. 7.

ganization of the Secretariat, which made additional recommendations for achieving a wider geographical distribution in the Secretariat, recognized that the effect of their proposals might be to increase the percentage of fixed-term appointments to as much as 25 percent by the end of 1962, but it did not regard this percentage as "an excessive proportion."[30]

As a result of these political pressures and ensuing recommendations, there has been a steady increase in the percentage of posts subject to geographical distribution filled by fixed-term appointments: 16.6 percent in 1959; 17.3 in 1960; 20.5 in 1961; 25.4 in 1962; and 29.7 in 1963.[31] Of the 176 appointments made to posts subject to geographical distribution in the year ending 31 August 1963, 147 were for fixed terms, and, of 59 appointments to posts with special language requirements, 37 were on a fixed-term basis. Thus 78.3 percent of the appointments made during the period in question to all P and D posts were for fixed terms.

All this suggests that the policy of the Secretary-General for achieving better geographical distribution was to allocate vacancies roughly on a fifty-fifty basis between internal promotion and outside recruitment and, of the vacancies allocated for outside recruitment, to use about 75 percent for fixed-term appointments and the rest for probationary permanent appointments. The Secretary-General indicated in his 1963 report that fixed-term appointments were "sometimes" converted to permanent appointments and that he intended to continue this practice "to bring within the career group an increased number of staff from the 'under-represented' regions," while maintaining the proportion of fixed-term staff "at about 25 percent of the total."[32]

The percentage of fixed-term appointments by itself need not be a cause of alarm, assuming the desirability of maintaining a career service. The requirements and conditions of an inter-

[20] A/4776, 14 June 1961, para. 92, p. 35.
[31] A/C.5/987, 11 October 1963, paras. 17–18.
[32] *Ibid.*

national administrative service are such that, as the Preparatory
Commission recognized, a considerable use of fixed-term appointments can be justified. Many UN posts require highly
specialized qualifications that cannot be filled from within, as
in the Department of Economic and Social Affairs. Furthermore, the kind and quality of competence desired can often be
obtained only on the basis of a fixed-term appointment, for a
highly skilled individual desired for a UN position may not be
willing to leave his career, for example, in a university, except
for a fixed period of time. Making international service a permanent career, moreover, does not always have the attraction
that the Preparatory Commission rather idealistically thought it
should. For many men to live with one's family in an urban
area, like New York, and in a foreign country has many disadvantages, especially if regarded as a permanent assignment.
In some cases the prospect of a career service may result not in
attracting the best candidates but in discouraging them. The
situation was somewhat different under the League of Nations
as it was primarily a European organization. Residence in Geneva
for people brought up in the European culture was not a great
inconvenience. Finally, there are a large number of new UN
members who are unable to spare permanently the services of
their qualified nationals but who can benefit from the experience
that their nationals may gain during short tours of duty in the
Secretariat. Whether the Secretariat benefits to the same degree
can be questioned, but there is undoubtedly merit in the argument that an international secretariat ought to comprise different
cultures and different points of view.

What is of particular concern to those who wish to see the
Secretariat maintained as a career service is that the increase in
fixed-term appointments has come so suddenly and been used so
largely for the one purpose of achieving a wider geographical
distribution, not just by those countries that cannot provide qualified personnel or cannot afford to have their nationals accept

permanent appointments but also, most significantly, by those countries that are unwilling to allow their nationals to accept permanent employment because of their objections to the principle of a career service. Without question the result has been to reduce to an excessive extent the promotional opportunities within the Secretariat, greatly to weaken the morale of those on permanent appointments, and to make the Secretariat less attractive as a career. It has also resulted in increased work loads for the experienced personnel who have had the added responsibility of supervising and assisting untrained people, in an increased turnover of personnel since many of the fixed-term appointees serve only short terms or leave before their terms are even completed, and in a dependence of fixed-term appointees on their national governments to which they return on completing their tours of duty.

The Problem of Loyalty

The Charter states clearly that the Secretary-General and his staff are to regard themselves as international officials who are to serve the UN exclusively and loyally. They are not to seek or receive instructions from any government, and they are to refrain from any action that might reflect on their position as "international officials responsible only to the Organization." Conversely, every member state undertakes to respect the international character of the Secretariat and not to seek to influence its officials in the discharge of their responsibilities. To fortify the position of members of the Secretariat as independent international officials, they are guaranteed privileges and immunities essential to the performance of their duties. In its *Report* the Preparatory Commission stated emphatically that the Secretariat could not be composed, "even in part, of national representatives, responsible to governments." [33] It declared that it is essential that officials should be inspired by a sense of loyalty to the UN,

---

[33] *Report of the Preparatory Commission*, p. 85, para. 3.

such loyalty being "in no way incompatible with an official's attachment to his own country, whose higher interest he is serving in serving the United Nations." [34] The Staff Regulations provide for an oath or declaration of loyalty by which the official undertakes to exercise the functions entrusted to him "as an international civil servant of the United Nations . . . with the interests of the United Nations only in view." [35]

The conception of the international official owing exclusive loyalty to the UN has come under attack largely as the result of the "cold war," and the suspicion and distrust inspired by it, although to some extent it also reflects an unwillingness on the part of some states to accept fully the idea of an international official performing an international function impartially and objectively. Members of the UN have challenged the establishment of an impartial and objective Secretariat in three ways: (1) an unwillingness to allow the Secretary-General full freedom in the choice of officials; (2) an insistence on forms of appointment that inevitably leave the officials in a state of dependence on his government, accompanied by a failure to respect in practice their obligation not to seek to influence the official; and (3) an insistence on holding the official to certain standards of conduct set by his national government and not necessarily dictated by his character as an international official.

The unwillingness to allow the Secretary-General full freedom in the choice of his staff has taken different forms and is sometimes difficult to distinguish from a natural dependence of the Secretary-General on member governments in the recruitment of personnel. Some governments have insisted on nominating persons for appointments or have prevented the Secretary-General from employing those whom it does not approve—actions that do not deny the principle of exclusive international loyalty but that create a UN atmosphere scarcely favorable to its realization. Likewise, the United States requirement of a pre-

[34] *Ibid.*, para. 4.
[35] Regulation 1.9.

liminary security clearance for its nationals before appointment is hardly in harmony with the conception of an international official whose loyalty is exclusively to the Organization.

Of necessity the Secretary-General is to a considerable extent dependent upon the assistance of the governments of member states in filling posts in the Secretariat. Whether this assistance has been rendered with due regard for the responsibilities of the Secretary-General and the exclusive international loyalty of the officials appointed can only be determined in the light of the facts. In a memorandum issued by President Johnson on 15 August 1964, to the heads of the executive departments and agencies, for example, he expressed his desire that "affirmative and continuing steps" be taken to "assist international organizations to obtain properly qualified United States citizens for employment." [36] This kind of constructive assistance can only be welcomed as positive support for the chief administrative officer of the UN, the Secretary-General, in the discharge of his onerous duties.

The practice of fixed-term appointments, however, particularly where it takes the form of seconding a government official to Secretariat service, weakens the sense of international loyalty. A national official seconded by his government for a limited period of service with the UN is obviously in a different position from an official on a permanent appointment who does not contemplate a subsequent career with his government. This was recognized by the Preparatory Commission when it stated that members of the staff cannot "be expected fully to subordinate the special interests of their countries to the international interest if they are merely detached temporarily from the national administrations and remain dependent upon them for the future." [37] Some of the governments favoring the practice of short-term

[36] U.S. Department of State, *Bulletin*, September 14, 1964, pp. 388–89. See also its *Staffing International Organizations: A Report of the Advisory Committee on International Organizations* (Washington, D.C., U.S. Government Printing Office, 1963).

[37] *Report of the Preparatory Commission*, p. 92, para. 59.

secondment do not in fact accept the idea of an independent international civil service but rather regard the Secretariat as a projection of the diplomatic process. Thus the Soviet representative in the Committee of Experts and in the discussions in the Fifth Committee openly argued that the entire staff of the Secretariat should be reorganized so as to reflect more accurately the balance of forces in the world today.[38] The advocacy of the Secretariat as an organ with representational functions, giving a legitimate role to the Secretariat official as a representative of the views of his government with its political tendencies, denies the original UN Charter concept of the nature of the obligation of the Secretariat official.

A final threat to the concept of international loyalty is the insistence of some governments on prescribing standards of conduct for their nationals who hold posts within the Secretariat that are contrary to or additional to those prescribed by the international organization. The 1952 and 1953 investigations of the loyalty of United States citizens in the Secretariat, the requirement of security clearance by United States authorities for United States citizens, the efforts of certain governments to obtain the removal of Secretariat officials on ideological grounds, and the close control exercised by some governments over their nationals while employed as Secretariat officials are cases in point. Such infringements upon the concept of exclusive responsibility and loyalty to the Organization have been encouraged by the ideological conflict of the postwar world. Tendencies in this direction have been strengthened as governments have become convinced that the Secretariat is an important center of power and influence in international relations.

Conclusion

The UN Secretariat is in a critical period of its development as the result of new and heavy demands upon it, the conditions

[38] A/4776, 14 June 1961, Appendix, p. 5.

under which it must perform its duties, and the political pressures flowing from postwar developments in international relations to which it has been subjected. Owing to the failure of the UN representative political organs and the states that constitute them to assume their full responsibilities in providing guidance to the Secretary-General and to the nature of the demands made upon the UN since World War II, the Secretary-General and his staff have either assumed, or been forced to assume, political responsibilities and powers of decision beyond what was anticipated at the time the UN Charter was written. With this development of the political role of the Secretariat, the consequent increased interest of the Soviet Union and its allies in the structure and composition of the organ, and the growing influence of the new and developing nations in the UN, demands have been made in respect to the recruitment and employment of personnel that directly or indirectly challenge the concept of an independent international career service.

Insistence that imbalances in the geographical distribution of staff be quickly remedied have led to the subordination of superior personal qualifications to nationality in the making of new appointments and to the large-scale use of fixed-term appointments, often for excessively short periods, in circumstances where the practice cannot be justified as the only means of obtaining the services of the best qualified people. As a result, excessively heavy burdens have been placed on the permanent staff, there has been a serious decline in efficiency in many areas, and the morale of the permanent staff has suffered from the substantial reduction of promotion opportunities.

Other considerations of a more basic nature also limit the application of the concept of an international career service. Conditions of living, particularly in the New York metropolitan area, are not satisfactory for many people from the diverse cultures represented in the UN. As a consequence some of the best qualified people have not been interested in making the commit-

ment of living in a foreign environment that permanent appointment implies. Moreover, the expansion of UN activities, particularly in the economic and social fields, has created the need for
specialized experts at posts that normally cannot be filled by
promotion and can only be satisfactorily filled by bringing in
persons on fixed-term appointments who will at the end of their
period of service be able to return to their original work. The
increasing need for recruitment from the outside and on fixed-
term appointments at higher levels in order to get the level of
competence desired obviously limits the possibilities of applying
the career principle even under the most favorable political conditions.

Once an equitable geographical distribution within the UN
Secretariat has been attained within the framework of the flexible 1963 formula, it should be possible to place primary emphasis on efficiency, competence, and integrity in the recruitment
and employment of personnel for the UN Secretariat and to
strengthen the career service as an indispensable element of continuity and commitment in the Organization. The conditions
under which an international administrative service is organized
and operates are different from those of a national administrative
service. Consequently, the same personnel principles cannot be
applied without modification. International organization, in the
form of the UN, is comparatively new and undeveloped as a
form of universal social control. It provides a fragile framework
for an administrative system and limited protection against the
buffetings of political pressures, conflicts, and ambitions. And
yet the success of the UN in the discharge of its varied and
increasingly important responsibilities depends upon the quality
of the Secretariat and the extent to which its members approach
in their technical competence, integrity, and devotion to the
UN the standards of a professional service.

By Theodor Meron

ADMINISTRATIVE AND BUDGETARY

COORDINATION BY THE

GENERAL ASSEMBLY

The United Nations system is a multifunctional set of organizations that, in the economic and social domain, now embrace a bewildering variety of complex tasks. Today the member states of the UN are not only required to contribute to the gradually increasing, regular annual budget of the UN, which is assessed by the General Assembly, but also to the regular budgets of the specialized agencies. In addition, they are exhorted to make contributions to several voluntary programs of the UN and the specialized agencies. In 1965 the expenditures of all UN agencies —not counting major peace-keeping operations—ran well above $400 million. Governments, therefore, have shown a growing concern about the budgetary trends of the UN system and have sought to improve its over-all administration.

All decisions on UN program matters involve administrative and budgetary considerations. To insure efficiency and the best economic utilization of the available resources, there must be a continuing process of coordination with respect to budget terminology and budget presentation, financial regulations, systems of personnel and exchange of personnel opportunities, the planning of conferences and meetings, and other matters within the UN system. All this requires the development of proper parliamentary procedures within and between the organs of the UN as well as their dependent or related agencies.

The United Nations and the Specialized Agencies

The basic pattern of relations between the UN and the specialized agencies is set by the UN Charter. Under Article 57 of the Charter, the specialized agencies, that is, agencies "established by inter-governmental agreement and having wide international responsibilities, as defined in their basic instruments, in economic, social, cultural, educational, health, and related fields" were to be brought into relationship with the UN. Article 63 provides that ECOSOC may enter into agreements with the various specialized agencies and define the terms on which the agency concerned shall be brought into relationship with the UN. Such agreements are subject to approval by the General Assembly. ECOSOC, moreover, may coordinate the activities of the specialized agencies "through consultation and recommendations" to such agencies and through recommendations to the General Assembly and the members of the UN. ECOSOC may also take appropriate steps to obtain regular reports from the agencies and may make arrangements with them to obtain reports on the steps taken to give effect to the recommendations of ECOSOC and of the General Assembly (Article 64), as well as make arrangements for representatives of the agencies and of ECOSOC to participate without vote in each other's deliberations (Article 70).

With regard to the General Assembly, Article 17 (3) provides that the General Assembly "shall consider and approve any financial and budgetary arrangements with the specialized agencies referred to in Article 57 and shall examine the administrative budgets of such specialized agencies with a view to making recommendations to the agencies concerned." Indeed, the UN was expected to make recommendations for the coordination of the policies and activities of the specialized agencies (Article 58), a responsibility vested in the General Assembly and, under its authority, in ECOSOC (Article 60).

The basic constitutional instruments of the specialized agencies provide for a general conference of all members, for a governing body of limited membership, and for an international secretariat under an executive head. In order to ensure the effective implementation of the agreements between the specialized agencies and the UN under Article 57, to facilitate the accommodation of any matters falling outside the area of such agreements, and to make recommendations regarding the improvement of relations between the UN and the specialized agencies, the Secretary-General of the UN established, in accordance with ECOSOC resolution 13 (III) of 21 September 1946, ACC, which is a standing committee consisting of himself, as Chairman, and the executive heads of the specialized agencies.

A realistic approach to the problem of coordination within the UN family of organizations, whether administrative, budgetary, or in program matters, must necessarily take into account the essential autonomy of the specialized agencies and IAEA in their respective fields of activity vis-à-vis each other and vis-à-vis the UN. Their autonomy indicates that any coordination must be of a horizontal consultative-persuasive nature and not a vertical *diktat*. This situation is further complicated by the fact that in the UN itself, as well as within the specialized agencies and the IAEA, there are a number of autonomous or semiautonomous legislative and executive organs. What is therefore required is not only coordination between the various organizations of the UN family, but also, and foremost, coordination within each organization. Intraorganizational and interorganizational coordination is urgent since the organizations belonging to the UN family often share the same objectives with respect to the advancement of international economic, social, cultural, health,

and human rights standards, as enumerated in Article 55 of the
UN Charter.

Responsibilities for Coordination in the United Nations

In its first report to ECOSOC, ACC explained that coordination was necessary in order to achieve "maximum efficiency"
and avoid "duplication and overlapping of activities." [1] This
involves, of course, the optimum utilization of the limited resources available for the advancement of the common objectives
of the UN family of organizations.

Later in 1947 the Secretary-General explained [2] the parliamentary implications of the provisions of the UN Charter dealing with administrative and budgetary coordination of the Organization and the specialized agencies as follows: Coordination
of program activities and the avoidance of duplication of functions are the responsibility of ECOSOC, which is assisted by
the regular reports of the agencies, provided for in Article 64
of the Charter. In administrative and budgetary matters, the
main procedure for coordination is the submission under Article 17 (3) of the administrative budgets of the agencies to the
General Assembly, which has delegated its function of review,
in the first instance, to ACABQ, whose twelve members are
chosen by the General Assembly on the basis of broad geographical representation and personal qualifications for three-year
terms.

The reports of the specialized agencies and of ACC are submitted to ECOSOC, which reports, in turn, to the General Assembly, whose General Committee refers such ECOSOC reports, as the need may be, to the Second (Economic and
Financial) Committee, or to the Third (Social, Humanitarian
and Cultural) Committee, or directly to the Plenary session.
Under the rules of procedure of the General Assembly the

[1] E/287, 26 February 1947.
[2] A/394/Rev. 1, 27 September 1947, para. 17.

main committees submit their recommendations to the Plenary session.* The administrative budgets of the specialized agencies, however, are communicated directly to the General Assembly and the General Committee refers them for consideration and report to the Fifth (Administrative and Budgetary) Committee of the General Assembly, which is assisted by ACABQ.

A division of responsibilities, therefore, exists between ECOSOC and the General Assembly and among the main committees of the General Assembly with regard to the consideration both of program matters and of administrative and budgetary matters. This division exists not only in matters concerning both the UN and the specialized agencies but also in the economic and social activities of the UN itself: their substantive aspects are considered by the Second or the Third Committee of the General Assembly, while their administrative and budgetary implications are studied by the Fifth Committee. This division of responsibilities has always been a major problem. Although the primary responsibility for the coordination of programs belongs to ECOSOC and the task of interorganizational coordination with regard to administrative and budgetary questions is reserved to the General Assembly, program matters and administrative and budgetary matters are—as pointed out by the Chairman of ACABQ at the 809th meeting of the Fifth Committee (fifteenth session of the General Assembly)—"two different aspects [that] go hand in hand. They are the two sides of the same coin and cannot be considered—must less coordinated—in complete isolation." [3]

* NOTE: During the twentieth session of the General Assembly, on the proposal of the Israel representative, the Fifth Committee expressed the hope that at future sessions the chapter of the annual report of ECOSOC entitled "Questions of co-ordination and relations with specialized agencies" would be referred to the Filfth Committee rather than directly ot the Plenary session. It was understood that a study of that chapter would enable the Committee to have a better understanding of the close relationship between substantive aspects of coordination and the budgetary and administrative aspects. A/C.5/L.863, 20 December 1965, para. 4.

[3] A/C.5/851, 8 December 1960, para. 3.

*Relationship Agreements between the United Nations
and the Specialized Agencies*

Article 17 (3) of the Charter provides that "the General
Assembly shall consider and approve any financial and budgetary
arrangements with specialized agencies referred to in Article
57 and shall examine the administrative budgets of such specialized agencies with a view to making recommendations to the
agencies concerned." As pointed out in the *Report* by the
Executive Committee to the Preparatory Commission of the
UN, "the first part of paragraph 3 of Article 17 envisages varying degrees of relationship, from complete financial integration
downwards, and the second part is conceived as the minimum
degree of relationship on the budgetary and financial side which
should be included in the agreements with the Specialized
Agencies." [4] The *Report* referred, of course, to the possibility
of attaining one consolidated budget for the UN and the
specialized agencies, to be voted upon by the General Assembly,
as the maximum degree of financial and administrative relationship and to the submission of the agencies' administrative budgets to the General Assembly for examination and recommendations as the minimum degree of relationship.

In pursuance of Article 57 of the Charter, so-called "relation-
ship" agreements were signed between the UN and ILO, FAO,
UNESCO, ICAO, WHO, IBRD,[5] IMF, UPU, ITU, WMO,
IMCO, and IAEA.[6] In addition, the UN and the contracting

[4] PC/EX/113/Rev. 1, 12 November 1945, Chapter VIII, para. 27.

[5] See agreements between the UN and the specialized agencies and IAEA,
ST/SG/14, 1961, as well as the agreements regarding the relations between
(*a*) the UN and IDA and (*b*) the UN and IFC.

[6] Although IAEA cannot be formally regarded as a specialized agency,
when its annual budget was first transmitted to the General Assembly in 1958,
the Assembly decided that the budget would be considered in connection with
the agenda item "Administrative and Budgetary Coordination between the
UN and the Specialized Agencies." The General Assembly further decided
that the normal procedures for review, within the UN, of the specialized
agencies' budgets would be applied in the case of the budget of IAEA. See
A/4016, 1 December 1958, para. 2. In general, IAEA coordinates its administrative arrangements with the UN much in the same way as the specialized
agencies.

parties to GATT cooperate through the GATT Secretariat, which was originally set up to serve as the Secretariat of the Interim Commission of the International Trade Organization and through the consultative machinery of ACC.

The relationship agreements deal with such matters as recognition of the agencies' status; reciprocal representation; reciprocal right to propose agenda items; the making of recommendations by the UN; the exchange of information and documentation and the submission of reports; assistance to the UN; personnel, statistical, administrative, and technical services; budgetary and financial arrangements, and so forth.[7]

Of particular interest are the provisions in the relationship agreements regarding personnel and budgetary and financial arrangements. The agreements generally recognize the desirability of developing a single unified international civil service and to that end provide for developing common personnel standards and common standards in conditions of employment, so as to avoid competition in recruitment and to facilitate the interchange of personnel. The agreements with ITU, UPU, WMO, and IAEA provide for the development of common personnel standards but do not refer to the eventual unification of the international civil service, whereas the agreements with IBRD and IMF provide only for consultations with the UN on personnel and administrative matters of mutual interest. With regard to budgetary and financial arrangements, the relationship agreements generally provide that the agencies should consult with the UN in the preparation of their budgets, transmit them to the UN General Assembly for examination and recommendations, and conform to standard practices and forms recommended by the UN.

A number of relationship agreements provide for consultations concerning the desirability of making appropriate arrangements

---

[7] See the useful "Summary of Internal Secretariat Studies of Constitutional Questions relating to Agencies within the Framework of the United Nations." A/C.1/758, 15 November 1954.

for the inclusion of the budget of the agency in a general budget of the UN. Such arrangements were to be defined in supplementary agreements.[8] The relationship agreement between the UN and IAEA provides merely for the transmittal by the agency of its annual budgets to the UN "for such recommendations as the General Assembly may wish to make on the administrative aspects thereof," and the agreements with ITU and UPU provide only for the transmittal of their budgets to the General Assembly, which can make recommendations thereon. The agreements with IBRD and IMF contain no provisions regarding the transmittal of their budgets, consultations to be held thereon, or the need to conform to standard practices recommended by the UN but merely provide for consultations to be held from time to time regarding personnel and administrative matters of mutual interest. While IBRD accepts that it furnish the UN with copies of its annual reports and of its quarterly financial statements, the UN agrees that, in the interpretation of Article 17 (3) of the Charter, it would take into consideration that IBRD does not rely for its annual budget upon contributions from its members and that it enjoys full autonomy in deciding the form and the content of its budget.

National Coordination

Most of the difficulties inherent in the problems of coordination could find a practical solution if the governments of the member states of the UN would succeed in coordinating the activities of their representatives in the various international organizations. Proper national governmental coordination would permit the achievement of some rational consistency between the various main committees of the General Assembly and between the latter and ECOSOC but would also strengthen consistency and coordination in administrative and budgetary

[8] See, for example, article XIV (2) of the Agreement between the UN and ILO.

matters between the UN and the specialized agencies, particularly as regards budgetary and personnel policies. For example, proper national coordination would make it possible to achieve rapidly a common system of salaries, allowances, and related benefits in the various organizations.

The various organizations constituting the UN family have essentially the same membership, the differences in membership among them being of little consequence. If the representatives of member states would pursue the same policies in the different legislative bodies of the UN family of organizations, consistency would be achieved. It has therefore always been recognized that it is essential that the representatives of a government in the various organizations speak with a single voice and take mutually consistent positions. As early as its second session, the General Assembly called upon the member states to take measures to ensure, on the national level, a coordinated policy of their delegations to the UN and to the different specialized agencies in order that full cooperation may be achieved between the Organization and the agencies.[9] The importance of national coordination had been reiterated by ECOSOC in such resolutions as 283 (X) of 8 February 1950; 590 A II (XX) of 5 August 1955; 630 A II (XXII) of 9 August 1956; and 694 B I (XXVI) of 31 July 1958. Special studies have been prepared by international organizations with the object of facilitating national coordination. In 1948, UNESCO and the International Institute of Administrative Sciences undertook a joint study of the administrative measures taken by governments for their participation in international organizations, and this resulted in the publication in 1951 of a report entitled "National Administration and International Organization, a Comparative Survey of Fourteen Countries." Pursuant to the ECOSOC resolution 630 A II (XXII) of 9 August 1956, the Secretary-General of the UN submitted to the twenty-sixth session of ECOSOC a compre-

[9] GA Resolution 125 (II), 20 November 1947.

hensive report based on information furnished by the governments of member states. This report on "Co-ordination on the National Level" [10] described means and methods for coordinating national policies with respect to the economic and social activities of the UN family, including the question of arrangements for representation at conferences and meetings. Time and again the importance of national coordination has been stressed at the meetings of the General Assembly, of ECOSOC, and of the various inter-secretariat bodies such as ACC. Despite some progress, the situation in this field is far from satisfactory. Were full national coordination achieved, it would not be difficult to find suitable procedures and machinery for ensuring interorgan and interorganizational coordination in administrative and budgetary matters. Without decisive national coordination, however, no machinery or procedures can give fully satisfactory results.

A Consolidated Budget

One procedure that could have contributed greatly to the solution of the problems of interorganizational coordination would have been the adoption of a consolidated budget for the UN and the specialized agencies. The *Report* by the Executive Committee to the Preparatory Commission of the UN mentioned the advantages of a consolidated budget that would enable the members of the UN to consider and vote at one time and in one place the budget of the Organization and of the agencies within the consolidated system and that would bring about a simplification of the complicated process of budget examination. The Committee noted that the League of Nations and ILO had had a similar financial arrangement, which had worked satisfactorily, but recognized the principal difficulties involved in realizing a consolidated budget: (1) the specialized agencies would have to adopt constitutional amendments empowering

[10] E/3107, 6 May 1958.

the General Assembly to vote their budgets; (2) the problem of the difference in membership between the UN and the specialized agencies would have to be solved. This problem could be dealt with by establishing a procedure whereby, initially, the budget section relating to each agency would be voted in the Budgetary Committee only by the states which are members of that agency. On the other hand, arrangements would have to be made to enable states which are not members of the UN to participate in the consideration of the budgets of the agencies to which they belong. Subsequently, the consolidated budget could be finally approved in a General Assembly plenary meeting. Such voting arrangements had proved satisfactory in the case of the consolidated League of Nations–ILO budget.[11]

At the time of the negotiation of the relationship agreements between the UN and the agencies, scepticism prevailed regarding the possibility of attaining a consolidated budget. The specialized agencies, whose full autonomy was recognized in their constitutions and in the system of the Charter, were wary of relinquishing one of the principal attributes of their autonomy. Consequently, as mentioned before, no relationship agreement provided for the immediate adoption of a consolidated budget. While the agreements with FAO and UNESCO provided for consultations "concerning appropriate arrangements for the inclusion of the budget of the Organization within a general budget of the United Nations," the agreements with ILO, ICAO, WHO, WMO, and IMCO provided only for consultations "concerning the desirability of making appropriate arrangements for the inclusion of the budget of the Organization within a general budget of the United Nations." The agreement with IAEA does not mention the possibility of adopting a consolidated budget, nor, of course, do the agreements with IBRD and IMF.

The possibility of adopting a consolidated budget was under

[11] PC/EX/113/Rev. 1, 12 November 1945, Chapter VIII, paras. 30–32.

active consideration by ACC in 1948–49. The technical aspects
of the question were considered by ACC's Consultative Committee on Budgetary and Financial Arrangements (subsequently
CCAQ). This active consideration followed the adoption by
the General Assembly of resolution 81 (I) of 14 December 1946,
whereby the Secretary-General was requested to explore, in
consultation with ACABQ, possible arrangements by which the
budgets of the specialized agencies might be presented to the
General Assembly for approval. In a report submitted to the
agencies in January, 1948, on the basis of replies received from
ILO, FAO, UNESCO, ICAO, the WHO Interim Commission,
and UPU, the Consultative Committee on Budgetary and Financial Arrangements discussed the technical problems involved,
assuming that no changes would be made in the structure of
the organizations. Thus, the legislative body of each agency
would have to approve its own budget prior to its approval by
the General Assembly. The Consultative Committee interpreted the General Assembly resolution as referring to total
budgets and not only to administrative budgets. The technical
problems that would arise would include: the coordination of
the budget calendars of the various agencies; the coordination
of the "financial year" of the various agencies; the relationship
of time of preparation of the budget to the financial year to
which it applies; uniformity in budget presentation; and common financial practices.[12] In its report of 20 July 1948, ACC
summed up the constitutional problems as follows: To achieve
a consolidated budget, it would be necessary to ensure (*a*) the
constitutional transfer of budget-making powers from the con-
stituent assemblies to the General Assembly of the UN, and
(*b*) changes in the character of the delegations to the General
Assembly. It would, moreover, be necessary to lengthen the sessions of the General Assembly, enabling it to perform at one
time and place the budgetary tasks now performed by the finan-

[12] E/614, Annex E, 29 January 1948.

cial committees, governing bodies, and conferences of the various individual agencies. Even if these policy questions were solved, complicated technical problems would remain, as pointed out by the Consultative Committee. ACC reiterated the view that an eventual consolidation of the budgets would require the creation of executive and legislative conditions for approving the budgets comparable to those applicable to a national government. Further steps towards a more integrated budgetary system could only be taken by government representatives in the UN and, parallelly, in the different bodies of the agencies.[13] In the view of ACC, a consolidated budget was not immediately practicable and the aim of such a budget—over-all economy and efficiency—should be obtained by other machinery. Collective efforts might more profitably be directed to developing alternative methods of coordination, such as the improvement of the process of agency budget examination by the General Assembly.

The question of a consolidated budget has often been raised in the Fifth Committee and in ACABQ. During the sixth session of the General Assembly, the Joint Second and Third Committee, meeting jointly with the Fifth Committee, considered a Norwegian draft resolution[14] that would have required the Secretary-General to report, through ACABQ, to the seventh session of the General Assembly, on the constitutional and practical problems connected with the adoption of a consolidated budget. The discussion revealed, however, that the time was not yet ripe for action, whereupon the draft resolution was withdrawn. The consolidated budget idea has continued to be raised from time to time. Thus, during the fifteenth session of the General Assembly hope was expressed in the Fifth Committee that the question could be considered before long. A consolidated budget, it was pointed out, would obviously facilitate the application of a rational scale of priorities to all the programs

---

[13] E/846, 8 February 1949.
[14] A/C.2&3/L.48–A/C.5/L.139, 14 December 1951.

of the organizations as well as the development of a concerted approach. But again the conclusion was that the adoption of a consolidated budget was not practicable and that means for co-ordination must be found without interfering with the constitutions of the various organizations.[15]

While a consolidated budget could be a major instrument for concerted action, it would not be realistic to expect that it could be achieved in the political circumstances prevailing today in the UN and in the agencies. As long as the autonomy of the agencies is maintained—and this is the reality of today—effective machinery for coordination must be found without a consolidated budget.

Outline of the Machinery for Coordination

The following is the main outline of the existing coordination machinery (see Chart II):

(*a*) Day-to-day administrative inter-secretariat consultations, including in particular the activities of the ECOSOC secretariat and those of the Office of the Deputy Under-Secretary—Personal Representative of the Secretary-General to the specialized agencies.

(*b*) The formal inter-secretariat consultative machinery of ACC with its Preparatory Committee and other subsidiary bodies (see their list in A/C.5/L.812, 27 November 1963, and their terms of reference in E/3368, Annex 3, 10 May 1960.)

(*c*) In the program field on the legislative level, the coordination machinery comprises ECOSOC and its various subsidiary bodies (see list in A/C.5/L.812). It may be observed, in passing, that there has been some mushrooming of these bodies, which brought the Secretary-General to observe at the 1,274th meeting of ECOSOC, on 9 July 1963, that, "the bodies recently concerned with the inter-dependent and largely over-lapping ques-

[15] A/4662, 16 December 1960, para. 6.

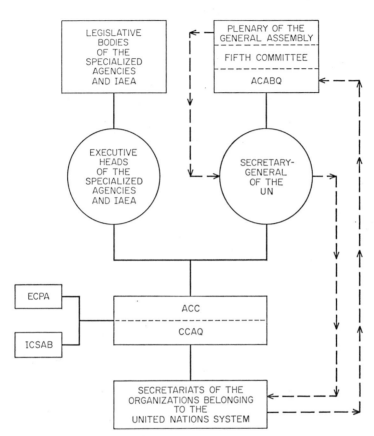

- - - - - administrative budgets of the agencies
———— channels of reporting and normal working relationships

Chart II. Principal Machinery for Administrative and Budgetary Coordination in the United Nations System

(*Not including the machinery relating to ECOSOC and to extra-budgetary programs*)

tions of organization and coordination in different fields had come to constitute a veritable labyrinth." [16]

Particularly concerned with administrative and budgetary co-ordination are the following:

(*a*) Within the framework of the ACC consultative ma-chinery, the CCAQ; the Expert Committee on Post Adjust-ments; and, in a rather special status, ICSAB.[17]

(*b*) On the legislative level, the Fifth Committee of the Gen-eral Assembly, as a general intergovernmental committee, and ACABQ, as an expert committee.

The foregoing description of the coordination machinery is incomplete, but it contains the principal elements, as indicated in Chart II.

The Fifth Committee of the General Assembly

The Fifth Committee of the General Assembly performs im-portant coordinating functions in connection with the examina-tion of the budget estimates, the budgetary implications of var-ious proposals, and other administrative and budgetary items on its agenda. Although in recent years the attention of the repre-sentatives on the Fifth Committee has been largely focused on the major political problems of peace-keeping operations and the so-called "geographical distribution" of the staff of the Sec-retariat, the Fifth Committee has, on the whole, performed its functions as a coordinating body, particularly with respect to the administrative activities of the Secretariat.

The two principal problems facing the Fifth Committee in the performance of its coordinating functions are the following:

(*a*) The difficulty of controlling the expenditure occasioned by decisions of the various Councils, Commissions, and Com-mittees of the UN, including such decisions of the General As-sembly as are taken upon recommendations of other main com-mittees.

[16] E/SR.1274, 9 July 1963, para. 17.
[17] A/C.5/L.804, 11 November 1963.

(*b*) The principle that the General Assembly, acting on the recommendations of the Fifth Committee, has exclusive administrative and budgetary responsibility has not been maintained with regard to economic and social programs financed from extrabudgetary funds. This is true as regards both UN and interagency programs. The Fifth Committee has, normally, little to do with the administrative and financial aspects of such programs, except review their audit reports. As pointed out by ACABQ in its "Report on Administrative and Budgetary Coordination between the United Nations and the Specialized Agencies," with particular reference to EPTA,[18] there has been a dispersion of the legislative direction of the various extrabudgetary programs. Although a subsidiary body of ECOSOC, TAC was responsible—subject only to the broad authority of the General Assembly—for both the substantive and the administrative and budgetary control of EPTA, and while ECOSOC assures program coordination regarding the various activities in social and economic fields—whether extrabudgetary or financed under the regular budget—"a central point of coordination, at the intergovernmental level, is lacking on the administrative and financial side."

Control of Financial Obligations Occasioned by Legislative Decisions

It is clear that the ability of the Fifth Committee to coordinate—on the administrative and budgetary level—the activities of the Organization through the process of budget examination depends upon the control it has over expenditures arising from decisions of other organs. The problem of expenditure occasioned by decisions of bodies other than the General Assembly is not an unexpected one. Already the Advisory Group of Experts on Administrative, Personnel and Budgetary Questions,

[18] A/4172, 25 August 1959, para. 5. The question of the consolidation of the Special Fund and EPTA in a United Nations Development Programme will not be considered here.

observed in its *Second Report* of October, 1946,[19] that under
"the General Provisions of the Charter of the United Nations
and of certain specific decisions of the General Assembly, the
various Councils, Commissions and Committees are given powers
to undertake investigations, surveys and studies. As a result,
these bodies take decisions . . . which have important budgetary consequences." The Committee observed that there was
a lack of specific budgetary limitations on the activities of the
various organs and that it would be desirable "that systems
should be devised to enable priorities to be established with due
regard for budgetary implications."[20] Similarly, ACABQ noted
in its "Report on the Budget Estimates of the United Nations
for 1948,"[21] that the

Secretariat is obviously placed in an intolerable position if administrative and budgetary committees call it to task over increasing
expenditures while other committees can increase the work load
with little or no restraint. The Committee has no doubt that a great
weakness in the UN financial system is the fact that projects can
be approved by bodies other than the General Assembly, which is
the only appropriating authority.[22]

In order to provide a measure of control over the decisions
taken by the Councils, by its main committees, and by other
committees, the General Assembly adopted, upon the recommendation of ACABQ, the financial regulations now numbered 13.1 and 13.2. These regulations concerning resolutions
involving expenditures provide as follows:

13.1: No council, commission or other competent body shall
take a decision involving expenditure unless it has before it a report
from the Secretary-General on the administrative and financial implications of the proposal.
13.2: Where, in the opinion of the Secretary-General, the pro-

[19] A/C.5/42, October 1946, para. 56.
[20] *Ibid.*
[21] A/336, 8 August 1947, GAOR, Second Session, Supplement No. 7.
[22] *Ibid.*, para. 26.

posed expenditure cannot be made from existing appropriations, it shall not be incurred until the General Assembly has made the necessary appropriations, unless the Secretary-General certifies that provision can be made under the conditions of the resolution of the General Assembly relating to unforeseen and extraordinary expenses. (ST/SGB/Financial Rules/1.1960).

During its Second Session, the General Assembly also adopted the provisional rule of procedure 142,[23] which is now numbered rule 154:

No resolution involving expenditure shall be recommended by a committee for approval by the General Assembly unless it is accompanied by an estimate of expenditures prepared by the Secretary-General. No resolution in respect of which expenditures are anticipated by the Secretary-General shall be voted by the General Assembly until the Administrative and Budgetary Committee has had an opportunity of stating the effect of the proposal upon the budget estimates of the United Nations.[24]

The related rule 155 of the Rules of Procedure requires the Secretary-General to keep all committees informed of the detailed estimated cost of all resolutions that have been recommended by them for General Assembly approval.* ECOSOC has a rule of procedure of its own concerning estimates of expenditure (rule 34) which reads as follows:

1. The Secretary-General shall circulate to the Council for its information at the beginning of its session immediately preceding the regular session of the General Assembly, an analysis, by fields of activity and by budget sections, of the estimated cost for the following financial year of the economic and social activities of the United Nations, prepared as an annex to his budget estimates.

[23] See GA Resolution 173 (II) of 17 November 1947, A/520, 12 December 1947, and rule 152 in A/520, Rev./1, 1 January 1950.
[24] A/520/Rev. 7, June 1964.
* NOTE: While Rule 154 applies to the General Assembly, Financial Regulations 13.1 and 13.2 apply similarly to other UN organs. Similar provisions concerning financial implications are to be found in the Rules of Procedure of the Trusteeship Council, the Functional Commissions of ECOSOC, and the Regional Economic Commissions, but not in the Provisional Rules of Procedure of the Security Council.

2. Before a proposal which involves expenditure from United Nations funds is approved by the Council or by any of its committees, the Secretary-General shall prepare and circulate to members . . . a separate estimate of the cost involved in each such proposal. . . . The President of the Council and the chairmen of committees shall draw the attention of members to these estimates and invite discussions on them when the proposal is considered by the Council or by a committee.

3. The Council shall take into account the estimates referred to in paragraph 2 before adopting any proposal involving expenditure from United Nations funds. If the proposal is adopted, the Council shall indicate, whenever appropriate, the priority or degree of urgency which it attaches to the projects and, as the case may be, which current projects may be deferred, modified or eliminated to ensure that the economic and social work of the United Nations and the specialized agencies will be carried on most effectively.

4. Whenever the Council wishes to recommend, in cases of exceptional urgency, that work for which no financial provision exists be started before the next regular session of the General Assembly, it shall include a specific indication to that effect to the Secretary-General in the resolution approving the proposal.[25]

The rules of procedure and the financial regulations referred to above, while contributing somewhat to the improvement of the situation, have not entirely achieved their basic objective. ECOSOC and the two main committees of the General Assembly concerned with the economic and social activities of the Organization have neither established a meaningful order of priorities nor given more than cursory attention to the above rules and regulations. Indeed, the interest and the know-how in administrative and budgetary questions shown by ECOSOC and by the Second and Third Committees of the General Assembly have been limited. The reports on the financial implications of draft resolutions submitted by the Secretary-General to the main committees, or to other organs of the General Assembly, under rule 155 and under the financial regulations have been of

[25] E/3063, March 1958.

necessity cautious statements of a technical or bookkeeping nature. Whereas related reports of ACABQ have usually been candid in the scope of their observations, the reports on financial implications submitted by the Fifth Committee to the plenary session of the General Assembly under rule 154 have tended to be of a cautious technical-informative nature, for the Fifth Committee is only required to state the effect of the proposal upon the budget estimates of the UN and is therefore reluctant to include in this type of report recommendations adverse to the policy decision made by another organ. With respect to the main budget estimates of the UN, however, which the Fifth Committee receives for consideration and recommendation, the Committee has been more willing to recommend to the Plenary session changes in the estimates, corresponding to its budgetary and administrative views, especially if such changes have been suggested by ACABQ.

In his foreword to the budget estimates for the financial year 1966, the Secretary-General referred to the recent intensification of the trend to take, in the subsidiary bodies of ECOSOC and of the General Assembly, decisions involving financial commitments that did not have the prior approval of the General Assembly and in a statement made at the 1,066th meeting of the Fifth Committee, the Chairman of ACABQ observed that this trend was found in organs that are somewhat isolated within the totality of the activities of the Organization and probably insufficiently aware of the relative influence the decisions they take may have on the over-all budget.[26] The Chairman further suggested that the representatives of the Secretary-General in the subsidiary organs of the United Nations, and the Committee Secretaries should play a more positive role than hitherto in bringing administrative and financial rules to the attention of the members of those organs before decisions were taken and that the Chairman of the Fifth Committee should write a letter to the

[26] A/C/5/1038, 11 October 1965, p. 8.

President of the General Assembly drawing his attention to Financial Regulation 13.1 and Rule 154. (This suggestion was followed. A/BUR/164, 3 November 1965. See similarly A/C.5/ 927, 10 October 1962.)

The United Nations Budget Cycle

The ability of the Fifth Committee to coordinate—on the administrative and budgetary level—the activities of the Organization through the process of budget examination is adversely affected by the timing of the submission of budget estimates. This is the problem of the so-called budget cycle, to which ACABQ has devoted particular attention in its "Report on the Budget Estimates of the Organization for 1964." [27] ACABQ pointed out that in a given year, the various commissions and committees of ECOSOC draw up their programs for the following year piecemeal. These programs are considered by ECOSOC only in July. Since the initial budget estimates of the Organization are submitted to ACABQ in May–June, it follows that an important part of the over-all program cannot be forecast at that time. As a result, the Secretary-General must submit revised estimates later in the year. Even these revised estimates are not final, because additional activities, financed initially under the Resolution relating to Unforeseen and Extraordinary Expenses are submitted to the General Assembly as supplementary estimates at the end of the year.

The uncertainty of the budget cycle is considerable. In 1962, apart from supplementary estimates, some $8.5 million were added to the budget, between the month of July, when ACABQ completed its examination of the budget estimates for 1963, and the month of December, when the General Assembly approved the appropriations, as a result, in part, of decisions taken by the General Assembly itself and, in part, of decisions taken by ECOSOC at its summer session. (See Table III.) Member gov-

[27] A/5507, August 1963.

TABLE III

UNITED NATIONS (REGULAR) BUDGET CYCLE

(In Dollars)

	1960	1961	1962	1963	1964
Secretary-General's initial estimates	61,863,200	67,453,750	73,533,500	86,649,500	96,611,350
Advisory Committee's recommendation	61,213,300	66,510,900	72,402,850	84,683,450	95,498,780
Appropriation approved by General Assembly following submission by Secretary-General of revised estimates[a]	63,149,700	72,969,300	82,144,740	93,911,050	101,327,600
Supplementary estimates[b]	2,585,200	(1,320,000)*	3,673,480	(1,034,500)*	1,621,377
Total appropriation	65,734,900	71,649,300	85,818,220	92,876,550	102,948,977

* Figures in parentheses indicate decrease.

[a] Between the time of the preparation of the original estimates and the time of their consideration by the General Assembly, new decisions entailing either additional expenditure and/or additional income are often taken by one or more of the organs of the UN, including ECOSOC and committees of the General Assembly. In each such case, revised estimates are prepared in the same way as the original estimates and are submitted to the General Assembly, which, after consideration and report by the Advisory Committee, eventually consolidates the amounts into a single appropriation resolution for the ensuing year.

[b] In addition to approving the budget estimates for the ensuing year, the General Assembly at its regular annual session may be required to consider estimates involving modifications to the appropriations for the current year. Such supplementary estimates are made necessary by the fact that, after the budget has been voted and during the financial year to which it relates, unforeseen and extraordinary expenses may arise which are incurred under the annual General Assembly resolution on unforeseen and extraordinary expenses. The Secretary-General is required to submit supplementary budget estimates at the subsequent session of the General Assembly to cover the expenses incurred. The supplementary estimates, as approved, are consolidated with the amounts approved at the previous session resulting in new appropriation figures for particular sections of the budget.

ernments were thus unable to obtain a complete picture of the program and budget for the following year and to determine the extent of the financial contributions they would be required to make.

ACABQ has stressed that the entire program of work of the Organization should be completed in time for its inclusion in the main budget estimates, so that the budget can coherently be reviewed by member governments, ACABQ, and the General Assembly. ACABQ has also recommended that the General Assembly and the various councils, commissions, and committees consider seriously the problem of the budget cycle and that ECOSOC, in particular, review its entire program cycle, as well as the schedule of meetings of its subsidiary organs, with a view to adopting the necessary measures to ensure that the whole program in the economic and social field for a given year is drawn up in time for its inclusion in the main budget estimates.

In this context the desirable objective is to ensure, by long-term planning and the establishment of priorities, that the program of all foreseeable activities for any given year is drawn up in time for inclusion in the main budget estimates. The present situation could be somewhat improved by considering the work program of ECOSOC earlier in the year. The General Assembly, in resolution 1987 (XVIII) of 17 December 1963 on "Pattern of Conferences," requested ECOSOC to consider the possibility of advancing its first session each year to January and its summer session to May or early June.

This, however, is not a simple matter, and it would require changes in the schedules of meetings of the subsidiary organs of ECOSOC. Of course, it would be best if the work program of ECOSOC could be planned several years ahead. Indeed, ECOSOC, in resolution 1046 (XXXVII) of 15 August 1964 on the "Work Program of the United Nations in the Economic, Social and Human Rights Fields" requested the Secretary-General, in view of the divergency between the program and the budget calendars, to study the possibility of presenting the work program on a biennial basis. By resolution 1093 (XXXIX) of 31 July 1965, ECOSOC reaffirmed "the interest it attaches to the possibility of having a programme of work presented on a biennial basis and adjusted periodically to conform to the annual budgetary cycle of the United Nations."

Controlling New Financial Obligations

The General Assembly has attempted in the past to minimize the number of requests for additional appropriations submitted after the Secretary-General had circulated his annual main budget estimates. Thus, in resolution 1096 (XI) of 27 February 1957, the Assembly requested, on an experimental basis, for the financial year 1958, that requests for additional appropriations be limited to (1) those needed urgently in the interest of peace and security; (2) projects certified by the Secretary-General to have been urgent and unforeseen at the time of the preparation of the main budget estimates; (3) decisions of the three Councils, provided that appropriate requests were circulated to member governments not later than twenty-one days before the opening date of the General Assembly; and (4) those required to meet decisions of the General Assembly. This resolution, which left so many doors open for additional requests for appropriations, was not an effective one.

A different approach to limiting requests for appropriations was used by the General Assembly in resolution 1449 (XIV) of 5 December 1959. Instead of attempting to enumerate matters with respect to which additional appropriations could be requested, the General Assembly requested "all organs of the United Nations to consider ways and means whereby new projects might be deferred until suitable provision for them can be made by the Secretary-General in the main budget estimates for a subsequent financial year, unless they are of major or urgent importance or unless they can be accommodated within approved expenditure levels by the postponement of projects of relatively low priority." The failure of this resolution to achieve the desired object resulted from the inability of the programming organs to establish a meaningful order of priorities and their lack of interest in budgetary considerations. Something more than exhortations by the Fifth Committee of the General Assembly was obviously necessary.

Another approach was taken by the Fifth Committee during the seventeenth session of the General Assembly, when upon its recommendation, resolution 1797 (XVII) of 11 December 1962 on "Integrated Programme and Budget Policy" was adopted. ECOSOC was requested, by this resolution, to establish a framework of priorities for UN programs in the economic, social, and human rights fields, to review regularly the order of priorities, to give due, timely, and adequate consideration to the financial implications of its actions in the light of information provided by the Secretary-General, and to consider the comments of ACABQ concerning the administrative and financial aspects of activities in the above fields. This resolution was thought to "represent an acceptable first step towards establishing a procedure for concording the decisions of the Economic and Social Council and the Second and Third Committees, on the one hand, and those of the Fifth Committee and the Advisory Committee, on the other, and for presenting to the General Assembly a coherent and mutually complementary picture of the programme and budgetary problems." [28]

General Assembly resolution 1797 (XVII) of 11 December 1962 was due to the concern expressed by many delegates at the inconsistency between the decisions of policy-making bodies and those of the Fifth Committee and by the feeling that the financial obligations incurred by the Organization as a result of some of the decisions of the policy-making bodies were inap-

[28] A/5328, 4 December 1962, p. 2.

propriate. Could this situation be remedied by the resolution concerned? It may be worth while citing here a skeptical view, expressed by one delegate at the 949th meeting of the Fifth Committee on 15 November 1962:

Before the situation could be remedied, however, it must be properly defined. The situation was, in fact, simple: United Nations bodies could take decisions on matters within their competence which bound the hands of the Fifth Committee when it came to consider the impact of those decisions on the budget of the Organization. The Fifth Committee, which was responsible for keeping the Organization's finances on a sound footing, could neither originate decisions in other bodies nor change the substance of their decisions once they had been made. It was constantly being faced with a fait accompli and was now very understandably suffering from a sense of frustration at its inability to discharge its vital responsibilities.

The draft resolution was not intended as more than a first step towards remedying that situation. . . . It did not do more than call upon the Economic and Social Council to exercise restraint in taking decisions which had financial implications. It did not provide for any effective action, if the Council chose to disregard that admonition . . . some way of enforcing it should be envisaged; a ceiling might, for instance, be imposed on expenditure on economic and social activities. Otherwise, the draft resolution might not only be ineffective but positively dangerous. If the Committee made a request to the Council to modify its procedure, the Council's reaction might very well be to question the Committee's competence in such matters. It would, of course, be for the General Assembly itself to decide such a conflict of competence; but the situation in the meantime would be highly uncomfortable.[29]

The same delegate went on to say that if the Committee chose merely to appeal to policy-making bodies to keep their projects within reasonable limits, dictated by budgetary resources,

it must ask itself whether the draft resolution would enable it to achieve its purpose; he had very serious doubts on that point.

[29] Statement by the representative of Israel. See A/C.5/SR.949, 15 November 1962, paras. 6–7.

The Council was being requested to do something which appeared very simple, to devise a framework and to establish within that framework an order of priorities; but what was simple for a subsidiary body working in a limited field, such as the Social Commission, would be far from simple for a body like the Council, which would not only have to assign priorities to projects within a single field, but would also have to decide whether projects in one field should have precedence over those in another. It might well find it impossible to decide whether the economic or the social aspects of its work should have priority.[30]

In its resolution 1046(XXXVII) of 15 August 1964, ECOSOC underlined the necessity to proceed each year to a careful analysis of the United Nations work program in relation to its budgetary implications and encouraged the Secretary-General to proceed with the preparation of a work program for the Council together with adequate information on its budgetary implications in each major area. The Secretary-General presented to the Council, at its thirty-ninth session, a work program for 1965–1966 listing the functions of the Department of Economic and Social Affairs of the Secretariat, together with annex tables showing the United Nations resources allocated to each major area of work in the fields of economic, social, and human rights. (E/4070, 24 June 1965, and Add. 1, 30 June 1965.) In its report on the budget estimates for the financial year 1966, ACABQ commended this first attempt at providing the Council with a document setting forth the work program in relation to budgetary implications and expressed the hope that the program part would be further consolidated with the budgetary part, for such a consolidated presentation would facilitate the appreciation of resources available for certain activities, as well as the establishment of priorities. ACABQ also commended the Secretary-General for his intention to present to the Council not only a listing of the activities in the economic, social, and human rights fields arranged by organizational units of the Sec-

[30] *Ibid.,* para. 10.

retariat but also a listing following the functional classifications approved by ECOSOC for the Development Decade. The ACABQ considered that the budget format and system of budget presentation had an important role to play in the achievement of the aims of resolution 1797(XVII), 11 December 1962 (that is, an integrated program and budget policy), and felt that another system of budget presentation could relate programs to costs more clearly and that, if programs were described in a functional classification, a greater measure of comparability could be possible with the programs and budgets of the specialized agencies.

The General Assembly has also considered suggestions for a consolidated budget and program document to be drawn up annually by the Secretary-General that could link ECOSOC decisions to the budgetary process of the Assembly.

The possibility of the Fifth Committee exercising its authority by placing a ceiling on expenditure on economic and social projects, as suggested in the above-cited passage, appears to be an unlikely course of action. The question has been raised a number of times in the course of the discussions in the Fifth Committee, but it has never been considered acceptable.[31] With the present UN emphasis on development in the economic and social fields—which finds expression in the declaration of the Development Decade—the placing of such a ceiling would not be acceptable to the majority of the delegations in the General Assembly, as some representatives of developing countries have frequently indicated in the Fifth Committee with respect to the Secretary-General's policy of budgetary consolidation and containment in his financial estimates for 1964.*

[31] See, for example, A/2107, 1 February 1952, para. 12.

* NOTE: See similarly the Report of the Fifth Committee on the French proposal for the establishment of an *ad hoc* committee of experts to examine the finances of the UN and the specialized agencies (Committee of Fourteen). A/6152, 10 December 1965. Budget ceilings were, however, acceptable for particular sections of the budget, such as those falling under Part V (Technical Programmes).

An important attempt to provide for the necessary coordination between the General Assembly, as the appropriating organ of the Organization, on the one hand, and the three Councils, on the other, was made by Belgium as early as the second session of the General Assembly. A Belgian draft resolution presented to the Fifth Committee[32] noted that under the Charter the three Councils could make, in their respective provinces, decisions on activities involving expenditure for which the necessary credits had not previously been voted by the General Assembly and that the General Assembly could not thus exercise freely the powers conferred upon it under Article 17 (1) of the Charter. It proposed the establishment of a permanent work-planning committee of the United Nations, composed of representatives of the General Assembly, appointed on the recommendation of the Fifth Committee, and of representatives of the three Councils. The task of the Committee would have been to prepare, with the assistance of ACABQ and of the Secretary-General, a plan of work of the Organization and to establish an order of priority. Before taking any decision involving expenditure for which no credit had been provided, each Council would have been required to consult the Committee, which could recommend to the Secretary-General and ACABQ that the necessary advances be made from the Working Capital Fund.

During the discussion of the Belgian proposal in the Fifth Committee, however, concern was expressed lest the creation of a new body should interfere with the prerogatives of the General Assembly and of the Secretary-General, with the delegates fearful of the complication that might arise as a result of the creation of an additional body between the General Assembly and the Fifth Committee and between the latter and ACABQ. The whole matter was referred to ACABQ for study. In its report presented to the third session of the General Assembly,[33]

[32] A/C.5/179, 24 October 1947.
[33] A/534, April 1948.

ACABQ expressed the view that it was premature to establish additional formal machinery for work-planning within the UN or between the UN and the specialized agencies. It believed that, given proper national coordination, as requested in General Assembly resolution 125 (II) of 20 November 1957, ECOSOC, the Secretary-General, and ACABQ could cope with problems of coordination.

Association of the Fifth Committee with Programming Committees

In its "Report on the Budget Estimates for 1948," ACABQ suggested the establishment of a special mixed committee consisting of the representatives of the Second, Third, and Fifth Committees of the General Assembly, with the object of determining the priorities between the various programs and activities of the UN. ACABQ added that a scheme of priorities should be evolved to cover both the UN and the specialized agencies.[34] The Chairmen of the two substantive programming committees (the Second and the Third) and the Fifth Committee initiated a new procedure during the second session of the General Assembly designed to bring about a comprehensive consideration of both the substantive and the administrative-budgetary aspects of coordination with the specialized agencies.

By a letter dated 17 October 1947, the Chairmen of the Joint Second and Third Committee and of the Fifth Committee advised the President of the General Assembly that the Fifth Committee had before it a draft resolution on coordination in the budgetary field, while before the Joint Second and Third Committee there were draft resolutions on the subject of general relations and coordination with the specialized agencies. The letter pointed out further that "the subjects of those parts of these resolutions which deal with questions of programming and

[34] A/336, 8 August 1947, para. 27.

of priorities, and with budgetary and financial coordination, are interlocked, and it is clear that some form of joint consideration of them is necessary in order that a comprehensive and consistent resolution may be framed for the General Assembly." [35] After consultations, the Chairmen decided to propose to their Committees, subject to the approval of the President of the General Assembly, that a joint meeting be held in order to discuss the various draft resolutions with a view to presenting a consolidated draft resolution to the Plenary session. The proposed technique was that "each Member should select one representative for the joint meeting, which would thus consist of fifty-seven representatives, with their advisers; that the Chairmen of the Fifth Committee and of the Joint Second and Third Committees should preside over the joint meeting in a manner to be agreed between themselves; and that the rapporteurs of the Fifth Committee and of the Joint Second and Third Committee should act as joint rapporteurs." [36] The proposed procedure was approved by the President of the General Assembly in a letter dated 18 October 1947. He suggested that the joint report be submitted directly to the Plenary session.[37]

During the third session of the General Assembly, the same procedure was followed. In a note dated 15 October 1948, the Chairmen of the Joint Second and Third Committee and of the Fifth Committee observed that "the subject of co-ordination of programmes and activities of the Specialized Agencies, which is primarily the responsibility of the Economic and Social Council, is from its nature interlocked with the aspects of administrative and budgetary co-ordination which are within the sphere of the Advisory Committee . . . and the Fifth Committee"

[35] A/C.2 & 3/55, 17 October 1947; A/C.5/173, 17 October 1947.
[36] *Ibid.*
[37] GA Resolution 125 (II), 20 November 1947, which dealt with both substantive and administrative and budgetary coordination with the specialized agencies was a product of the joint consideration of the different and interlocked aspects of the problem during the second session of the General Assembly.

and proposed that the Joint Second and Third Committee, and the Fifth Committee consider jointly the several questions involving relations and coordination with the specialized agencies, in their administrative, budgetary and program aspects.[38] During the fourth, fifth and sixth sessions of the General Assembly, joint meetings of the Fifth Committee with the Second and the Third Committees were also held.[39] In the second part of the first session of the General Assembly, moreover, certain arrangements regarding the International Court of Justice at the Hague and the proposed agreement with the Carnegie Foundation were discussed by a joint Sub-Committee of the Fifth and Sixth (Legal) Committees, leading to resolutions 84 (I), 85 (I), and 86 (I), all of 11 December 1946, that were adopted on the joint reports.[40]

The procedure consisting of joint meetings of the Fifth Committee with the committees concerned with the substantive work in the economic and social fields was very important, for it enabled the Fifth Committee to be associated during the early phase of the decision-making process with the substantive aspects of the work of the Organization. It could thus introduce the applicable budgetary and administrative considerations as relevant factors in the discussion of the program of the work of the Organization and play more fully its role as the main legislative organ responsible for administrative and budgetary coordination. There was also particular value in the joint discussion of the reports of ECOSOC and the comprehensive consideration of both the program and the budgetary and administrative relations with the specialized agencies.

[38] A/C.2 & 3/72 and Corr. 1, 15 October 1948, paras. 2–3. See also the correspondence between the chairmen of the Second, Third, and Fifth Committees and the President of the General Assembly, A/C.2 & 3/78–A/C.5/244, 27 October 1948.

[39] Regarding the fourth session, see A/C.2 & 3/L.1, 21 October 1949, A/C.2 & 3/L.5, A/C.5/L.24, 4 November 1949, A/C.2 & 3/L.5, 4 November 1949. Regarding the fifth session, see Annexes, Agenda item 29. Regarding the sixth session, see Annexes, Agenda item 28.

[40] A/217, A/219, November 1946.

Despite its obvious merits, the joint meetings procedure did not prove successful in practice. The principal reason for the failure of this procedure is to be found in that perennial failing of UN coordination: the lack of national coordination. The above procedure could have worked if there had been proper coordination on the level of each delegation, between the representatives to the three committees concerned, and if the representative at the joint meeting had been adequately assisted by his colleagues and advisers experienced in the work of the two committees with which he was not personally acquainted. It appears, however, that uncertainty prevailed in many delegations as to who should be the representative at the joint meeting and how he should be assisted. In fact, the "strong" men in the various delegations, often regardless of their qualifications, represented their respective delegations in the joint meetings. There was hardly any common language between the delegates from the three committees concerned. Conflicting personalities trained in different disciplines clashed below the surface.

In the sixty-fourth meeting of the Fifth Committee, on 21 January 1952, during the sixth session of the General Assembly, the representative of Denmark expressed serious doubts regarding the usefulness of the joint meeting procedure. In his view,

such meetings complicated the heavy meeting schedule of the Assembly. Many of the points that had been made at joint meetings, many of the decisions that had been taken, could have been made or taken equally well at meetings of the Fifth Committee; others could have been taken at meetings of the Joint Second and Third Committee, or of the Second Committee or of the Third Committee. . . . If joint meetings were to be held in the future, they should be limited strictly to the discussion of specific proposals submitted preferably in advance and relating to points in the annual reports of the Administrative Committee on Co-ordination.[41]

[41] A/C.5/SR.64, 21 January 1952, paras. 74–75.

The reservations expressed by the Danish representative reflected broad dissatisfaction with the joint meetings' procedure, which, indeed, has not been resorted to since the sixth session of the General Assembly. It is doubtful whether the joint meetings' procedure, which did not work when the UN had a membership of fifty-seven (1952), would be helpful in an Organization comprising 117 member states (1965).

During the ninth session of the General Assembly the agenda item "Programmes of Technical Assistance" was allocated to the Second Committee, which, at its 289th meeting, requested its Chairman to make arrangements with the Chairman of the Fifth Committee concerning the consideration of a report on EPTA.[42] The report had been proposed by ACABQ under General Assembly resolution 722 (VIII) of 23 October 1953, following a recommendation of the Second Committee. The proposed arrangement was that the Fifth Committee should first consider ACABQ report and forward its comments to the Second Committee in time for the latter's consideration of the relevant agenda item. This did not work, owing to the fact that the Second Committee decided to advance the consideration of that item. Instead, the President of the General Assembly, in a letter addressed to the Chairman of the Fifth Committee, drew the Committee's attention to the fact that it could formulate such comments as it might deem necessary on the draft resolution adopted in the Second Committee. The reports both of the Second Committee[43] and of the Fifth Committee[44] were presented to the Plenary session, and the draft resolution recommended by the Fifth Committee was included, in an amended form, in the resolution adopted by the General Assembly mainly on the recommendation of the Second Committee.[45]

[42] A/2661, 25 June 1954.
[43] A/2803, 25 November 1954.
[44] A/2804, 25 November 1954.
[45] See GA Resolution 831 D (IX), 26 November 1954.

In its report of 1960 to the General Assembly on Administrative and Budgetary Co-ordination with the specialized agencies, ACABQ had devoted considerable attention to the question of program appraisals in the light of administrative and budgetary considerations and stressed the necessity for proper coordination of program aspects, on the one hand, and administrative and budgetary aspects, on the other.[46] During the fourteenth session of the General Assembly, it was observed in the Fifth Committee, in the course of the discussion of administrative and budgetary coordination with the specialized agencies, that the chapter of the 1960 report of ECOSOC to the General Assembly, dealing with the consolidated report of the ECOSOC Committee on Programme Appraisals, should be referred to the Fifth Committee or, alternatively, to a joint session of the three main committees primarily concerned, so that the Fifth Committee could be associated with the consideration by the General Assembly of the consolidated report.

During the fifteenth session of the General Assembly, the wish of the Fifth Committee to be associated with the budgetary and administrative aspects of the substantive program of work of the UN family was granted by means of another procedure: the General Committee of the General Assembly accepted the recommendation of the Secretary-General that Section 1 of the ECOSOC report entitled "Programme Appraisals in the Economic, Social and Human Rights Fields" be referred to the Fifth Committee and be made available also to the Second and Third Committees.[47] The relevant section of the ECOSOC Report was indeed discussed not only in the Fifth Committee but also, from the substantive point of view, in both the Second and Third Committees. The Chairmen of the Second and Third Committees apprised the Fifth Committee of the gist of the discussions that had taken place in their respective commit-

---

[46] A/4599, 28 November 1960; A/C.5/851, 8 December 1960.
[47] A/BUR/152, 14 September 1960, para. 8.

tees by means of letters addressed to the President of the General Assembly for communication to the Chairman of the Fifth Committee. These letters, which formed part of the Fifth Committee documentation,[48] enabled this committee to view in a comprehensive way the question before it. Upon the recommendations of the Fifth Committee, the General Assembly adopted resolution 1554 (XV), of 18 December 1960, on "Program Appraisals in the Economic, Social and Human Rights Fields." This interesting and simple method of associating the Fifth Committee with the program committees at the decision-making stage by referring the item concerned to one committee and making it available also to the other committees, whose views are then communicated to the committee responsible for the item by means of correspondence, deserves to be studied with a view to its further application.

Another simple and potentially effective means of associating the Fifth Committee with the work of the main committees of the General Assembly responsible for the economic and social activities of the Organization might be developed through more energetic exercise of the functions of the General Committee. As pointed out in the report of the *Ad Hoc* Committee on the Improvement of the Methods of Work of the General Assembly, "the General Committee should try in particular to ensure better coordination of the proceedings of all committees of the General Assembly." [49] Whatever the particular technique may be, it is widely realized that some kind of dialogue is necessary between the Fifth Committee and the organ concerned with the substantive activities of the Organization, for in recent years the impact of the decisions of substantive bodies of the United Nations on the discussions of the Fifth Committee has become increasingly clear.

[48] A/C.5/841, 11 November 1960, A/C.5/847, 1 December 1960, A/C.5/847/Add.1, 7 December 1960.
[49] A/5423, 28 May 1963, para. 37.

Administrative and Budgetary Control
over the Expanded Program
of Technical Assistance

In its general report on administrative and budgetary coordination between the UN and the specialized agencies, submitted to the fourteenth session of the General Assembly, ACABQ had pointed out that administrative and budgetary responsibility with respect to EPTA had been vested in TAC. ACABQ had stated that

even where the General Assembly is involved, as in the matter of confirmation of allocations made by TAC, the Fifth Committee has no defined responsibilities in regard to the programme. [These allocations are confirmed by the Second Committee.] It may be argued that, together with an integration of programmes and of programming procedures, there should be an integration of administrative and budgetary procedures at the legislative level. Some progress has been made towards such integration by the present arrangements for the review of various administrative and budgetary aspects of the Expanded Programme by the Advisory Committee. . . . Further progress in this matter would seem to lie in the direction of associating the Administrative and Budgetary Committee of the General Assembly with the legislative review of those aspects.[50]

The above comments of ACABQ were discussed by the Fifth Committee during the fourteenth session of the General Assembly. In his statement before the Fifth Committee on 16 November 1959, the Chairman of ACABQ recalled that ECOSOC was responsible for the program aspects of economic and social activities financed from the regular budget, although the administrative and budgetary responsibility for those activities belonged to the General Assembly, and specifically to the Fifth Committee. With respect to the special programs, including EPTA, ECOSOC or its subsidiary bodies were responsible

[50] A/4172, 25 August 1959, para. 14.

both for the program and the budgetary aspects.[51] One of the principal questions discussed was that of the need—pointed out by ACABQ—to associate more closely the Fifth Committee, as a single legislative body, with the administrative and budgetary matters, so as to ensure that administrative and budgetary coordination embraced both the regular and the special programs of the Organization.

The discussions of the suggestions of ACABQ in the Fifth Committee were cautious. The representative of the Netherlands presented the main critical appraisal, stressing that, while the Fifth Committee was supposed to deal with the administrative and budgetary questions arising in the UN, it was impossible to consider such matters in a responsible way without reference to the substantive background and activities of the specialized agencies. In order to achieve a comprehensive discussion by the General Assembly of the programs and activities of the UN and its organs, structural changes might be necessary, such as a change in the terms of reference of the main committees, a broadening of the powers and authority of ACABQ, or the establishment of an advisory programming committee to work in cooperation with ACABQ. The Netherlands representative considered that the proposal to transfer to the Fifth Committee certain responsibilities of TAC and ECOSOC regarding EPTA would serve no purpose since it would deprive TAC of responsibilities with which it was coping satisfactorily and that the whole Fifth Committee could not do the job as well as TAC, a body of twenty-four members, which often handled certain of its problems in even smaller working groups. He felt that it was impossible to separate the closely interwoven programming and administrative and budgetary problems, that there might arise a risk of duplication of activities between TAC and the Fifth Committee, and that difficulties would arise in connection with the proper representation in the Fifth Com-

[51] A/C.5/SR.744, 16 November 1959, para. 5.

mittee debates of the organizations and nonmember states participating in EPTA. In his view, the step that the Fifth Committee could take immediately was to extend the terms of reference of ACABQ so as to enable this body to respond to direct requests for advice in the administrative and budgetary fields from organs of the UN concerned with the administration and execution of special programs.[52] This was indeed the action taken by the Fifth Committee, as shown in the following pages.

There was obvious reluctance on the part of the Fifth Committee to take action that might conflict with the autonomy of the specialized agencies, and the feeling was that the coordination of interagency programs should be left to ECOSOC, assisted, where appropriate, by ACABQ as the expert administrative and budgetary body. One of the reasons for the cautious attitude taken seemed to be the reluctance to broaden the basis of control over programs that depended primarily on voluntary contributions. Another consideration seemed to be that the Fifth Committee has very limited know-how of substantive problems concerning programs in the economic and social field, although the Fifth Committee, which at one time was composed to a considerable extent of treasury experts, has today many representatives with experience with economic and social programs. Indeed, to the contrary, it may be argued that ECOSOC has little know-how or interest in budgetary and administrative problems.

*Questions of Administrative and Budgetary Coordination
with the Specialized Agencies*

It has already been observed that the General Assembly, and particularly the Fifth Committee, has little authority over the special programs of the UN family of organizations. What functions does the Fifth Committee actually perform in the field of coordination with the specialized agencies? It considers

---

[52] *Ibid.*, paras. 10–14.

administrative and budgetary relations with the specialized agencies in matters such as the administrative budgets of the agencies, the development of common personnel standards (common systems of salaries, allowances, and related benefits) for the secretariats, common staff regulations and financial regulations, uniformity in budget terminology and presentation, arrangements for coordination in schedules of conferences, and approval of the terms of reference of certain types of machinery for coordination such as ICSAB. Important and necessary as these matters are, one is forced to admit that their consideration by the Fifth Committee is generally perfunctory and seldom amounts to more than giving the required legislative approval to the results of work accomplished through the patient labors of CCAQ machinery. The successful performance by CCAQ can best be attributed to the high authority of the representatives of the participating organizations, that is, directors of personnel and controllers, and to the good preparatory work done by the CCAQ secretariat.

On the part of the General Assembly, these administrative and budgetary matters are examined in some detail by ACABQ, mostly from the point of view of the UN rather than by the Fifth Committee. There has indeed been considerable progress in coordination between the UN and the specialized agencies, but much of the credit should go to the ACC consultative machinery, and particularly to CCAQ.

The limited role of the Fifth Committee with respect to interorganizational administrative and budgetary coordination is understandable in view of the considerable complexity of the matters involved and the increasing orientation of the Fifth Committee toward political questions. The considerable delegation of powers to ACABQ has on the whole been successful, for this small expert body can conduct a dialogue with ACC and the secretariats and may go deeper into difficult questions than the Fifth Committee as a whole.

In the last few years the delegates to the Fifth Committee have shown a growing appreciation of the importance of inter-organizational coordination, partly as a result of the greater comprehensiveness and improved presentation by ACABQ of reports on the administrative budgets of the agencies, which have thus become more useful to the Fifth Committee. The better ACABQ reporting has been possible in part because of the improvements in the budget presentation by the agencies themselves and the interest of ECOSOC and ACC in developing a uniform budget layout. (See ECOSOC Resolution 1090 D (XXXIX) of 31 July 1965.)

There has been considerable heart-searching in ACABQ and in the Fifth Committee about whether the way in which the Fifth Committee examines the administrative budgets of the agencies constitutes adequate performance by the Fifth Committee of the mandate given to the General Assembly in Article 17 (3) of the Charter. The representatives in the Fifth Committee have often complained that the reports of ACABQ on agency budgets have been presented too late and so close to the end of the sessions of the General Assembly that no thorough consideration was possible. At times, ACABQ attributed the delay in the submissions of the report to the lengthy process of consultations with each of the agencies which had to precede the preparation of the final text of the report.[53]

The question whether the cursory examination of the administrative budgets constituted adequate implementation of Article 17 (3) of the Charter was clearly raised in the ACABQ report on the administrative budgets of the specialized agencies for 1956, submitted to the tenth session of the General Assembly. ACABQ stated:

24. Under its term of reference, the Committee has, in each year since 1947, examined the administrative budgets of the agencies. Summary statements of the various budgets, together with informa-

[53] See, for example, A/5064, 19 December 1961, para. 6.

tion on relevant administrative and financial developments, are prepared for the use of the Committee by the United Nations Secretariat. To the extent practicable, the Committee also examines the basic budget submission of each agency, and normally has an opportunity of consulting with the executive head or his representative. The Advisory Committee then submits a report to which the Fifth Committee gives a rather brief and general consideration.

25. The practices that have been developed in this regard both in the Advisory Committee and in the Fifth Committee constitute no more than a cursory review of the agency budgets. It is doubtful whether such a review can be regarded as an adequate implementation of Article 17, paragraph 3, of the Charter. The time has perhaps come when this question should be reconsidered.

26. While a decision on this matter rests with the General Assembly, the Advisory Committee wonders whether it might not be possible, in order to meet this situation, to substitute for the present procedure a more thorough review, to be made at regular intervals of a few years, with only one or, at most, two agencies coming under review in a given year. In submitting this tentative suggestion, the Committee takes account of the other duties assigned to it under its terms of reference, the discharge of which takes up a very large part of its time. The Committee also recognizes that a departure from present practice should be the subject of careful prior study.[54]

The Fifth Committee was not of one mind with regard to the suggestion made by ACABQ. While some delegates supported the suggestion, others appealed for a cautious attitude to ensure that the autonomy of the specialized agencies in their proper fields of activity was not impaired. No action was taken.[55]

During the twelfth session of the General Assembly, reference was made to the above suggestion of ACABQ, and it was suggested that at the thirteenth session of the General Assembly, formal and detailed consideration be given to the matter. In the course of the discussions that took place during the thirteenth session of the General Assembly, the representative of Canada

[54] A/3023, 11 November 1955.
[55] See A/3098, 14 December 1955.

in the Fifth Committee welcomed the special studies which ACABQ had undertaken, at the invitation of the specialized agencies, regarding administrative and budgetary coordination between the UN and these agencies, with special reference to EPTA, but he pointed out that a broader type of review was needed, in which all the administrative and budgetary aspects of the agencies' activities would be examined.[56] Although ACABQ was well qualified to undertake such studies, such a detailed review was not practicable on an annual basis in view of its work-load, and the Canadian delegation had proposed, at the tenth session of the World Health Assembly, that WHO should invite ACABQ to undertake, at two or three years' intervals, a review of the administrative aspects of WHO's program and budget estimates. Both the Executive Board of WHO and the World Health Assembly, however, had recommended to defer any decision on the matter until the General Assembly of the UN had made known its views, although ACABQ would have had no authority to make value judgements about the programs themselves and the agency could, of course, have rejected at will ACABQ's comments. In arguing in favor of appropriate action, the Canadian representative criticized the "excessive sensitivity to the autonomy of the specialized agencies," which in his view overlooked the formal responsibility of the General Assembly to examine the budgets of the agencies and the fact that the membership of the UN and the agencies was essentially the same.

No action was taken on the suggestions made by the Canadian representative; the Fifth Committee displayed once more the attitude of great caution towards the autonomy of the specialized agencies. The position regarding the discharge by the Fifth Committee of the mandate given to the General Assembly under Article 17 (3) of the Charter has since remained basically the same, although there has been, as pointed out above,

[56] See A/C.5/SR.702, 9 December 1958.

an increased interest in the matter on the part of the delegations due to the improvement in the comprehensiveness and in the methods of presentation of the data on the administrative budgets of the specialized agencies. At the twentieth session of the General Assembly, however, the Fifth Committee was less sensitive to the question of the autonomy of the specialized agencies and adopted a French proposal for the establishment of an *ad hoc* committee of experts to examine the finances of the UN and the specialized agencies (General Assembly resolution 2049(XX) of 13 December 1965.)

Coordination Consciousness

In order that the Fifth Committee may perform more fully its role as an instrument of administrative and budgetary coordination, two things seem necessary: first, a further improvement in national coordination, particularly on the level of the delegations to the UN; and, second, a greater awareness and consciousness of problems of coordination on the part of the Fifth Committee delegates.

Just as the representatives to ECOSOC and the Second and the Third Committees must fully take into account the budgetary and administrative repercussions of their decisions, so the Fifth Committee delegates must be conscious of the repercussions of their decisions upon the programs of the Organization in the economic and social fields and upon the development of greater uniformity, efficiency, and economy as regards the UN and the specialized agencies.

It is only natural that ACABQ and the Fifth Committee should be first and foremost interested in the UN view of administrative and budgetary matters. What is, however, of the greatest importance is that in the absence of overwhelming reasons, the Fifth Committee should be prepared to postpone legislative action in order to enable the CCAQ-ACC consultative machinery to work out mature and satisfactory inter-secretariat arrangements for legislative approval in the UN and in the legislative bodies of the specialized agencies. ACABQ and the Fifth Committee should also be willing to consider carefully and sympathetically the recommendations of the Secretariat in matters such as the wording of common staff regulations and financial regulations, where such wording has been proposed with the object of achieving greater interorganizational coordination and coordination consciousness. In order to encourage coordination consciousness on the part of the delegates to the Fifth Committee, it may be worth while studying the possibility of submitting to the Fifth Committee, as General Assembly documents, parts of the ACC reports to ECOSOC, particularly those relating to administrative and budgetary matters.[57] It may also be helpful to encourage the Secretary-General to prepare and submit from time to time to the General Assembly progress reports on interorganizational coordination in administrative and budgetary matters, and it has been suggested that ACABQ present an annual progress report on coordination along with the budget estimates.[58]

Coordination and Policy

The problem of coordination was emphasized during the eighteenth session of the General Assembly when the Third Committee adopted a resolution recommending that ECOSOC reconsider its previously adopted calendar of conferences for 1964 and include in it a session of the Human Rights Commission, despite the adverse recommendation of the Secretary-General, which had been based on administrative and budgetary considerations.[59] The question then came to the Fifth Committee, which was asked to report on the financial implications, under

[57] This has sometimes been done. An excerpt from the ACC Report on its second session, for example, was submitted to the Fifth Committee, as document A/404, 4 October 1947.

[58] A/C./5/SR.1071, 19 October 1965.

[59] See E/3741, 4 April 1963; A/C.3/L.1136/Rev.1, 31 October 1963; A/5611, 18 November 1963; A/C.5/994, 5 November 1963.

rule 154 of the Rules of Procedure. After some discussion, the Fifth Committee went along with the Third Committee, despite the apprehensions of certain delegates, and submitted the required report to the Plenary session. A rather similar situation had occurred in the Fifth Committee during the fifth session of the General Assembly with regard to a decision of the Third Committee inviting ECOSOC to reconsider its resolution 336 (XI) of 16 August 1950 with a view to including in its calendar of conferences for 1951 a session of the Sub-Commission on Freedom of Information and of the Press, as well as a session of the Sub-Commission on Prevention of Discrimination and Protection of Minorities.[60] In principle, a decision of the General Assembly *recommending* to ECOSOC that it reconsider its decision regarding the calendar of conferences, whereas perfectly legitimate, is, of course, undesirable. It would be a simplification to attribute this type of decision merely to the lack of inter-organ coordination. Partly responsible is the lack of adequate coordination on the national-delegation level, but contributing to the difficulty is the difference in membership between ECOSOC and the General Assembly. Legitimate differences of opinion between them are bound to occur, for the General Assembly, with its broader representation, yields more easily to the majority political opinion and its sense of the importance of certain meetings regardless of the administrative or budgetary implications.

The Advisory Committee on Administrative and Budgetary Questions

ACABQ was established under Part A of General Assembly resolution 14 (I), of 13 February 1946, on budgetary and financial arrangements, which reads as follows:

To facilitate the consideration of administrative and budgetary questions by the General Assembly and its Administrative and

[60] See A/1562, 29 November 1950.

Budgetary Committee, there be appointed at the beginning of the second part of the first session of the General Assembly, an Advisory Committee on Administrative and Budgetary Questions of nine members . . . with the following functions:

(*a*) to examine and report on the budget submitted by the Secretary-General to the General Assembly;

(*b*) to advise the General Assembly concerning any administrative and budgetary matters referred to it;

(*c*) to examine on behalf of the General Assembly the administrative budgets of specialized agencies and proposals for financial arrangements with such agencies;

(*d*) to consider and report to the General Assembly on the auditors' reports on the accounts of the United Nations and of the specialized agencies.

The Committee shall deal with personnel matters only in their budgetary aspects, and the representatives of the staff shall have the right to be heard by the Committee.

General Assembly resolution 1659 (XVI) of 29 November 1961, increased the membership of ACABQ to twelve members and amended rules 156 and 157 of the Rules of Procedure of the General Assembly. The Rules of Procedure, governing the status and the activities of ACABQ, read, in their present version, as follows:

Rule 156

The General Assembly shall appoint an Advisory Committee on Administrative and Budgetary Questions (hereinafter called the "Advisory Committee") with a membership of twelve, including at least three financial experts of recognized standing.

Rule 157

The members of the Advisory Committee, no two of whom shall be nationals of the same State, shall be selected on the basis of broad geographical representation, personal qualifications and experience, and shall serve for three years corresponding to three financial years, as defined in the regulations for the financial administration of the United Nations. Members shall retire by rotation and shall be eligible for reappointment. The three financial experts shall not retire simultaneously. The General Assembly shall appoint the members of the Advisory Committee at the regular session immediately preceding the expiration of the term of office of the members, or, in the case of vacancies, at the next session.

Rule 158

The Advisory Committee shall be responsible for expert examination of the budget of the United Nations, and shall assist the Administrative and Budgetary Committee of the General Assembly. At the commencement of each regular session it shall submit to the General Assembly a detailed report on the budget for the next financial year and on the accounts of the last financial year. It shall also examine on behalf of the General Assembly the administrative budgets of specialized agencies and proposals for financial and budgetary arrangements with such agencies. It shall perform such other duties as may be assigned to it under the regulations for the financial administration of the United Nations.

The above resolutions and rules make it clear that ACABQ was originally established as an expert body to assist the General Assembly, and particularly the Fifth Committee, in three major areas: (*a*) examination of the budget of the UN; (*b*) examination of the budgets of the specialized agencies; (*c*) in an advisory capacity, in other administrative and budgetary matters.

In the course of time, ACABQ has been given—by General Assembly resolutions—additional functions, including the important tasks of legislative supervision of expenditures under the annual resolutions concerning (*a*) Unforeseen and Extraordinary Expenses; (*b*) Working Capital Fund. The most interesting development regarding ACABQ has been the pragmatic and gradual extension of its functions into the field of the programs of the Organization, including programs financed from extrabudgetary funds. In fact, ACABQ has become not only the principal link between the Fifth Committee, on the one hand, and ECOSOC, the Second Committee, and other organs responsible for the special programs of the Organization in the economic and social fields, on the other, but also a major advisory organ regarding the administrative and financial aspects of extrabudgetary programs.

The Advisory Committee and the Fifth Committee

ACABQ is actually elected by the Fifth Committee and only in a formal sense by the Plenary session. The item concerning elections to ACABQ is referred by the General Committee to the Fifth Committee, which proceeds to elect the members of ACABQ by simple majority. A report on the elections made is then submitted to the Plenary session, which approves the report. This procedure reveals the close relationship between the Fifth Committee and ACABQ. This relationship is further emphasized by the fact that every year the Fifth Committee agrees to give the floor to the Chairman of ACABQ to participate in the debates, as appropriate. The Chairman of ACABQ thus shares the dais with the Committee officers and senior Seretariat officials.

Owing to the considerable complexity of the subjects on the agenda of the Fifth Committee, ACABQ performs the vital function of an expert body, which is small enough and has the necessary technical expertise to examine the various subjects and advise the Fifth Committee on them. ACABQ is able to hold frequent meetings with senior administrative officers of the Secretariat, including the Controller, the Director of the Budget Division, and the Director of Personnel, as well as with ACC, the executive heads of the various specialized agencies, or their administrative assistants, the officers of CCAQ, and other officers concerned with various aspects of administrative and budgetary coordination. These contacts enable ACABQ to obtain the additional data and clarifications that it needs in order to gain a well-informed opinion. The Fifth Committee itself also conducts in the course of its meetings a constant and productive dialogue with senior Secretariat officials concerned with administrative and budgetary matters. But the Fifth Committee is, of course, much more limited in this respect than ACABQ, which not only is a small group but also holds closed meetings. Members of ACABQ, moreover, are often relected, so that much expertise is accumulated and its Chairman is normally one of the "senior statesmen" of the Fifth Committee. On the whole, ACABQ enjoys great prestige in the Fifth Committee and its recommendations are nearly always followed. During the eighteenth session of the General Assembly, ACABQ, after expert examination, presented altogether thirty-six reports.

The influence enjoyed by ACABQ in the Fifth Committee has some negative aspects. ACABQ is, naturally, so concerned with considerations of economy and other administrative and budgetary considerations that it may sometimes not attach enough importance to program or political considerations. Indeed, ACABQ is often criticized for putting excessive stress on economy at the expense of other considerations. ACABQ has acquired lately greater insight into the economic and social activities of the UN, which will, no doubt, contribute to its greater appreciation of program matters, but in any case, its reports, distinctly coordination-oriented, help to foster coordination consciousness among the Fifth Committee delegates.

The Advisory Committee and the Regular Budget Estimates of the United Nations

In the examination of the regular budget estimates of the UN, ACABQ has tried to be sensitive to the program content of the estimates, as in its report on the budget estimates of the Organization for 1959:

The Advisory Committee's approach to budget examination is based generally on the belief that a review of the budget is meaningful only when it is related to an understanding and appraisal of the programmes of which the budget is an expression in financial terms. While, therefore, the Committee's recommendations in the present report are given, as indeed they must be, under individual budget sections, the Committee has devoted attention in its consultations with representatives of the Secretary-General, to the programme content of the estimates, especially where new projects are involved.[61]

This approach of ACABQ, relating budget review to an understanding and appraisal of the programs, has enabled the Fifth Committee to exercise more meaningfully its coordinating functions in so far as the regular programs of the Organization are concerned. Moreover, the reports submitted by ACABQ to the General Assembly show the devotion of ACABQ to effective administrative and budgetary coordination in the UN, with efforts to rationalize the budget cycle, to limit supplementary estimates, to press for an introduction of a meaningful order of priorities in the economic and social fields, to rationalize the arrangements for meetings and conferences, to improve public information activities, and to use the staff resources of the Organization efficiently.

The Advisory Committee and the Administrative Budgets of the Specialized Agencies

The basic procedures for the review by ACABQ of the budgets of the specialized agencies, under resolution 14 (I) of the General Assembly, have been established by resolutions 81 (I) and 125 (II) and by the relevant provisions of the relationship agreements. ACABQ has rightly been of the opinion that,

Although each of the specialized agencies has assumed an individual responsibility for a specific field of activity, it forms part of a community of international organizations and shares in a common endeavor to attain the aims and ideals enunciated in the Charter of the United Nations. This basic unity of purpose should be reflected, not only in a concerted development of work programmes, but also in the co-ordination of administrative and other services.[62]

[61] A/3860, August 1958, para. 29.
[62] A/3023, 11 November 1955, para. 15.

The review of the administrative budgets of the agencies has been regarded by ACABQ as the principal means of developing administration and budgetary coordination between the UN and the agencies. In its reports to the General Assembly on the administrative budgets, ACABQ has insisted on constant improvement in the simplicity, uniformity, and comprehensiveness of budget presentation, so as to make sound budget analysis and budget comparison possible. As with the UN, ACABQ has emphasized that budgetary and administrative coordination can only be meaningful if considered in relation to the programs of work of the agencies. Moreover, as regards the extrabudgetary programs of the agencies, ACABQ has made constructive recommendations, such as in its report on the administrative budgets of the specialized agencies for 1951:

8. Of these problems, perhaps the most important concerns the control of technical assistance funds and other extra-budgetary funds, as well as the form of presentation of the relevant estimates. At present, such funds are not incorporated in the annual budgets of the agencies and, except in the case of WHO, even the presentation of the estimates for technical assistance is entirely separate from the annual budgets.

9. As a consequence of this procedure, the annual budgets do not reflect the whole of the activities of the Organization for the year to which they refer, and a comprehensive appraisal can be made only by reference to a number of separate documents.

10. The Advisory Committee therefore suggests that the specialized agencies should be requested to include, as information annexes to their annual budget documents, the estimates and plans for expenditure of any other funds which may be available for use during the year covered by the regular budget estimates.[63]

This recommendation of ACABQ was approved by General Assembly resolution 411 (V) of 1 December 1950 upon the recommendation of the Joint Second and Third Committee and the Fifth Committee, and the specialized agencies participating in the technical assistance program were thus requested "to

[63] A/1441, 16 October 1950.

provide information concerning the estimates for expenditure of technical assistance funds, as well as other extra-budgetary funds, in their regular budget documents." The reports presented by ACABQ to the General Assembly on the budgets of the agencies now contain data on the financing of the special projects by the agencies.[64]

As already observed, during the last few years ACABQ has made great progress in the technique of reporting on the agency budgets, which has thus made possible a more meaningful consideration of the subject by the Fifth Committee. In view of the growing complexity of the matters involved, ACABQ decided in 1962 to reorganize the form of its annual report on the administrative budgets of the specialized agencies. Broad policy questions in the administrative and financial field were singled out for consideration in one part of the report, in another part a summary review of the administrative budgets was presented, while the detailed comments on the budget of each agency appeared in the annexes to the report.[65] Policy problems discussed—with considerable stress on program of work matters —have included the general budgetary trends in the UN and the agencies; the increased emphasis on operational activities (including a discussion of the institution of UN resident representatives); a critical discussion of the central machinery for coordination; the administrative and financial implications with respect to the agencies of decisions taken by the UN bodies (including the need for prior consultations before decisions are taken on new activities in fields of direct concern to the agencies); and problems of coordination of conference and meetings schedule. The observations and recommendations of ACABQ are communicated to the specialized agencies by means of appropriate resolutions adopted by the General Assembly, upon the recommendations of the Fifth Committee, and drafted usually

[64] See, for example, A/5599, 14 November 1963, paras. 77, 147.
[65] A/5332, 5 December 1962, para. 2.

in accordance with the suggested outlines contained in the ACABQ reports.

The Advisory Committee and Extrabudgetary Programs

In its coordinating functions with regard to the budgets of the specialized agencies, the budget of the UN, and other administrative and budgetary questions, ACABQ acts primarily as a subsidiary expert organ of the Fifth Committee. But ACABQ also has coordinating functions with regard to the special extrabudgetary programs falling under the primary responsibility of ECOSOC and the Second Committee of the General Assembly. This development has been gradual and pragmatic, indicating that ACABQ has become a much-needed link between the Fifth Committee and the organs responsible for the special programs of the Organization in the economic and social fields.

ACABQ has acquired a rather special status as an advisory body on administrative and budgetary matters, perhaps beginning with the sixth session of the General Assembly and the adoption of resolution 594 (VI) of 4 February 1952 on "Operational Programmes under Responsibility of the United Nations, Financed by Voluntary Contributions." It was resolved that the administrative part of the technical assistance programs financed by voluntary contributions and executed by the UN "should be subject by the ACABQ to the same scrutiny as that applied to expenses proposed under the regular budget." [66] The next step was taken by the General Assembly during its eighth session. On the recommendation of the Second Committee, the General Assembly adopted resolution 722 (VIII) of 23 October 1953 on "The Expanded Programme of Technical Assistance for the Economic Development of Under-Developed Coun-

[66] See also GA Resolution 519A (VI), 12 January 1952, on EPTA for the Economic Development of Under-Developed Countries, regarding the review of audit reports relating to expenditure by the specialized agencies of technical assistance funds allocated from the Special Account.

tries," which requested ACABQ to review the administrative procedures of TAB and those of the participating organizations as well as their administrative expenditures so far as those were financed from the Special Account.[67]

New Terms of Reference for the Advisory Committee

ACABQ's report on EPTA, submitted to the ninth session of the General Assembly,[68] followed by General Assembly resolution 831 D (IX) of 26 November 1954 requesting ECOSOC to report to the tenth session of the General Assembly on the progress made in the consideration of the questions raised in the report of ACABQ, led to a discussion in the Fifth Committee on the terms of reference of ACABQ.

During the 481st meeting of the Fifth Committee, the representative of Argentina stressed that the General Assembly resolution recognized the competence of ACABQ regarding administrative questions affecting technical assistance programs and proposed that the Fifth Committee should request ACABQ "to continue its study of the questions raised in its first report . . . such study to be carried out at the headquarters of each of the specialized agencies participating in the Expanded Programme of Technical Assistance." [69] The Chairman of ACABQ, who participated in the discussion of the Argentine proposal, insisted, however, that, having regard to the provisions of the Charter and the relationship agreements, such studies should only be undertaken at the request of the General Assembly *and* on the basis of an express invitation from the specialized agency concerned. Caution would have to be exercised so as not to impinge on the system of relationships with the agencies. Sim-

[67] Regarding the authority for the examination by ACABQ of the budget estimates of the TAB secretariat, see A/3996, 13 November 1958; A/4032, 5 December 1958, para. 27; and A/5598, 8 November 1963, para. 1. See also A/2582, 1 December 1953, para. 48, and A/2619, 8 December 1953, para. 7.
[68] A/2661, 25 June 1954.
[69] A/C.5/L.319, 8 December 1954.

ilar constitutional questions were raised also by a number of delegates. It was further suggested that any on-the-spot study should cover also the review, already provided for in ACABQ's terms of reference, of the regular administrative budgets of the specialized agencies.

Following this discussion, the Fifth Committee agreed to the following text:

> The Fifth Committee authorizes the ACABQ to respond favourably to any invitation received from a specialized agency to continue at the headquarters of such agency the study of administrative and budgetary coordination between the United Nations and the Specialized Agencies, including the questions raised in its first report . . . if in its judgment such a course would be desirable and practicable in the light of the Advisory Committee's existing responsibilities under its terms of reference.[70]

This formulation, which was included in the report of the Fifth Committee to the Plenary session, was to be transmitted by the Secretary-General to the agencies.

The authorization granted to ACABQ during the ninth session of the General Assembly to respond to invitations of the specialized agencies was expressly reiterated during the tenth session[71] and subsequently. Such invitations were indeed extended, and ACABQ prepared, at the headquarters of the various agencies, studies on administrative and budgetary coordination, with particular reference to the working of EPTA, between the UN and ILO, UNESCO, WHO, WMO, FAO, and ICAO, respectively. Reports were also prepared on the administrative and budgetary coordination with IAEA and ITU.[72]

The observations made by ACABQ in these special reports were brought to the attention of the specialized agencies con-

---

[70] A/2861, 11 December 1954, para. 10.
[71] A/3098, 14 December 1955, para. 8.
[72] The relevant documents are, respectively, A/3142, 10 July 1956; A/3166, 22 August 1956; A/3596, 9 July 1957; A/3597, 9 July 1957; A/3598, 9 July 1957; A/3861, 20 August 1958; A/4135, 8 July 1959; and A/4148, 17 July 1959.

cerned by means of appropriate General Assembly resolutions while ACABQ also prepared one general report.[73] The special reports examined the whole administrative structure of the agencies, the regular and the special programs and their mutual relationship, and various problems of coordination and of administrative and budgetary controls. An important question raised in the reports was that of the allocation of the costs of the administrative and operational services of technical assistance between the regular budgets of the agencies and the Special Account of EPTA. The general report afforded the Fifth Committee an opportunity to extend the steadily developing terms of reference of ACABQ. The ACABQ report contained certain suggestions regarding the legislative control over the administrative and budgetary aspects of the special programs, but the Fifth Committee hesitated to extend directly its own power over the administrative and budgetary aspects of special programs. It was, however, attentive to the suggestion made to broaden further the terms of reference of ACABQ "so as to enable it to respond to direct requests for advice in the administrative and budgetary field from organs of the United Nations concerned with the administration and execution of special programmes."[74] Better coordination could be achieved without giving rise to constitutional difficulties, by enabling ACABQ to respond to requests for advice from such organs and committees of the UN.

By resolution 1437 (XIV) of 5 December 1959 adopted by the General Assembly on the recommendation of the Fifth Committee, ACABQ was authorized to "examine and report on co-ordination and on the administrative and budgetary aspects of special programmes of the United Nations, at the request of a principal organ or of the body responsible for the special programme." ACABQ was also authorized "in fulfilment of its

---

[73] A/4172, 25 August 1959.
[74] A/C.5/SR/744, 16 November 1959, para. 11.

function under rule 158 of the rules of procedure of the General Assembly, to meet as it deems necessary and appropriate at the various offices of the United Nations and at the headquarters of the specialized agencies and the International Atomic Energy Agency and, at the request of those agencies, to advise them on administrative and financial matters." One of the sponsors of the draft resolution explained that its object was to "convert into a permanent duty of the Advisory Committee a function assigned to it experimentally at the ninth and tenth sessions," and another sponsor explained that it "would give the Advisory Committee general authority to undertake a type of activity it had already been empowered to perform in three special cases," [75] which were: (*a*) the authorization granted to ACABQ by the General Assembly to render such advice to TAC, or any administrative review group established by it, as may be requested by the Committee in the review of the administrative and operational services costs of EPTA; (*b*) the request to ACABQ by ECOSOC to consider the question of the allocation, between the regular budgets of the participating agencies and EPTA special account, of the administrative and operational services costs of EPTA; and (*c*) the authorization granted to ACABQ by the General Assembly to comment on the administrative budget of the Special Fund.

Responsibilities of the Advisory Committee

In order to give a general idea of the actual increase in the functions of ACABQ, some of its duties—present and past—have been enumerated below:

(*a*) To examine the work programs of ECOSOC.[76]

---

[75] A/C.5/SR.745, 17 November 1959, paras. 4, 14.
[76] See GA Resolution 1094 (XI), 27 February 1957, and ECOSOC Resolution 665 (XXIV), 2 August 1957. Regarding the continuing interest of ACABQ in the question of program appraisals and coordination, see, for example, its report on the administrative budgets of the specialized agencies for 1962, A/5007, 4 December 1961.

(*b*) To make studies on decentralization of the economic and social activities of the UN, strengthening of the regional economic commissions, the role of resident representatives, and coordination in the field.[77]

(*c*) To conduct studies on the allocation of the administrative and operational services costs of technical assistance between the regular and the EPTA budgets.[78]

(*d*) To make studies on the budget estimates of the TAB Secretariat.[79]

(*e*) To make studies on the administrative budgets of the Special Fund.[80]

(*f*) To study the possible effects on the activities of the UN, the specialized agencies, and IAEA of an increase in the operations of EPTA and the Special Fund.[81]

(*g*) To study, in collaboration with the ACC, the possibility of utilizing a uniform layout for the preparation and presentation of the budgets of the specialized agencies.[82]

(*h*) To allow the Chairman of ACABQ to participate in meetings of the ACC, and of the Special Committee on Coordination, upon invitation.[83]

(*i*) To make available to ECOSOC at its summer sessions

[77] See the GA Resolutions 1446 (XIV), 5 December 1959; 1437 (XIV), 5 December 1959; 1709 (XVI), 19 December 1961; and 1823 (XVII), 18 December 1962; and ECOSOC Resolutions 856 (XXXII), 4 August 1961, and 955 (XXXVI), 5 July 1963. See also the reports of ACABQ on the role of Resident Representatives, A/5138, 21 June 1962, and on decentralization, A/5584, 30 October 1963.
[78] See ECOSOC Resolution 737 (XXVIII), 30 July 1959, and ACABQ report, A/4774, 9 June 1961.
[79] See, for example, A/4966, 14 November 1961; A/5598, 8 November 1963.
[80] See, for example, A/5021, 27 November 1963.
[81] By resolution 794 (XXX), 3 August 1960 ECOSOC requested ACC to prepare this study, but GA resolution 1554 B (XV), 18 December 1960 adopted on the recommendation of the Fifth Committee, requested ACC to transmit the results of its study to ACABQ for whatever administrative and budgetary comments it may deem desirable and further requested ACABQ to submit its comments in time for their consideration by ECOSOC together with ACC study.
[82] ECOSOC Resolution 1090 D (XXXIX), 31 July 1965.
[83] ECOSOC Resolution 1090 G (XXXIX), 31 July 1965, para. 2.

comments on the administrative and financial aspects of activities in the economic, social and human rights fields.[84]

Although General Assembly resolution 1437 (XIV) of 5 December 1959 had formulated in general terms the terms of reference of ACABQ with respect to the examination of the special programs of the UN, ACABQ still depended on the willingness of the organs or agencies concerned to associate ACABQ with their work. Although the basis of ACABQ's advice to organs responsible for the special programs has remained voluntary, the actual scope of the functions of ACABQ has been steadily increasing, owing to the prestige and expertise of ACABQ, the need for skilled advice about the special programs, and the importance that the General Assembly—the Fifth Committee and, in a growing measure, the Second Committee—attach to the recommendations of ACABQ. The Secretary-General and ACC in the future may also wish to encourage resort to ACABQ in regard to the extrabudgetary programs. So far ACABQ has not been given any functions—except as regards the audit review—in respect to UNICEF, UNHCR, and UNRWA.

The good performance of ACABQ must be continued, of course, if further resort to its advice is sought. Both the procedure and composition of ACABQ will have to be kept under observation, and the possibility of including in it some experts in the economic and social field may have to be considered at an appropriate time. One question that may be worth exploring further is the possibility of allowing oral interventions by the Chairman of ACABQ in the various organs of the UN (such as ECOSOC or the Second and Third Committees) whenever his comments on the administrative and budgetary aspects of the matters under discussion may be timely. This again would, of course, have to be a voluntary arrangement, so as not to impinge on the authority of the organs concerned. But past

[84] ECOSOC Resolution 1093 (XXXIX), 31 July 1965.

experience has shown that the element of timing in the submission of administrative and budgetary comments may be essential, particularly when urgent draft resolutions are considered.[85]

Conclusions

In order to improve UN economic and social administration the following suggestions are offered, not as panaceas but as courses of action that might help the Fifth Committee and ACABQ in their responsibilities for administrative and budgetary coordination:

(*a*) National coordination should be improved. It is essential that the representatives of a particular government on the various committees of the General Assembly, in other organs of the UN, and in the specialized agencies should follow consistent policies. The governments should define their policies and formulate them in clear directives issued to their representatives in all the organizations belonging to the UN family. There is a particular need for improved coordination on the level of delegations to the UN. In order to foster the improvement of national coordination, it may be worth while reaffirming, both in the General Assembly and in ECOSOC, some of the past resolutions on the subject. The Secretary-General might wish to examine whether his report of 6 May 1958 on "Coordination on the National Level" needs to be brought up to date. He might also consider issuing periodically special progress reports on national coordination.

(*b*) Coordination consciousness should be developed in all the organs of the UN and the specialized agencies. Delegates in the various organs should be aware that their acts or omissions to act affect, for better or for worse, the prospects for more effective coordination between the committees of the General Assembly, between the organs of the UN, and between the

---

[85] It is interesting to observe that ACC and the Special Committee on Coordination have in fact invited the Chairman of ACABQ to participate in some of their meetings.

UN and the specialized agencies. The delegates should act, taking into full consideration the interests of effective coordination. The presiding officers of all the organs, including the Fifth Committee, as well as officials of the Secretariat, should develop and maintain coordination consciousness in the various organs and keep alive the idea that each organ is duty-bound to take into due consideration the activities of other organs. In order to encourage coordination consciousness on the part of the delegates to the Fifth Committee, it may be worth while studying the possibility of submitting to the Fifth Committee, as General Assembly documents, parts of the ACC reports to ECOSOC. The Secretary-General may also wish to submit to the General Assembly progress reports on administrative and budgetary coordination.

(*c*) As regards the General Assembly, flexible procedures should be developed with a view to achieving proper inter-committee cooperation, particularly between the Fifth Committee on the one hand, and the Second and the Third Committee, on the other. The draft resolutions presented to the Plenary session should be based on both program considerations and on administrative and budgetary considerations. Although it is unlikely that the cumbersome procedure of joint meetings of the main committees concerned would work, coordinated and comprehensive intercommittee action can be developed through simpler procedures, as indicated in previous pages. Such procedures, which would not require changes in the Rules of Procedure of the General Assembly, could be effective if the General Committee of the General Assembly fully performs its function of coordinating the work of the main committees. These procedures could include either (1) the allocation of an item first to the program committee concerned, for prior consideration, and then to the Fifth Committee, which would take into full consideration the preceding discussions and the positions taken, or (2) the reference of an item first to the Fifth Committee and then to the program committee concerned, as the need may be; intercommittee communications through exchange of letters between the chairmen, cooperation between the chairmen within the framework of the General Committee, and so forth. These procedures would require a coordinated timing of the consideration of the relevant items by the main committees concerned. It is important that the Second or the Third Committee, as the case may be, be prepared to postpone the adoption of a particular draft resolution having administrative or budgetary implications until the Fifth Committee has been given the possibility to consider the matter and bring its views to the attention of the Committee concerned. Indeed, there must be willingness to postpone final action until the budgetary and administrative implications can be taken into account. The Fifth Committee should not be placed before a *fait accompli*.

(*d*) The possibility of amending rule 154 of the Rules of Procedure of the General Assembly might be studied in order to enable the Fifth Committee to perform more effectively the function of administrative and budgetary coordination through the process of budget examination. The amended rule 154 might authorize the Fifth Committee to make recommendations regarding the advisability of adopting the proposed draft resolution, and not merely state, as it is bound to do now, the effect of the proposed measure on the budget estimates of the UN. The report on financial implications submitted by the Fifth Committee to the Plenary session would thus become a more substantive paper, which would be considered by the Plenary together with the report of the program committee concerned. Such a change in rule 154 could result in conflicting recommendations from two main committees of the General Assembly.

(*e*) Both in the General Assembly and in ECOSOC, the Secretary-General should be encouraged, within the context and framework of the present rules requiring him to report to the organ concerned on the administrative and financial implications of the proposal, to make substantive recommendations on the administrative and budgetary advisability of adopting the proposed measure. Such an action would of course have to be purely discretionary, and the Secretary-General should not be formally required to do more than report on the financial implications of the proposal, for he might otherwise become involved in controversies. Today the Secretary-General submits substantive recommendations whenever he deems it desirable, and he should bring to the attention of committees the financial rules before any decisions are taken by them.

(*f*) As regards ACABQ, further resort to its advice may be encouraged, especially as regards those extrabudgetary programs with which it has not been associated so far. Also, it may be worth considering the advisability of inviting the Chairman of ACABQ to appear and make statements before the organs of the UN, such as ECOSOC and the Second and the Third Committees of the General Assembly, whenever critical administrative and budgetary advice may be timely. This could be done within the existing terms of reference of ACABQ and would, of course, necessitate an express invitation from the organ concerned. The good will of the presiding officer of such an organ, and of the organ itself, would be essential.

(*g*) As regards ECOSOC, it would be desirable that the program of work and the schedule of meetings of the Council and its subsidiary organs be arranged in such a way that the whole program of work in the economic and social fields for the following year be prepared in time for its inclusion in the main budget estimates presented by the Secretary-General. ECOSOC, finally, should try to plan its program of work for several years ahead, with a view toward postponing final decisions until the Fifth Committee has examined the related budgetary estimates, but such an achievement must ultimately depend upon improved program coordination.

By Walter R. Sharp

PROGRAM COORDINATION AND THE ECONOMIC AND SOCIAL COUNCIL

Under the impact of science and technology the United Nations system is gradually assuming new functions in order to meet the growing demands of the economically less advanced countries of the world for development. Orderly and effective working relationships between the UN itself and the related specialized agencies are needed to pursue the goal of world-wide economic and social progress as efficiently as possible. In recent years the creation of machinery and the improvement of procedures have often been studied and discussed, leading slowly to constructive modifications in the relationships between the several organs and agencies of the UN system. The process of coordination, however, centering around ECOSOC must continue to adjust to what has become, in effect, a revolutionary world environment, if some of the high ideals of economic and social progress set forth in the Charter are eventually to be realized.

The constitutional framework of the UN system, fortunately, allows for considerable flexibility and experimentation. Consisting of a congeries of quasi-autonomous agencies and organs, the system can operate coherently only if its various parts are amenable to persuasion and will accept wise guidance from the appropriate general policy centers. The unique pattern adopted at San Francisco in 1945 makes this possible but by no means easy. Now, after some twenty years' experience, it seems time to take stock of the problem in its present contours and to project, however tentatively, what may feasibly be done to strengthen the UN family of agencies for their *cooperative* attack on poverty, disease, and ignorance.

The San Francisco pattern, as elaborated in Chapters IX and X of the Charter, reflects a somewhat blurred compromise between the acceptance of a cluster of completely independent intergovernmental agencies and the development of a hierarchy of functional institutions under UN control. The text of the Charter, on the one hand, sets forth in sweeping but imprecise terms various economic and social functions for which the UN itself is made responsible, while providing, on the other, no clearly defined means of assuring that the economic and social activities of the total "system" will constitute an integrated whole.

Within the scheme of "coordination," as envisaged by the Charter, ECOSOC was to play the key role at the intergovernmental level. It was expected to bring into an orderly relationship the economic and social work of the UN and the various specialized agencies by consultation, the promotion of "partnership" agreements, the examination of agency reports and the issuance of recommendations. But, as H. G. Nicholas has observed, since the specialized agencies

fell very short of covering all the topics appropriate for UN treatment, ECOSOC was made into a kind of hold-all for the residue of specialist activities in the economic and social fields. Thus it suffered . . . from having to be both coordinator and part of the coordinated. This dual nature of ECOSOC, part specialist agency, part "super-agency," has made it much more difficult to establish a satisfactory relationship between it and the General Assembly.[1]

This situation has also hampered relationships between the specialized agencies and ECOSOC.

[1] H. G. Nicholas, *The United Nations as a Political Institution* (London, Oxford University Press, 1959), p. 129.

The status of ECOSOC vis-à-vis the General Assembly was left equivocal. Although a "principal" organ, in Charter terms, it was to operate "under the authority" of the Assembly, as indicated in Chart III. Yet it was accorded a substantial range of initiative and it could issue recommendations to the Assembly or by-pass it by forwarding recommendations directly to member states. Actually, there has developed a two-way flow of decisions between the two bodies, resulting in much repetition of discussion and much duplication of documentation. The Charter arrangement was further complicated by the division of responsibility between ECOSOC and the Assembly for scrutinizing the programs of the specialized agencies: the former was to examine their substantive reports while the latter was given the duty of reviewing their administrative budgets. Apparently, the architects of the Charter did not conceive of budgets as "program instruments."

Expansion and Change of United Nations Economic and Social Activities

At San Francisco there was little or no expectation of the vast array of economic, social, and welfare tasks the UN system has undertaken during the first two decades of its existence. Except for IBRD and IMF (which were then held to be virtually independent of the central UN organization), the specialized agencies were originally assumed to be essentially technical, clearinghouse, research-promoting, and standard-setting bodies. Accordingly, the process of seeing to it that their activities did not unduly overlap or conflict was thought to be a relatively simple matter. Not only has the range of economic and social functions exceeded the expectations of 1946, in part because of the establishment of additional agencies such as WMO and IAEA, but the character of these functions has taken on significant new aspects with the emergence of far-flung *operational* programs financed mainly by voluntary contribu-

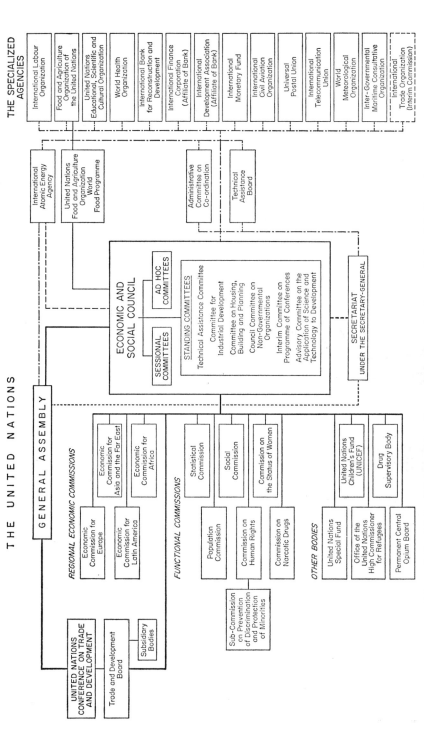

Chart III. Main Organs Dealing with Economic and Social Questions

Adapted from the chart in YEARBOOK OF THE UNITED NATIONS, 1964
(New York, 1966); copyright, United Nations, 1966

tions. These programs—EPTA and the Special Fund in particular—have in effect transformed the principal specialized agencies from technical and informational bodies into purveyors of
a wide variety of services to governments and peoples throughout the economically underdeveloped world. Concurrently, the
UN itself, through its Department of Economic and Social Affairs, has become an active agent of technical assistance in fields
often closely related to those claimed by certain specialized
agencies to be within their constitutional province.

Around two thirds of the annual expenditures of the UN
family of agencies (not counting major "peace-keeping" operations) now fall within the economic and social category, while
nearly four fifths of the total personnel on the payroll of the
over-all system are handling tasks in this domain. During recent
years the regular annual budgets of the specialized agencies have
aggregated more than the total regular budget of the UN while
the various voluntary programs in 1965 accounted for a total
almost equal to that of all the regular budgets combined.[2]

The specialized agencies have felt the impact of the new
field programs in several different ways. First, their secretariats
at headquarters have had to assume a heavy burden of administration for planning, field recruitment, briefing, supervision, and
evaluation, which in some cases goes beyond the allocation for
overhead costs provided by the extrabudgetary program concerned. Some agency secretariats, in the words of one observant
UN official, have become "constipated" with operational activities. The two major voluntary programs, moreover, EPTA and
the Special Fund, were managed differently: in the former case,
it was on an interagency basis, and, in the latter, on a UN sys-
tem-centralized basis, where program formulation in the substan-

---

[2] For 1964, the approximate figures were: UN Regular Budget, $96 million;
regular budgets of nine specialized agencies and IAEA, $111 million; volun-
tary programs (EPTA, Special Fund, UNICEF, UNCHR, UNRWA), $200
million.

tive sense was largely removed from the arena of agency bargaining.

Second, the locus of interagency relationships on program development and execution has substantially shifted from headquarters to the field. The problem of coordination has thus taken on three dimensions: (1) laterally, between agency headquarters; (2) vertically, from headquarters to regional and country level operations; and (3) laterally, again, between field projects of related agencies. This trend toward geographic decentralization has not only been a feature of specialized agency evolution, with extensive field machinery developed by WHO, FAO, ILO, and, to a lesser degree, by UNESCO and ICAO, but recently, within the UN itself, there has been considerable devolution of program-making and program-execution functions to the UN regional economic commissions, whose terms of reference now include social as well as economic matters.[3] This development is bringing the major specialized agencies into closer contact with the UN in the field. Certain of the agencies, notably FAO, are outposting staff to the regional commission secretariats, thus tending to turn the latter into interagency groups. At the country level the resident representatives of TAB, since their assumption of the additional responsibility as directors for Special Fund programs and the general upgrading of their roles, seemed to be on the way to becoming *de facto* program coordinators of all UN economic and social agencies in the field.

Third, the availability of resources in the expanding UN system, as a result of the voluntary programs, has provided an impetus for incursions into new functional areas, many of which by their nature fall outside the province of any existing specialized agency and require cooperative action usually under

---

[3] See W. R. Malinowski, "Centralization and Decentralization in the United Nations Economic and Social Activities," *International Organization*, XVI (Summer, 1962), 521–41.

UN leadership. Foremost among such emerging areas are economic development planning, involving the establishment of regional institutes for research and training in this field; the development and conservation of water resources; the application of science and technology for the benefit of the developing countries; the peaceful uses of atomic energy and the development of other forms of energy (for example, solar and wind); and the stimulation of research and exchange of information on population control methods. The inauguration of the UN Development Decade in 1961, providing a central focus and target for interagency action, has encouraged a more integrated approach to major UN welfare goals. This trend is particularly noticeable in such agencies as FAO, where as much as two thirds of its total expenditure in 1963 came from the extra-budgetary sources of EPTA and the Special Fund, and UNESCO, whose regular budget expenditures are virtually matched by allocations from these two voluntary programs. A somewhat similar distribution of resources now characterizes the financing of the substantive work managed through the UN Department of Economic and Social Affairs.

All of this is not to say that there is no longer any problem of interagency coordination but rather that its contours have changed enormously since the early days of the UN. In certain respects the major activities of the UN family in the economic and social domain tend to "integrate" themselves by their technical character, as will be shown later. At the same time, as the pressure on UN system resources becomes constantly heavier, the difficulty of determining the most urgent economic-social problems calling for UN attention and their order of priority remains crucial. The primary purpose of coordination should be to ensure that the available resources, always too little, are utilized to maximum advantage for the achievement of the major objectives that have been agreed upon. "This requires not only that duplication of activities and conflicts of policy should be eliminated but also that the activities should be coherently related and that resources should be concentrated on areas in which the needs and opportunities for international action are greatest." [4] Indeed, the danger of serious overlaps seems less likely in view of the inadequacy of resources available to UN agencies than the peril of important gaps left unfilled for want of appropriations.

To what extent can machinery and procedures facilitate such coordination short of a drastic transformation in the constitutional framework of the UN system? Are existing machinery and procedures as effective as they might be? How might they be made more effective?

The Processes of Coordination in the United Nations System

THE ROLE OF ECOSOC. Over the years ECOSOC has tackled the problem of program coordination through a variety of methods. During the earlier period it tended to view coordination "as something restrictive." The Council seemed to assume rather naively that one could go through a "catalogue of projects" and with a red pencil strike out certain items, while promoting others to a higher place in a hierarchy of priorities. Typical of this attitude was a resolution of 1952 proposing six major priority program objectives, as follows: [5]

Increased food production and distribution
Promotion of domestic full employment and economic stability
Increased production in fields other than food
Acceleration of welfare, social security and basic public health
Development of education and science
Formulation and wider observance of human rights
The trouble with this type of exhortation to agency program-

---

[4] Quotation from the Report of the *Ad Hoc* Working Group on Coordination, E/3647, 4 June 1962.
[5] E/2332, 28 July 1952.

makers was that the guidelines were too broad to be really helpful. They were, in fact, little more than generalities. Even this
effort, however, had one salutary effect: it tended to demon-
strate to governments that there was really little overlapping and
that the salient problem was how to obtain more resources.

Beginning in 1956 the Council examined rather closely the
annual review of the economic, social, and human rights programs and other activities of the UN and the specialized
agencies as a whole, prepared for it by the Secretary-General
and his staff. The purpose of the review and observations by
the Secretary-General was to enable the Council to consider
how best to use the limited resources available in the light of
changing requirements. In 1962, at its thirty-fourth session, the
Council went a step further and asked the Secretary-General
to prepare a "consolidated statement of work programs . . .
listing projects according to a functional classification," in lieu
of an agency-by-agency approach. A year later such a classification was submitted to the Council.[6] Unfortunately since
the classification was based merely on project titles it did not
penetrate very deeply the labyrinth of studies, reports, and
operations covering the UN family of agencies, but it did include useful functional indicators of program content, as follows:

Planning for economic and social development
Economic growth
Social advancement
Development finance
Institutional and administrative development
Development of national and international statistics
Human rights
Basic information

Practicable criteria for selecting priorities among and within

[6] See Annex to E/3788, 14 June 1963. An elaboration of this classification
appears in the Twenty-ninth Report of ACC, E/3886/Add.1, 6 May 1964.

these classifications in more specific terms still remain to be devised.

A different line of attack on agency program coordination has stressed the desirability of "concentrating" activities into a limited number of substantive areas on the basis of planning ahead for a period of years. These "streamlining" efforts, marked by a series of resolutions since 1949, led to an ambitious undertaking by ECOSOC to obtain an across-the-board appraisal of "the scope, trends and costs of programs in the economic, social, and human rights fields." The appraisal reports, which were prepared by each agency, were analyzed by a special Council committee, and a consolidated report was issued in 1960.[7] This impressive document endeavored to project program trends, their costs and significance over the five-year period 1959–64. At the outset of this appraisal some of the specialized agencies were fearful of having some "master plan" imposed upon them, but their concern gradually turned into a grudging admission of the usefulness of the forward appraisal exercise. In certain cases, notably FAO, significant subsequent shifts in the allocation of budgetary resources for program purposes can be traced to suggestions emanating from the ECOSOC consolidated report.

Concurrent with the above efforts for program coordination, a still different approach has been tried since the middle 1950s; namely, the "concerted action" technique, where the joint effort of several agencies is required both at the planning and the execution stages for complex projects. The initiative for this approach came primarily from the Social Commission of ECOSOC under the impetus of the Bureau of Social Affairs of the UN Secretariat. It was first applied in the field of "community development" (later, at the instance of FAO, called "rural and community development"), and it has since been projected into such areas as urbanization, industrialization,

[7] E/3347, 5 May 1960.

oceanography, and housing.[8] In specialized agency circles there
has been a tendency to criticize these programs, especially that
of community development, for their "fuzziness" of definition.
Perhaps their chief merit has been to stimulate interagency cooperation at the field level through joint projects and the
utilization of interdisciplinary teams.

Another development has been the establishment within the
UN Secretariat, with ECOSOC's approval, of so-called "centers" designed to facilitate integrated planning by the UN
and related agencies in selected crucial functional areas. In
1964 three such centers were in operation: one for water resources development, another for industrial development, and a
third for economic projections and programming. A fourth
center, for housing, building, and planning, has been proposed
by the newly created ECOSOC committee under this name.[9]
These centers appear to have been accorded a higher hierarchical status than other major functional units in the Department
of Economic and Social Affairs. One of them, the center for
industrial development, seemed to reflect a compromise solution in lieu of the establishment of a new agency to handle
program activities in an area allegedly not covered adequately
by the UN and ILO, although in 1964 ECOSOC endorsed by
a close vote the establishment of a new specialized agency for
industrial development. As for water resources development,
in which FAO has a major interest and WHO and UNESCO
a minor but significant stake, the UN center has been charged
by certain officers of these interested agencies of having developed "imperialistic" tendencies.[10]

[8] For a review of this experience see the *Report of the Social Commission*,
15th Session, E/3769, May 1963.

[9] See E/3719/Rev.1, March, 1963, E/3918, 16 June 1964, and ECOSOC Resolution 976 (XXXVI), 1 August 1963

[10] In interviews by the writer with senior officials of FAO, UNESCO, and
WHO. During the summer of 1964, the Water Resources Development Center was "downgraded" by the Secretary-General by being reabsorbed into
the Resources and Transport Division of the Department of Economic and
Social Affairs. See E/3894/Rev.1, 19 May 1964.

For the most part, the various coordination devices cited above have been hortatory only, lacking any really effective sanction. Without doubt the most far-reaching impact by ECOSOC on interagency program relations was the establishment of the two major technical cooperation programs: EPTA and the Special Fund. These two operational programs added significantly to agency resources under ground rules laid down by special UN organs, and, on a much narrower front, WFP, administered jointly by FAO and the UN, has done the same.[11] As requests from governments for technical services have mounted with new resources available from EPTA and the Special Fund, interagency rivalry, although it has by no means entirely disappeared, has distinctly diminished. ECOSOC's role in relation to the substantive content of EPTA and the Special Fund up to 1965 mainly took the form of urging governments to initiate aid requests in fields calling for special attention (for example, economic development planning, education and training, land reform, and so forth) or suggesting to the control authorities of these programs, TAB, TAC, and the Special Fund Governing Council, the desirability of shifting a larger portion of the available program resources to a particular regional area, such as Africa.

Otherwise, it cannot be said that ECOSOC has played a leadership role of any marked significance. Its general debates on the World Economic Report and the Report on the World Social Situation occasionally produce interesting exchanges on broad policy issues, but these scarcely touch the operational provinces of the UN family in the economic and social domains. Ideological overtones sometimes detract from any material impact such talkfests might have on UN system program activities, let alone on national government policies. But another reason why the Council has only rarely exercised important policy leadership stems from the fact that it has become overshadowed

[11] GA Resolution 1714 (XVI), 19 December 1961.

by the General Assembly, especially since the great influx of new nonwestern members in the last decade. Whether enlargement of the Council's membership in 1966 will help to swing the pendulum of policy leadership back to the Council is a matter that will be considered later.

THE ROLE OF THE GENERAL ASSEMBLY. As indicated earlier, the relations of the General Assembly and ECOSOC are not precisely defined under the UN Charter as regards economic and social matters. Under Article 13 of the Charter, the General Assembly *"shall* [not may] initiate studies and make recommendations of the purpose of . . . (*b*) promoting international cooperation in the economic, social, cultural, educational, and health fields [italics added]," thus allowing the Assembly to extend its interests into the domain of various specialized agencies. Article 17 added an injunction "to examine the administrative budgets of such . . . specialized agencies with a view to making recommendations to the agencies concerned." Finally, by Article 60, the Assembly was given general responsibility for the discharge of Charter functions in respect of international economic and social cooperation, both directly and, "under its authority," through the Economic and Social Council.

The General Assembly's use of its power to review specialized agency budgets, including the approval of budgetary and financial arrangements with the agencies, which was discussed in the preceding essay, shows that the Assembly's impact has been limited almost entirely to administrative and financial practices and procedures. Rarely has its scrutiny of agency budgets dealt with the program implications of financial expenditures.

In relation to ECOSOC, the General Assembly has played a dual role. First, it has not hesitated, on occasion, to initiate new undertakings and to issue to ECOSOC more or less definite directives as to how such undertakings should be carried out. Sometimes these directives have been given concurrently to the Secretary-General, ECOSOC, and the specialized agencies involved, or to the Secretary-General "in consultation with the heads of the specialized agencies." The frequency of such initiatives appears to have grown as the balance of voting power in the Assembly has shifted to the new developing states of Asia and Africa.

Second, the General Assembly has ratified, often without substantial change but usually after extended talk, the program decisions taken by ECOSOC. Seldom has the Assembly gone so far as to reject an ECOSOC policy decision involving the UN system: during recent years, on the contrary, the tendency has been to expand the scope, and cost, of ECOSOC proposals, especially those involving the interests of the developing nations. Certain of these actions have taken on rather grandiose dimensions without regard to the feasibility of obtaining revenues for their execution. In this fashion the working relations of the two bodies have evolved pragmatically, without any effort by the General Assembly to work out an orderly delegation of responsibility to ECOSOC so as to minimize the duplication of discussion and action by the two organs.

A few concrete cases may help to illustrate this pattern. The proposal for the UN Development Decade originated in the General Assembly, largely on the initiative of the United States delegation following President Kennedy's speech before the Assembly in 1961. The resolution calling for this long-range undertaking requested the specialized agencies to prepare proposals indicating how each of them might best contribute to the success of the decade's objectives, which were to be formulated in some detail by the Secretary-General for consideration a year hence. This the Secretary-General did in the form of a comprehensive report entitled *The United Nations Development Decade: Proposals for Action.*[12] These proposals were

[12] UN Publication Sales No.: 62.II.B.2. The Secretary-General proposed as a minimum target an annual economic growth rate of 5 percent for the developing countries by the end of the decade.

forwarded to ECOSOC for consideration at its 1962 summer session. Meanwhile, the Council had set up a Special Committee on Coordination to study in particular what the priority areas should be with a view to accelerating progress toward the objectives of the Decade. A flow of progress reports has issued since then from ECOSOC and, by request, from the specialized agencies.

As already suggested, the Development Decade idea was intended to set forth a central theme and goal for the over-all economic and social development programs already under way or to be initiated within the UN family of agencies. The fact that it did not, however, provide for any additional resources led a considerable number of international officials to set it down mainly as a publicity gimmick and a breeder of unnecessary reports. On the whole, however, the idea was favorably received by the specialized agencies.

A second example of General Assembly initiative may be seen in its recent proposal for a world literacy campaign.[13] Literacy clearly falls within the province of UNESCO, and the agency has done a great deal of valuable technical work in this field over the years. The Assembly's proposal asked UNESCO to prepare a report on plans and costs of a worldwide attack designed to eradicate illiteracy within the foreseeable future (that is, within ten years or so). This report, *World Campaign for Universal Literacy*, was briefly considered by ECOSOC and then referred to the General Assembly at its 1963 session. The Assembly, by resolution, adopted a sweeping and somewhat emotional appeal to national governments, nongovernmental organizations, and UNESCO itself to contribute technical and financial assistance for the conduct of the campaign, estimated to cost some $10 million a year for ten years.[14] Since there was little likelihood that any such amount

---

[13] See GA Resolution 1677 (XVI), 18 December 1961.
[14] GA Resolution 1937 (XVIII), 11 December 1963.

could be raised through voluntary channels, the net practical effect was probably a modestly increased appropriation from UNESCO's regular budget to support various anti-illiteracy pilot projects, although it is possible that the General Assembly, by focusing world attention on the problem of illiteracy, may have stimulated certain national education ministries to do more than they otherwise would have done to reduce its dimensions.

A third illustration involves the General Assembly only indirectly. The source of action was a report of the Assembly's Scientific Advisory Committee calling for the convening of a full-dress UN conference on the Application of Science and Technology for the Benefit of the Less Developed Areas.[15] Reacting favorably to this proposal, ECOSOC set in motion plans for such a conference, which took place in Geneva early in 1963.[16] Out of this meeting flowed numerous suggestions as to how UN system resources might be better related to the use of science and technology in industrial, agricultural, and social development programs. A minority group in the conference, moreover, took the position that a new specialized agency was needed to carry forward the objectives of the conference; whereupon UNESCO was aroused to action, making it widely known that it had been devoting a major share of its resources for years to the promotion of science and its application. Ultimately ECOSOC, on the recommendation of the UN Secretary-General, decided to set up a permanent Advisory Committee on the Application of Science and Technology to Development.[17] By way of reaction UNESCO proceeded to magnify the role of science in its own range of activities: (1) by raising the budgetary level of science up to that of education, and (2) by creating, largely at the expense of the social sci-

[15] E/3510, 24 May 1961.
[16] E/3772, 21 May 1963, contains the Secretary-General's report on the work and recommendations of this conference.
[17] For details see ECOSOC Resolution 980 A (XXXVI), 1 August 1963.

ences, a new secretariat department for the Application of Science to Development.[18] This is a clear example of how an initiative taken by a UN policy organ may prompt a specialized agency to alter the internal allocation of its resources in a particular functional direction.

This kind of impact may operate even more indirectly, as in the case of the creation of OPEX by the General Assembly on the recommendation of the Secretary-General in 1958.[19] A novel type of technical assistance, the UN's part in this experiment was at first financed wholly out of the UN regular budget and administered exclusively by the UN Secretariat. It soon became so popular with governments, however, and its scope was so widened that certain specialized agencies found it expedient to introduce OPEX-type arrangements into their own programs. By 1963 ECOSOC was persuaded, subject to the General Assembly's approval, to authorize the use of funds for such purposes from EPTA. This was a particularly constructive, if unusual, case of UN creativity that influenced and furthered the coordination of UN and specialized agency field programming.

Other illustrations are available. One rather different type of ECOSOC–General Assembly interaction arises in the twilight zone between the economic and political, where ECOSOC, after batting the ball back and forth for a number of sessions, may request the Secretary-General to place an item on the Assembly's agenda, seemingly with a view to getting rid of further responsibility for it. That happened in the 1962 session of ECOSOC, when such action was taken with reference to long-debated plans for studies of "the economic and social consequences of disarmament." [20] Another case that illustrates one of

[18] See UNESCO Document 13 C/5. The UNESCO Director-General and several delegates to the Executive Board (sixty-fifth session) contended that the Geneva Conference on Science and Technology should have been convoked by UNESCO and cited authority in UNESCO's Constitution to support this view.

[19] GA Resolution 1256 (XIII), 14 November 1958.

[20] ECOSOC Resolution 891 (XXXIV), 26 July 1962.

the rare reminders by ECOSOC to the General Assembly that the Assembly, too, has a responsibility for aiding the program coordination process occurred when ECOSOC recommended that the Assembly should conduct prior consultations with the specialized agencies before adopting any project or proposal relating to matters of important concern to such agency or agencies.[21] It seems, however, that the consequences of this resolution have thus far been negligible.

To sum up: the part played by the General Assembly in formulating and integrating policy in the economic and social domain has grown in impact especially since the middle 1950s. Its Second and Third Committees have tended to become the arena for a variety of initiatives, a good many of which reflect a lack of awareness of the structural characteristics and limited resources of the UN functional agencies. Frequently directives are given to ECOSOC as well as to the specialized agencies, which regard them as weird or unrealistic, or, at best, wasteful of time and energy.[22] Some of the Assembly's proposals would appear to be politically inspired, and others suggest the motivations of propaganda rather than any expectation of achievement.

[21] ECOSOC Resolution 800 (XXXIV), 3 August 1960. ECOSOC itself is obligated to do this as regards its own actions by rule 80 of its Rules of Procedure.

[22] For example, the proposal for a "World Campaign against Hunger, Disease and Ignorance" adopted by GA Resolution 1943 (XVIII), 11 December 1963, was a grandiose emotional appeal to governments, specialized agencies, and the non-governmental organizations to mobilize their efforts and public opinion for a laudable end, but with no financial provision to enable the UN family to make any significant contribution. ACC, to which the proposal was referred, indicated a certain annoyance over its "make work" features and the lack of any earmarked resources for its implementation, pointedly noting that world campaigns were already under way, or projected, against hunger and illiteracy. Similarly, WHO was embarrassed by General Assembly action in two other recent instances: (1) a resolution calling for an "International Medical Year," and (2) another proposing the establishment of international cancer research prizes. The first idea was received coolly as being "too spectacular" and of little utility, whereupon the UN let it drop. While WHO had reservations concerning the cancer research prizes as the best way to promote research in this field, it reluctantly agreed to serve as the nominating body.

At the same time, the Assembly consumes endless hours of debate on fairly routine ECOSOC program decisions, which more often than not end in their formal ratification without change. What is needed, among other things, is a more rational division of labor between the General Assembly and ECOSOC.

INTERAGENCY COORDINATION DEVICES. As the volume and complexity of international economic and social action under the sponsorship of the UN system has grown, its internal coordination has depended increasingly on arrangements taken at the staff level. At most, the intergovernmental control organs can only provide general guidelines and broad directives; it is in the *implementation* of programs that the occasions for confusion, conflict, and a dissipation of resources are most likely to occur. Without effective, continuing staff consultation and agreement between agencies, nothing ECOSOC (or the General Assembly) does by way of formal decisions on programs can serve as more than façade.

This point was clearly recognized early in the history of the UN system with the establishment by ECOSOC of ACC, which was designed to serve the functions of an administrative quasi-cabinet, although without collective responsibility to any single policy control body. Consisting of the executive heads of the specialized agencies and IAEA, under the chairmanship of the UN Secretary-General, ACC performs (or is responsible for) top-level staff work for the Council on both administrative and substantive matters. It provides for the Council periodic reviews of developments in interagency program relations and, in addition, offers advice as to how emerging fields of activity that cut across agency boundaries (for example, the peaceful uses of atomic energy, oceanography, and so forth) should be handled. It also at times acts as a kind of staff-level referee when serious jurisdictional disputes arise.

To facilitate its tasks, ACC has developed considerable subsidiary machinery. The busy heads of the specialized agencies, meeting only twice a year for two or three days at most, could hardly deal with the bulging agenda of ACC without the help of a Preparatory Committee of Deputies. This committee, consisting of agency representatives at the second or third hierarchical level, sits for four or five days prior to the meeting of ACC itself, sifts through the material assembled for ACC consideration, and, according to reliable information, draws up in skeleton form ACC's Report to ECOSOC and leaves only the more controversial items to be filled in after discussion by ACC itself.[23] ACC meets in private. Neither a verbatim nor a summary record of its discussions is made public, only a report in essay form, often with numerous special annexes and appendices. ACC's decisions are arrived at by consensus, which is often watered down, for, as one senior official has said, the agency heads have preferred to settle differences around their own private table rather than in a public intergovernmental forum like ECOSOC.

In addition to the Preparatory Committee, there has been a small staff unit in the UN Department of Economic and Social Affairs to perform the year round spade work for the semi-annual meetings of ACC, a unit recently under some criticism in ECOSOC for not being entirely adequate for its job. Also, ACC has created as needed, either on *ad hoc* or a continuing basis, a cluster of subcommittees, working groups, and interagency "meetings" in specific subject-matter areas. A few of these subgroups deal with common administrative matters and the most important of them is CCAQ. But most of them are concerned with interagency substantive problems. During the year 1963, for example, the list of such subsidiary groups included the following:

Sub-committee on science and technology

Working groups on housing and related community facilities

[23] According to one perceptive staff official, "The ACC is only as good as its Preparatory Committee."

and on urbanization (combined in 1964 into one group on
housing, building, and planning)
Interagency meeting on water resources
Working party to establish a draft framework of functional
classifications for UN system activities
Working group on evaluation of programs
Interagency meeting on juvenile delinquency
Interagency meeting on the peaceful uses of outer space
Subcommittee on oceanography
Subcommittee on education and training
Working group on rural and community development
Ad hoc interagency meeting on the rehabilitation of the
handicapped

In previous years there were similar groups on commodity
problems, on land reform (a chronic bone of contention between FAO and ILO), on social programs, on migration, and
on atomic energy, to mention only some. The year 1964
brought into existence a committee of agency representatives
on a program of studies of the economic and social consequences of disarmament.

Most of these subsidiary groups report to the Preparatory
Committee of Deputies. Since their proceedings are for the
most part private, it is difficult for an outsider to form a judgment of their value. But they do bring together the staff people who "get their hands dirty" in the planning and conduct of
cooperative activities. Reportedly, such persons, while initially
viewing themselves as "instructed" agency delegates, tend for
the most part to develop a wider, "UN Community" point of
view.

Not only through the staff machinery evolved by ACC but
by many kinds of information arrangements on their own
initiative the secretariats of the UN and the specialized agencies
conduct day-to-day consultation on a host of operational matters, without which the loose, cumbersome UN machine might

at times grind to a halt. In this connection, agency liaison offices at UN Headquarters play an important role. The volume of consultation has constantly grown since the inception of EPTA in 1949. The advent of the Special Fund nine years later multiplied still further the points of contact—and potential friction—among the agencies.

Interagency Competition

Notwithstanding substantial improvement during the past five or six years, there still persist pockets of rivalry among certain of the agencies and an inclination to expand agency prerogatives when an opportunity presents itself. The more strictly technical the province of an agency, the less prone it is to seek jurisdictional expansion. Such agencies as WHO, ICAO, ITU, and WMO fall in this class, though even they may sometimes display suspicion over any threatened "encroachment" on their domain. It tends to be the agencies with broadly or vaguely delimited economic and social functions, not excluding the UN itself, that at times exhibit "expansionist" behavior, as it is called by their rivals. The following statement, however, in a 1960 and quite properly praised volume now seems exaggerated: "In practice the specialized agencies negotiate together over any piece of work involving their collaboration in the high manner of independent sovereign states, whose basically friendly relations are constantly in jeopardy because their spheres of influence abut on one another." [24] Such a state of affairs may have existed during the early years of UN development but agency secretariats have learned to work together on friendly and cooperative terms most of the time.

In 1965 interagency competition was still fairly keen in such fields as the following: (1) land reform, involving mainly FAO and ILO; (2) water resources, where the main issue is how the

[24] Andrew Shonfield, *The Attack on World Poverty* (New York, Random House, 1960), p. 187.

control over river basin and ground water projects should be divided, FAO contending that agriculture is the most important interest, the UN contesting this view, and WHO claiming a stake in view of its concern for ensuring pure water supplies;[25] (3) rural development, where the leading contenders are FAO, ILO, and UNESCO;[26] (4) industrial development, where the labor-oriented ILO seems to fear the encroachment of the management-oriented UN on its constitutional preserves, and where, indeed, there has been a considerable body of opinion in favor of establishing a new agency to focus upon industrialization problems in their entirety;[27] and finally, (5) science and technology, where potential rivalry between UNESCO and IAEA may give rise to jurisdictional disputes, the situation being complicated by the fact that several other agencies, notably FAO, WHO, WMO, ITU, and the UN itself have definite interests in specific phases of the development of atomic as well as other newer forms of energy.[28]

The resolution of jurisdictional differences between cognate agencies has often best been promoted by bilateral or multilateral agreements. In large part it is through these agreements,

[25] FAO reluctantly supported the creation of the UN Water Resources Development Center on the understanding that it would only "coordinate." But, as intimated earlier, the center itself soon became a competitor for water projects financed by the Special Fund. Dissatisfaction with the center led ACC in its 1964 report to recommend that the development of a coordinated water resources program should be left to the ACC sub-committee on water resources, thereby diminishing the UN's role vis-à-vis FAO and other agencies. See E/3886, 6 May 1964.

[26] ACC has tried to resolve the knotty problem of jurisdiction on this subject through a series of interagency meetings that defined areas of "primary responsibility" and of "common interest." But the concept of "rural development," as distinct from "community development," remains a confused one, and there has been much resistance from ILO (and to some extent WHO) to recognizing rural development as a separate program area.

[27] See, for details, E/3781, Annex VIII, May 1963.

[28] At the IAEA headquarters some officials believe that this agency's province represents "the wave of the future" through the far-reaching effects of science and technology. In 1963 an intersecretariat working group was established by IAEA and UNESCO with a view to reaching agreement on arrangements for "cooperation in research, training, and scientific abstracts." See E/3886, Annex XII, 6 May 1964.

both formal and informal, that coordination difficulties are smoothed out. There have been almost innumerable examples of interagency agreements over the years, most of them stemming from joint secretariat initiative and a few consisting of joint committees of experts appointed by the policy-making organs of the institutions concerned. A notable illustration of the latter arrangement is the joint WHO/FAO Committee on Nutrition, which has functioned successfully from the very beginning of the two agencies. A comparably successful early agreement was that relating to occupational health, with WHO and ILO as the participating parties.

EDUCATION AND TRAINING. As a field for technical assistance activity, education and training has given rise to a succession of fairly stubborn jurisdictional problems, most of which have by now been ironed out by interagency understandings at the staff level. Here, of course, one is dealing with subject matter that cuts across the entire gamut of the UN family in one way or another: primary, secondary, higher, adult, technical, and vocational education—all relate to the manpower aspects of the UN's central theme of development. In the field of agricultural education, three agencies, FAO, ILO, and UNESCO, held a series of interstaff meetings from 1960 to 1962, out of which emerged a memorandum of agreement on future consultations, the division of responsibility, and arrangements for joint surveys and other projects.

As regards public administration, a series of working agreements that allocate jurisdiction has been concluded between the UN Division for Public Administration and the interested specialized agencies:[29]

United Nations: the training of personnel specialized in a particular branch and the in-service training of administrative grades of the public service (for example, the establishment of schools and institutes)

[29] See E/3765, May 1963, for the full text.

UNESCO: the advancement of the social sciences through the development of higher education and research in public administration in the university context

ILO: pre-entry and post-entry training of the lower grades and general responsibility for technical training

All specialized agencies to deal with administrative problems that concern public organizations specializing in the spheres of the agency in question (for example, education, labor, health, aviation, and so forth)

Notwithstanding the complicated nature of this understanding, it is reported to be proving reasonably effective in preventing duplicatory efforts and actions at cross purposes. Coordination in this all-embracing domain was aided by the appointment of a full-time UN consultant "to serve as liaison and to develop joint projects" between the UN and specific agencies. Public administration advisers were also being posted to the staffs of the regional commissions as a means of keeping in proper perspective the public administration needs of each region, with due regard for specialized agency roles.

Under the general rubric of interagency coordination devices, special mention is in order here of two new factors in the UN picture that may extend markedly the range of international action in educational development. One of these factors was the establishment of regional institutes on economic development planning under the aegis of the UN regional commissions. Within each institute there has been a section on the role of educational planning in general economic and social development, bringing together the economists and the educators in a joint endeavor. In 1964 ECOSOC took note of the desirability of close working interrelationships being developed among these regional economic planning institutes.[30] The other factor was the creation of an International Institute for Educa-

[30] ECOSOC Resolution 1036 (XXXVII), 17 August 1964.

tional Planning in Paris under UNESCO auspices, which has been partly financed by a grant from IBRD, indicating the Bank's emerging interest in education and an intention to make loans and possibly grants for education and training purposes. To paraphrase ACC's language, the various regional institutes, together with the Paris Institute, should help to keep education and training projects in line with the aims of the Development Decade.

LAND REFORM. Another field with a long history of inter-agency problems within the UN framework is land reform. Beginning in 1960, however, a General Assembly resolution led to the initiation of a series of reports on the progress of land reform prepared jointly by the UN Secretariat, FAO, and ILO. Meanwhile, over the years, FAO has carried on a continuing program of research, serviced technical meetings, and conducted numerous field surveys of land tenure and land settlement conditions, and agricultural credit. In 1961 the General Assembly decided to designate FAO as having *major* responsibility for work in this field. The Assembly also endorsed an ECOSOC resolution of 1962 that requested the Secretary-General to assign high priority to services for facilitating the execution of reform plans. The UN role has been mainly the study of agrarian reform questions in the broad context of planning for economic and social development.

The various UN resolutions on this subject have had a modest practical effect: namely, stimulating governments to give policy support to land reform in a limited number of countries. The priority attached by the UN to activities in this controversial field has also tended to lure ILO into claiming a substantial stake in it, with special reference to the status of the independent farmer and worker and to the development of rural cooperatives. In the eyes of FAO's professional staff, this represented a violation of the spirit of the Assembly's action in assigning major responsibility to FAO. Unlike most of the other

overlapping fields noted above, no interagency staff agreement
or *modus operandi* had been reached by 1964, although ILO
was then preparing a large-scale conference on agrarian reform
to which FAO and the UN were invited.[31]

TRADE AND COMMODITY PROBLEMS. In no area has international
machinery proliferated so much, chiefly on an ad hoc basis, as
in that of trade and commodity problems. A study made by a
group of UN experts in 1963 pointed out that the number of
international organizations and suborganizations dealing with
such problems had increased from only eight in 1945 to forty-
three in 1963.[32] Yet there exists no general, global organization
for trade. The FAO's province clearly encompasses *agricultural*
commodities, and it has had since 1949 a standing advisory Committee on Commodity Problems. The secretariat in the headquarters at Rome, moreover, carries on commodity research of
high quality. Study groups on specific commodities have been
set up on the initiative of the FAO Committee and of governments. The Secretary-General of the UN has also convened
various conferences to deal with individual commodities, such
as tin, sugar, wheat, olive oil, lead, zinc, coffee, and cocoa. International commodity agreements are now in force for sugar,
tin, wheat, olive oil, and coffee.

As early as 1947 ECOSOC indicated its concern over the
un-coordinated character of international action in the commodities field by setting up an "Interim Coordinating Committee for International Commodity Arrangements," with four
expert members. But it was not until after the sharp decline in
raw materials prices, following the Korean war, that pressure
in the UN from the underdeveloped countries led to further
action. Thus, in 1954 ECOSOC established a Commission on

[31] For a full account of the background of UN system action in this field,
see the Working Paper prepared by the Technical Advisory Group on
Agrarian Reform for ILO. Document Ag Rf/1, Geneva, October 1963.
[32] E/3756, 27 June 1963. Chapter 2 of this report summarizes the tortuous
history of actions by UN system and other machinery in this field.

International Commodity Trade. Four years later its terms of reference were broadened so as to cover the study of developments and trends in international commodity trade, including excessive fluctuations in terms of trade and their effects on economic development. This Commission has been served by a small unit in the UN Bureau of General Economic Research and Policies. Since the functions of the Commission overlapped to some extent those of the FAO Committee, the two bodies held a joint session in 1962. A joint report, dealing with the prospective production of and the demand for primary commodities, national marketing boards and price stabilization funds, and international compensatory financing, was issued and submitted to the two parent bodies, ECOSOC and the Council of FAO.[33]

The FAO Commission has continued to make a report to ECOSOC annually, drawing heavily on FAO and GATT activities, but it has been written independently of the UN World Economic Survey. Thus the UN has received two separate and sometimes duplicating or partially conflicting sets of conclusions on commodity problems. In the past, the staff work by FAO in this area has been regarded as somewhat more solidly based than that by the UN; FAO seems to have kept in closer touch with other agencies concerned with commodity problems than the UN.

The foregoing commentary on the UN system's role in the field of international trade and commodity problems is intended to reveal the institutional and functional confusion that can arise from the absence of any adequate mandate to deal with one of the most complex policy questions now facing the rapidly changing world community. In their effort to fill in the partial vacuum, the UN, FAO, as well as IMF and other intergovernmental actions, had by 1964 spawned a congeries of com-

[33] See the *Report of the Thirty-fifth Session of the Committee on Commodity Problems*, FAO Document CCP 62/68: CL 39/4 (Rome, 1962).

missions, committees, study groups, and special agreements without any effective integration. This state of affairs was marked by a free-swinging discussion of basic trade issues in ECOSOC and still more in the Second Committee of the General Assembly with a substantial amount of research, but singularly little multilateral action by governments, leaving aside GATT by the noncommunist "advanced" countries.

The lack of any central intergovernmental institution endowed with some degree of authority in the field of trade and commodity problems generally prompted the movement, which was spearheaded by the communist bloc and strongly seconded by the Afro-Asian countries, to hold a UN World Conference on Trade and Development at the intergovernmental level. A decision to convene such a conference was taken by ECOSOC at its 1962 summer session and endorsed by the General Assembly the same year.[34] Although FAO took no official position with regard to the utility of a world trade conclave, at the outset some of its senior professional staff were flatly opposed on the ground that the idea was "politically inspired" and was likely to lead only to another "world debating forum." Gradually, however, the FAO secretariat came around to the view that such a meeting might perhaps help to streamline international machinery in the trade field. A portion of the massive documentation for the Trade and Development Conference was prepared by the FAO staff, with some of the papers written in consultation with the UN Secretariat.

Whether any additional, or reorganized, international machinery can help much without some real *rapprochement* on trade policies between the North and South countries, as well as between the communists and the free world, is debatable, but, with a view to satisfying in some degree the insistent demands of the developing countries and communist bloc for special new

[34] ECOSOC Resolution 917 (XXXIV), 3 August 1962, and GA Resolution 1785 (XVII), 8 December 1962.

international machinery in the trade field under UN auspices, the UN Conference on Trade and Development in 1964 recommended (1) that the Conference be established as "an organ of the General Assembly," to meet at least every three years, (2) that there be set up a Trade and Development Board of fifty-five members to serve as the standing committee for the Conference and to report annually to the Assembly *through ECOSOC*, and (3) that within the UN Secretariat an "adequate, permanent and full-time secretariat" be created to service the Conference and the Board.[35] These hybrid and decidedly top-heavy arrangements were approved by the General Assembly. New problems of program coordination can be foreseen in the need to mesh the staff roles of the UNCTAD secretariat, the UN Department of Economic and Social Affairs, and the FAO and IMF staffs, as well as harmonizing the policy roles of the Trade Conference, the Trade Development Board, the General Assembly, and ECOSOC.

Secondment of Staff and Interagency Management

At a lower order of coordinative action, specialized agency staff have been seconded to the UN Secretariat in cooperative programs in recent years. For example, FAO has sent a member of its staff to serve on the UN Center for Industrial Development in order to explain the FAO's concern that the role of the farm machinery, fertilizer, seed, and food-processing industries not be overlooked in any realistic industrial development program, while FAO, WHO, and the WMO staff have been assigned to the Water Resources Development Center in New York, but the results have not always been happy.

Another coordinative device is the unique management of WFP. This program, authorized originally by the General Assembly in 1960, received FAO's official endorsement shortly thereafter. The FAO Director-General, on request, then pro-

[35] E/CONF.46/L.28, Annex A, 16 June 1964.

duced a comprehensive report on the potentialities of *Development through Food—a Strategy for Surplus Utilization.*[36] On
the basis of this study, the General Assembly approved in the
following year the establishment of an "experimental World
Food Program to be undertaken jointly" by the UN and FAO
and to be controlled by a joint UN/FAO Intergovernmental
Committee. Under the guidance of this Committee a joint UN/
FAO administrative unit was devised to manage the program.
This unit, headed by an executive director responsible jointly
to the Secretary-General of the UN and the Director-General
of FAO, included staff assigned from FAO and the UN, with
recent additions from ILO and WHO. The office is in Rome,
but there has been a tiny liaison group at UN Headquarters in
New York and a small field staff posted to countries where
WFP projects are under way.

From the administrative standpoint there would appear to be
no reason why WFP could not have been managed just as well
by FAO alone, for it is the principal agency dealing with food
policies in the UN family. Although the UN's initial blessing
of the program may have had psychological value and may have
helped to stimulate voluntary contributions from governments,
the handling of food shipments to aid development projects
has not involved any technique in which the UN itself has a
special competence. In the field, moreover, WFP has been
making use of the UN Resident Representatives, just as FAO
itself has done.

In sum, under the broad rubric "inter-agency coordinative
devices" a whole range of procedures have been evolved,
largely at the headquarters administrative level, with a view to
bringing related agency activities into some sort of cooperative
setting. As the United States delegate to ECOSOC noted some
years ago: "All this has been achieved not by way of centraliza-

[36] Published by FAO (Rome, 1961)

tion, not by directives and orders, but by consultation and persuasion." [37]

Coordination at the field level has also been markedly furthered, as will be shown in the following pages, not only by the expanded role of the UN resident representatives at the country level, but by the regional economic commissions as a consequence of devolution of program functions to them by ECOSOC and their closer working relations with specialized agency field staffs.

Improvements in Coordination Arrangements

Are there inherent weaknesses, or deficiencies, in the processes of program coordination, that are susceptible to elimination or improvement? Both ECOSOC, as the key coordinating organ at the policy level, and ACC with its auxiliary machinery need to be examined.

A MORE EFFECTIVE ECOSOC. The comments on ECOSOC's limitations that follow are based in considerable part on direct observation of the proceedings of its 1963 summer session in Geneva and a survey of secretariat opinion carried out between February and November of 1963, which involved interviews with approximately seventy staff officials of the UN, FAO, UNESCO, ILO, and WHO. This survey was designed to discover, first, what kind of program impact these officials believed ECOSOC had had on their respective agencies as well as on the UN system as a whole, and, second, how they would assess ECOSOC's utility, difficulties, and potentialities for improvement. As far as possible, the officials selected for interview were experienced persons of middle or senior grade who had participated importantly in various aspects of interagency program coordination.

[37] Statement by Walter Kotschnig to ECOSOC, 11 July 1958, as reproduced in the U.S. Department of State *Bulletin*, 1 September 1958.

The most striking impression derived from this survey was that specialized agency officialdom had comparatively little respect for ECOSOC and its elaborate committee system. This attitude, based on reasonably conclusive evidence, appeared to have intensified in 1964. With few exceptions the interviewees concurred that the quality of ECOSOC personnel, especially the delegates, was "low" and that it had "declined" appreciably within recent years. More specifically, certain officials noted that there were fewer top-flight economists on the delegations than formerly. Only a small group of delegations, perhaps five at most, were believed to do much, if any, homework on the massive documentation before the Council. One ILO official remarked that not only were most of the delegations lacking in technical competence but also in political sensitivity and that many of them had inadequate knowledge of the nature of the UN system or how it really functioned in the economic and social sphere. Part of this may be explained by the tendency of the smaller countries on ECOSOC to draw upon second- and third-level staff members from their New York UN missions for participation in the Council's work, whereas the Western European countries, in answering the claims of the new regional institutions for talent, may have adversely affected the level of their representation to ECOSOC.

The mediocre quality of ECOSOC personnel and its alleged recent deterioration may also be related to the existing "unrepresentativeness" of the membership of the Council. In 1946 the membership of ECOSOC represented slightly over a third of the entire membership of the UN; eighteen years later the figure had dropped to about 16 percent. Many of the newer countries, therefore, have not taken ECOSOC very seriously and felt that they could make a greater impact upon the General Assembly where they can "get something" for themselves.

Proposals for enlarging the size of the Council had been introduced repeatedly for more than a decade, only to die chiefly because of the Soviet Union's opposition to any amendment of the Charter until the People's Republic of China was admitted to the UN.[38] During the 1963 session of the Assembly, however, a resolution was adopted formally proposing an amendment by which nine additional members would be added to ECOSOC, to be chosen as follows: seven from the African and Asian states, one from Latin America, and one from Western European and other states.[39] This amendment was ratified by more than two-thirds of the members of the UN, including all the permanent members of the Security Council, by August 1965 and provides more equitable representation in the Council. It should allow the *major* developing countries to exert a more responsible influence there than in the Second and Third Committees of the Assembly, where the Afro-Asian majority has often produced "sterile" decisions. Assuming an enhancement of ECOSOC's prestige, some improvement in the general quality of its personnel may also be anticipated.

AGENDA AND DOCUMENTATION. The improved effectiveness of ECOSOC, however, would depend on certain other changes as well. One of its chronic problems stems from an overloaded agenda and massive supporting documentation that must be faced at the major session each summer. Ever since the largely abortive effort of 1951 to "reorganize" the work of ECOSOC, there have been recurring clamors for some practicable way of "controlling" the agenda. Proposals for a standing "agenda committee" have been put forward—and rejected. Meanwhile, the agenda has continued to swell, partly owing to the proliferation of UN bodies concerned with economic and social problems and partly owing to the increasing variety and complexity of international functions in this field.

Supporting documentation for the agenda has increased phe-

[38] For an excellent discussion of the problem of enlarging ECOSOC's membership, see Norman J. Padelford, "Politics and the Future of ECOSOC," *International Organization*, XV (Autumn, 1961), 564–80.
[39] GA Resolution 1991 (XVIII), 17 December 1963.

nomenally. At the 1963 summer session, for example, this
amounted to some 8,000 pages, less than half of which was dis-
tributed to governments within the time limit laid down by the
Council's own Rules of Procedure.[40] Small wonder so little advance homework has been done by ECOSOC delegates or that
"briefing" has become such a difficult operation! An examination of this mass of paper reveals that the bulk of it consists, in
part, of reports of other bodies to ECOSOC and, in part,
of reports by the UN Secretariat and expert groups, called for
by the Council itself at the request of one or more member delegations.[41] Indeed, the governments themselves are largely responsible for the overflow of studies and reports from the administrative bureaucracies. The burden of having to produce so much
documentation of this kind, a lot of which is not given serious
consideration, even if read, has a harmful effect on staff morale.
It is also expensive and time-consuming. Within the Council,
when a stalemate is reached, or there is no sign of any consensus
emerging on the matter under consideration, a move to bring
the discussion to a close by asking for a report—or "another"
report for consideration a year or so later—has often been the
easiest way out. Commenting on this circular behavior, one
wise participant confided that "in reading ECOSOC documents
one has the impression of having already seen the contents in
other documents!"

Although no one, even in the national delegations, contests
the desirability of reducing ECOSOC documentation and the
agenda *in principle*, self-curtailment, in the form of an en-
forceable rule, has not materialized. Nor will this be easy in an
association of sovereign states where each member, no matter its
size or economic contribution, insists on its "equal" rights to

[40] A/5599, 14 November 1963.
[41] The proposed Trade and Development Board will add still another
yearly report to ECOSOC documentation.

introduce business into the meeting.[42] A similar malady, of course, afflicts national parliamentary bodies, except that in the better disciplined ones the executive branch has been able to lay down reasonably effective controls.

Lacking an "executive branch" and being itself composed of dispersed, quasi-autonomous bodies, is it possible for the UN system to contrive any feasible expedient for curtailing the workload of ECOSOC? So far as the volume of documentation is concerned, the UN Secretariat has tried to protect itself somewhat by producing shorter studies, including "background" papers. On the other hand, with a view to saving its own staff time, the Secretariat no longer summarizes the replies of governments to UN inquiries but submits the comments *in extenso* "so that governments can see what other governments think." This procedure only adds to the length of the report.

No substantial remedy for long agenda and massive documentation seems likely without simplifying ECOSOC machinery and procedure and rationalizing its position vis-à-vis the General Assembly. It might, however, be worth while experimenting with a hybrid agenda-control group consisting of ACC plus the outgoing president and vice-presidents of the Council. This arrangement would bring together the special competence of the agency heads and the procedural experience of Council leaders. Such a joint committee might find it useful to meet shortly after the close of the Council's summer session in order to sketch out preliminary agenda for the following year, allocating intersession work and possibly meeting again, after correspondence, to complete its agenda preparation. By qualified

[42] The General Assembly is faced with a similar problem of excessive documentation which, because of its unwieldiness, is even more frustrating. A not inconsiderable portion of the ECOSOC docket consists of inquiries and reports requested by the Assembly. See GA Resolution 1272 (XIII), 14 November 1958, for an attempt, largely ineffective, to control and limit the Assembly's own documentation by exhorting UN organs and by proposing editorial control machinery within the UN Secretariat.

majority vote it might be given the authority to determine the
exclusion, postponement, and/or modification of agenda items,
with two provisos: (1) the Secretary-General or any specialized
agency head would have the right to appeal to the full Council
which might, by a two-thirds vote, overrule the committee on
its action in excluding an item, and (2) the Council itself would
have the right to add items urgently requested by any delegation shortly before or during the session *provided* the request
was supported by two thirds of its membership, after a delay of
at least twenty-four hours between the introduction of the item
and the vote of the Council.

Many objections, sincere and otherwise, would be raised to
such a proposal, and admittedly its chances of adoption on the
first round would be poor. But it would have the merit of bringing the question up sharply and forcing government representatives to stand up and be counted. Some more acceptable arrangement might emerge from the arena of debate, but in any
case ACC members would have to make clear their willingness
to assume this added responsibility and give it serious attention,
for otherwise the scheme would fail.

COMMISSIONS AND COMMITTEES. Useful as the foregoing device might be, reform of the ECOSOC subsidiary machinery
and internal procedures goes more directly to the heart of its
difficulties. In 1959 H. G. Nicholas observed that

Encouraged by the loose language of the Charter, the infant
ECOSOC began by pursuing every social and economic objective
in sight, with an extravagant faith in the virtue of words and
resolutions and in the value of proliferating committees and commissions. . . . Since 1952 some of the categories . . . have been
trimmed, but others have expanded, so that the total structure is
hardly less complex than before.[43]

The situation has not improved during the intervening years.

[43] Nicholas, *United Nations as a Political Institution*, p. 124.

Three new standing (intersessional) committees have come into being: namely, the Committee on Industrial Development in 1960; the Committee on Housing, Building, and Planning in 1962; and the Committee on the Application of Science and Technology in 1963. In 1965, in addition to its four regional commissions, the Council's structure embraced ten functional commissions and standing committees.

Standing committees in certain specialized areas are justified because they provide expertise lacking in ECOSOC and have at their disposal time for deliberation or study not possible within the Council's own crowded timetable. What is more, membership on the commissions and committees has been extended to governments not represented on the parent body. Unfortunately, the history of ECOSOC reveals a strong tendency on the part of several of its functional commissions to behave as policy-initiating rather than as technical advisory bodies because of their predominantly "governmental" composition.[44] One commission, moreover, may spawn another committee: for example, the Committee on Housing, Building, and Planning was recommended to the Council by its own Social Commission. ECOSOC functional commissions tend at times to act as if they were a law unto themselves, drawing up ambitious programs of work and adopting proposals involving financial expenditure. Accordingly, commission reports often provoke prolonged discussion in the Council and then their substantive recommendations must receive formal approval by the parent body, thus leading to a third round of discussions, often in the

[44] A long and at times acrimonious argument took place during the 1963 summer session of ECOSOC over the make-up of the proposed Advisory Committee on Science and Technology, whether it should consist of experts in their private capacity or of governmental appointees (the Soviet position). The upshot was a compromise: appointment by ECOSOC on nomination by the Secretary-General after consultation with governments, on the basis of personal qualifications, knowledge or experience in this field, but "with due regard for geographic representation." ECOSOC Resolution 980 (XXXVI), 1 August 1963. In this case, the appointees were clearly scientists and technologists.

Second or Third Committee of the General Assembly, where some of the very same people participate.

The multiplicity of ECOSOC's subsidiary bodies causes difficulty in scheduling meetings. During recent years, as one means of relieving pressure for meeting space, meetings of certain commissions have been shifted from an annual to a biennial basis. But the problem still remains, due to the mushrooming of ad hoc committees, study groups, and experts' panels. Within a span of two years (1960–62), for instance, the Council set up three different ad hoc committees to study coordination problems, the second of these groups taking over the functions of the first, while the third, with terms of reference restricted to the coordination of "technical assistance" activities, went its own way despite the unreality of separating out technical assistance as a problem of coordination from the problem as a whole.[45] Each such group must not only find a place to hold its sessions but a time that will conflict as little as possible with other international meetings.

The ACABQ of the General Assembly has more than once called attention to the difficulty of incorporating the programs of various ECOSOC commissions and committees into the overall UN budget estimates because of the time cycle under which these groups operate. ECOSOC has not been able to consider their recommendations until its July session, which is too late for ACABQ to scrutinize them during its examination of the UN budget in May–June. "The Secretary General is consequently obliged to submit revised estimates later in the year with the result that it is not until the closing months of the year that member governments are able to obtain a complete picture of the program and budget for the following year."[46] ACABQ

[45] See ECOSOC Resolutions 798 (XXX), 2 August 1960, 851 (XXXII), 4 August 1961, and 920 (XXXIV), 3 August 1962.
[46] See the ACABQ Fifth Report to the eighteenth session of the Assembly, A/5507, August 1963; also its Seventh Report to the nineteenth session, A/5807, September 1964.

has proposed that ECOSOC "undertake a comprehensive review of its entire program cycle, including the meetings schedule of its commissions and committees, with a view to adopting such measures as are necessary to ensure that the complete program in the economic and social field for a given year is drawn up in time for its inclusion in the Secretary-General's budget estimates for that year." Yet it is hard to see how this can be done without eliminating and/or consolidating some of ECOSOC's substructure: there are only so many weeks in the year and a limited number of meeting facilities, let alone the limitations of personnel for international committee work.

ORGANIZATION AND PROCEDURE OF ECOSOC SESSIONS. The *internal* organization and procedure of the Council sessions, while considerably more orderly than a decade ago, has been marked by a good deal of lost motion, confusion, and ineffectiveness. The Council handles its business (apart from the general debates in plenary session) by means of three sessional committees-of-the-whole: the Economic, the Social, and the Coordination Committees. Attendance at these committees has ranged from good to poor depending on the availability of delegation personnel and the degree of interest in the committee's immediate docket. Not infrequently only a little more than a quorum have shown up for a committee meeting, which is usually a sign of general apathy. The committee framework, moreover, has been poorly adapted to the dominant theme of "development." For the 1963 session, the Council secretariat allocated development items to the Coordination Committee, since development had both economic and social aspects, but the substance of development proposals interested the more active delegates, rather than their procedural aspects, and a development committee, instead of the existing committees, would have been a more rational arrangement.

A second shortcoming of the ECOSOC sessional organization has been the perfunctory way in which chairmen have been chosen. Customarily, the UN Secretariat has drawn up a slate of countries among which chairmen might be rotated for the Council and its committees, with little regard for the qualifications of individuals for the difficult post of chairman. This method of constructing the slate for a chairman has produced a disproportionate number of weak, inexperienced chairmen. Nor have they always been adequately advised by committee secretaries on parliamentary procedure. In a few sessions of the Council, for example, several procedural tangles might have been avoided by sophisticated chairmen with timely staff counsel.

The arrangement of agenda items, moreover, has not encouraged sustained, orderly consideration of a problem in ECOSOC. Executive heads of the specialized agencies have often presented their reports with explanatory comments without any real give-and-take discussion between the agency executives and the Council members, and the remarks have tended to be dispersed and spotty, with little attempt by the chairman to keep the speakers "on the beam." [47] Nor has the agenda been well arranged with a view to economizing the time of busy officials. Too many delegates seem bent on delivering "set" speeches on topics that may or may not be relevant to the day's business. All too often, moreover, Council committees seem to "run out

[47] An illustration of the annoying impact of political propaganda on the ECOSOC discussions may be cited from the 1963 summer session. During the Plenary session, while the Executive Secretaries of the regional commissions were reporting, the Soviet Union's delegate tried repeatedly to bring up the charge of "genocide" against the Kurds in Iraq. On a point of order made by the Jordanian delegate, the Soviet delegate was called to order by the Chairman of the Council, but he persisted and eventually produced a "draft resolution" on which he asked immediate consideration. The Chairman, apparently not properly advised by the Council's secretary, put to vote whether the Council's work program should be interrupted, and so forth. The Council decided 13 votes to 0, with 3 abstentions, against interruption, whereupon the Soviet delegate charged the vote was "illegal" and tried again to "motivate" his resolution. On a point of order, the United States delegate said that his Soviet colleague could not explain a "non-vote"! Finally the Soviet delegate subsided but only after threatening to bring up the Kurdish question in every subsequent meeting of the Council and its committees. A full hour had been lost in procedural wrangling that an effective chairman might well have checked.

of steam" in the middle of a session, for, despite the heavy docket, no one has anything to say on the item at hand and the meeting adjourns out of sheer frustration. To cite a typical case: on the afternoon of 17 July 1963, the Coordination Committee of the Council experienced a humiliating state of affairs when no speakers could be produced for a discussion of a UN development decade report that was the principal item before the meeting. Either the delegates had a general lack of interest in this important topic or they had not yet had time to read the document and prepare their remarks, although they were already midway through the ECOSOC session.

It is only fair to note that there are certain small signs of improvement in the offing. The Secretariat in New York has realized the importance of putting forward to the Council the names of persons equipped for the tasks of chairmanship, if such individuals can be spotted in advance, and the Council itself is perhaps becoming aware of the need of "coordinating" its own procedures. A tiny but not entirely insignificant indication of this took place at the 1963 summer session when attention was directed to the labyrinth of substantive resolutions the Council had produced over the years and the difficulty governments were having in finding their way among these many hundreds of declarations, exhortations, requests, recommendations, and program proposals. After seventy-five minutes of discussion, it was decided that since the "multiplicity" of ECOSOC resolutions "was causing considerable confusion especially among the developing countries," the Secretary-General should examine the problems arising therefrom and suggest methods for dealing with these problems, including the preparation of an "annotated index" or a "compendium" on economic, social, and human rights questions.[48]

ECOSOC RELATIONSHIP TO THE GENERAL ASSEMBLY. In a more

[48] ECOSOC Resolution 988 (XXXVI), 2 August 1963. The Secretary-General subsequently advised ECOSOC that an annotated index would be "both more economical to produce and easier to use" than a compendium. E/3880, 25 June 1964.

basic sense, the ECOSOC dilemma may be attributed to the ambiguity of its Charter mandate and the imprecise definition of its relationship to the General Assembly. Can anything constructive, not involving formal amendment of the Charter, be done about it? Over a decade ago Alexander Loveday put forward the suggestion that one way to lessen somewhat the overcharged workload of ECOSOC would be to transfer the consideration of human rights to the Assembly simply by having ECOSOC appoint the Commission on Human Rights and then arranging to have the Commission report directly and only to the Assembly.[49] The long, dreary, and intricate effort to draft acceptable human rights covenants has since then reinforced the soundness of Loveday's proposal, which has won the support of a number of other observers. In effect, ECOSOC has served merely as an unnecessary cog in the chain of discussion from its Commission up through the Third Committee of the Assembly, which has done little more than accentuate in its covenant debates the ideological cleavages already obvious in the Commission. This is of the very stuff of politics, not economic and social cooperation.

The work of two other ECOSOC commissions, those on narcotic drugs and on the status of women, might also be shifted to the General Assembly. The essence of their problems is political, although the economic and social aspects are not without importance. Concurrently, consideration might be given to the advisability of amalgamating the Commission on the Status of Women with the Commission on Human Rights, as it would contribute to the streamlining of UN committee machinery and would not detract from the scope or value of UN action on behalf of women.

The foregoing changes would not appreciably add to the workload of the General Assembly, while they would relieve

[49] Alexander Loveday, "Suggestions for the Reform of the United Nations Economic and Social Machinery," *International Organization*, VII (August, 1953), 325–41.

the agenda of ECOSOC considerably. At the same time the relations of the Assembly and ECOSOC ought to be rationalized further by the Assembly's formally delegating to ECOSOC, through some self-denying ordinance, the right to act *with finality* on all matters affecting interagency relations, economic and social program coordination and evaluation, and the like. Whereas the Assembly would, of course, still be free to adopt broad declarations of policy direction, such as the UN Development Decade, ECOSOC would no longer have to refer decisions on program operation to the Assembly for approval: in other words, ECOSOC would cease acting as an "agenda item factory" for the Assembly, and adding, as Eric Stein pointed out, to the burdens of that "already overburdened and not very efficient" body.[50] The membership base of ECOSOC was widened in 1966 so as to reflect more realistically the political map of the world, and it may be hoped that a revitalized Council will try to measure up to its tasks in a more orderly and responsible manner than heretofore. Perhaps it will feel more disposed to make constructive recommendations to member states and other UN agencies and to curtail its proneness to indulge in vague and innocuous, but "make-work," *pronunciamentos.*

A STRENGTHENED ACC STRUCTURE. Notwithstanding the importance attached to the various proposals put forward in the preceding pages, the ECOSOC problem derives fundamentally from a "crisis" of leadership or, to put the matter more pointedly, from lack of effective staff leadership. In this regard its position is unlike that of the executive boards and general conferences of the specialized agencies: there the key substantive role played by the agency head is to formulate and drive through the policy-control organs a draft program and budget. The Secretary-General of the United Nations is not in a position to assume any

---

[50] Eric Stein, *Some Implications of Expanding United Nations Membership* (New York, Carnegie Endowment for International Peace, 1956).

such role vis-à-vis ECOSOC, because, first, he is too preoccupied with political matters and, second, he represents only a part of ECOSOC's "constituency." Nor can the UN Under Secretary for Economic and Social Affairs do so, again because he represents only a part of ECOSOC's constituency and also because he neither enjoys sufficient "rank" prestige nor is his administrative department staffed on an *interagency* basis. ECOSOC has no substantive staff of its own. The only available leadership instrument is ACC in its collective capacity, and it has not been supplying the kind of strong, sustained leadership that a pluralistic organ like ECOSOC must have if it is to perform its tasks effectively.

Although ACC, in the form of its annual reports to ECOSOC, admittedly provides a lot of valuable "grist for the ECOSOC mill," it has not succeeded in establishing the kind of close, continuing *rapport* with the Council that a national cabinet normally enjoys with parliament. This gap in communication has from time to time evoked comments from the more perceptive Council members, leading to expressions of hope that somehow there might be developed a closer "partnership" between the two groups. Not many ECOSOC delegates may have the prestige, skill, and knowledge to communicate easily with the executive heads of the UN agencies, but this barrier might be overcome if ACC tried to cultivate informal contacts with Council delegates. The fact that ACC, acting like a jury, does not reveal to the Council its internal policy differences but presents a united front, has tended to encourage aloofness. If the minutes of ACC meetings were made public, however, they might consist merely of carefully guarded statements, so that there is no easy way out of this dilemma of ACC and ECOSOC relationships.

A second factor affecting ACC's role relates to its own staff support. Until quite recently, ACC back-stopping by the UN staff was handled by a single man, although he could draw as necessary on the subject-matter bureaus of the Secretariat for assistance. The Preparatory Committee of Deputies has reportedly come in for some criticism from agency heads because it has sometimes been late in getting its reports ready for the ACC meeting—a reflection, probably, of slow or poor staff work.

In ECOSOC circles, various suggestions have also been put forward that a stronger staff for ACC and ECOSOC should be created on a truly interagency basis. Short of this, it has been proposed that the specialized agencies should second staff to the ACC staff for specific periods and tasks. This idea appears to have been greeted without enthusiasm in New York on the ground that the subject-matter units, to which specialized agency staff have already been assigned to some extent, now provide a sufficient channel for interagency consultation. ECOSOC took official cognizance of ACC's staff situation by adopting a resolution to the effect that ACC study the possibilities of strengthening its secretariat, including agency secondment if feasible, and also requested the Chairman of ACC (the Secretary-General) to arrange a meeting between ACC and the officers of the Council "to discuss practical and effective means to bring about a closer relationship between the two bodies." [51]

Since this action, two promising developments have taken place: first, ACC has slightly enlarged its New York staff and established in Geneva a small unit headed by a Director for Coordination and ACC Matters in Europe, which ought to facilitate direct contacts with the specialized agencies whose headquarters are located on that side of the Atlantic; second, ACC met with the ECOSOC officers in Geneva during the 1964 session of the Council for consultation "on important current issues within the Council's purview." [52] These are small steps in the right direction.

[51] ECOSOC Resolution 992 (XXXVI), 2 August 1963.
[52] E/3886, 6 May 1964. Also see E/3957, 27 July 1964, for a report on the ACC/ECOSOC meeting at Geneva. Out of this meeting came an agreement that ACC should explain more fully the reasons underlying its recommendations to ECOSOC.

It is to be hoped that the members of ACC will arrange to give more active attention to ECOSOC strategy. ACC might usefully confer with the officers and committee chairmen of the Council as a kind of over-all steering group during its summer session. The pressure of other (agency) business might not make it possible for the entire membership of ACC to be present throughout the Council's summer session, but at least a working nucleus might be on hand. Such a steering group could, for example, offer advice as to when it would be desirable to resort to informal working parties or individual rapporteurs as expeditious procedural devices for handling controversial matters on the Council's agenda, which, as indicated earlier, would be drawn up initially by ACC and ex-officers of the Council.

Finally, in view of the inevitably and constantly heavy pressure on the UN Secretary-General from the political and peace-keeping responsibilities, which must remain his central concern, he ought to establish as part of his entourage a new post of Under Secretary for Economic and Social Affairs, with some slightly different title, which would have a status comparable to that of the existing "political" under secretaries without portfolio. There is, of course, an under secretary already assigned to this domain, but he is loaded down with the heavy administrative responsibility of running the largest UN subject-matter department. A new official, assuming he had the stature of a Paul Hoffman or a Ralph Bunche, could not only serve as the Secretary-General's trouble-shooter or roving ambassador in connection with economic and social programming involving the UN family, but also act as his *alter ego* in ACC matters, substituting for the Secretary-General during Council sessions when he is unavoidably absent. In addition, such an official, who should be chosen in consultation with the specialized agency heads, might appropriately provide general supervision over the work of the immediate ACC and auxiliary staff dealing with over-all program analysis, planning, and evaluation, as outlined below.

THE NEED FOR BASIC OVER-ALL PLANNING. The revolution in science and technology will continue to throw up new problems and tasks toward the solution of which the UN family of agencies can and should make a significant contribution. The available world machinery, while admittedly loose and cumbersome, is probably the best we can hope for in the foreseeable future. It is not additional institutional machinery that is needed, so much as a strengthened *system-wide* center at the high staff level for sustained over-all analysis and an appraisal of the changing economic, social, and technological context affecting UN system action. Such a center should not engage directly in research itself but should rather synthesize and interpret research from wherever in the UN framework or outside sources it seemed useful and relevant, with the result, it is to be hoped, of reducing the area of confusion that still exists as to what really makes for effective development. It would be essentially a "think" unit concerned primarily with long-range trends and basic planning. It should clearly develop the closest possible liaison with the professional staffs of IBRD and its affiliated institutions, especially in view of the Special Fund's interest in stimulating capital investment on the one hand, and the Bank's growing participation in general development and educational planning on the other.

Administratively the proposed center should be attached to the Secretary-General's office rather than to the Department of Economic and Social Affairs. It would also serve, of course, as part of the staff back-stopping for ACC, and it should be manned partly on an *interagency* basis by a careful, selective process which, it is hoped, would produce a permanent nucleus of highly qualified social scientists (mainly economists, sociologists, statisticians) together with a limited inflow (and outflow) of outstanding subject-matter specialists, including physical scientists, from the relevant agencies. Without some such cross-agency orientation the confidence of the specialized institutions in its findings might be difficult to assure.

In this connection, one *caveat* is in order: care would need to be taken not to appear to be imposing on the functional agencies a "master plan," which they would resent and resist. The planning center, however, might properly move a step beyond the "draft framework of functional classifications" for the economic and social activities of the UN system submitted in revised form by ACC to ECOSOC at its 1964 session,[53] by making recommendations on how the combined resources of closely related agencies might most effectively and economically be applied to high priority problems and by identifying existing gaps and emerging needs. Such a center, as well, should also attempt to keep abreast of non-UN assistance programs and of the current status of major national development plans by maintaining some sort of registry.

In short, the new center would be a frame of reference for fairly long-range program strategy. Interagency policy differences, where serious, might thus more easily be spotted and adjusted as early as the planning stage instead of after program patterns are set. Finally, such a center should help to strengthen the framework for a wider consensus within agency policy bodies as to economic and social action without unduly disturbing agency constitutional prerogatives. It is axiomatic that the quality of policy decisions by representative organs can rise no higher than the quality of basic staff work. This does not mean a surrender to "technocracy" but a recognition of a realistic allocation of functional roles in the total UN decision process in view of the complexity of the subject-matter.

Centralization as a Radical Solution?

The coordinative process within the UN confederative system has been reviewed from two angles: first, how does it actually work? and, second, what might be done to improve the effectiveness of the process short of altering the constitutional

[53] E/3886, Annex I, 6 May 1964.

framework of the system? It has been assumed that coordination is not an end in itself but a means to an end. It has also been recognized that within a decentralized institutional system of sovereign states the range of choices in respect of program integration is a narrow one. Critics of this approach may ask whether tinkering with the existing machinery and procedure is enough, whether the alternative of a drastic overhauling of the system should not be squarely faced. This is a perfectly proper question, particularly since UN member states are growing increasingly restive over the mutiplicity of programs, intricacy of procedures, and seemingly high overhead costs now confronting them.

BUDGET CONSOLIDATION? Here and there are signs that a movement for a single consolidated budget for the UN system may be reviving. One discovers voices contending that UN *control* over specialized agency budgets would not only promote administrative economy but help to eliminate program overlaps, duplication, conflicts, and so forth. In a rough sort of way budget consolidation might yield this kind of dividend, but at a considerable price. Even if resistance could be overcome to the amendment of specialized agency constitutions that any such change would involve, it is highly doubtful whether financial support for the solid if nonspectacular work of these agencies would be forthcoming in the same proportions as now. Each of the major agencies has its own professional clientele, highly organized in the case of labor, agriculture, health, and education, on which it can usually count for sustained budgetary support "back home" as well as in the agency's budget control organ. This special support might largely be dissipated if the specialized program budgets were submerged in a general UN system budget. Nor is there reason to suppose that the Fifth Committee of the UN General Assembly would allocate financial resources any more wisely than is the case under the existing plurality of bodies. Few of the national delegations to the Assembly would be likely to include the specialist personnel capable of making

informed judgments on programs ranging from aviation to telecommunications to metereology to public health to educational
planning to agriculture, forestry and fisheries, and on to labor
standards, to industrialization, energy development, transport,
and water resources. Nor is the Fifth Committee any more im-
mune to "log-rolling" than the comparable committees of the
general conferences of the individual agencies.

The case for budgetary consolidation is further weakened
by the fact that over half of the total expenditure for the economic and social activities in the UN system is now derived
from *voluntary* contributions and earmarked for special programs that are subject to UN control to a substantially greater
degree than the regularly financed agency programs. It would
be surprising if the major contributors could be induced to
approve the incorporation of these programs, EPTA and the
Special Fund in particular, into a general UN system budget,
where voting would be subject to heavy pressure from underdeveloped country majorities. The position of the chief contributors has been better protected through smaller control units
like TAC and the Governing Council of the Special Fund.

CONSTITUTIONAL CENTRALIZATION? Leaving the purely budgetary aspect of the situation and moving to the most advanced
point on the centralization scale, one can conceive of a constitutional reform that would reduce the specialized agencies to
subordinate units in a federalistic structure of world cooperation.
Despite isolated voices calling for such a "revolution," it seems
clearly beyond the range of political feasibility for a long time
to come, considering the vested interests involved and the difficulty of obtaining a political consensus as to the institutional
framework and voting arrangements for a reformed system.
But even if it were politically feasible, a good case could be
made against it because much of the vitality and creative experi-
mentalism now associated with the principal specialized agencies

might well be lost because complete centralization would be apt
to increase the impact of politics upon a wide range of problems
that are essentially technical in character. As C. W. Jenks re-
minded ECOSOC, the "grand design" of the San Francisco
Charter was to decentralize authority so as to remove politics
from the maximum area of UN system action.[54] Although the
Soviet bloc is now ensconced in several of the specialized
agencies, its influence on their policy decisions has not been
nearly so pervasive or obstructive as in the central organs of
the UN. And the Soviet boycott of the specialized agencies
working in the field of international trade and finance, civil
aviation, and agriculture has meant that much of the activity
of the UN system outside the peace and security domain is
still not markedly "politicized." [55]

It is worth noting, moreover, that even within the existing
UN structure the economic and social activities of the "core"
organization itself remain only partially coordinated. As
ACABQ has repeatedly complained, the "great weakness of
the UN financial system is the fact that projects can be approved
by bodies [that is, councils and committees] other than the
General Assembly, which is the only appropriating authority." [56]
The point is that a constitutionally centralized system does not
necessarily assure complete functional orderliness. Even in the
United States government, instances of clashes of departmental
and bureau special interests are not lacking in the formulation, enactment, and implementation of federal legislative programs, despite the concentration of appropriating power in the
single legislative body of Congress. In sum, the achievement of

[54] Comments made on ILO's annual report before ECOSOC, 9 July 1963.
A senior official of WHO has remarked that "ECOSOC helps to keep politics out of WHO."
[55] See Harold Jacobson, *The USSR and the UN's Economic and Social
Activities* (Notre Dame, Ind., University of Notre Dame Press, 1963), Chap.
9, for an illuminating interpretation of the Soviet impact.
[56] A/5507, August 1963.

program coordination depends far less on how policy-making power is legally allocated than on a host of flexible consultative and procedural arrangements under effective staff leadership.

OPERATIONAL PROGRAM MERGERS? Intermediate between largely uncontrolled agency and program proliferation and institutional centralization certain measures of partial consolidation may be practicable. Among these, the merger of the two major operational programs, EPTA and the Special Fund, approved by the General Assembly in 1965, was a significant step. It was felt (1) that the amalgamation would simplify contacts with recipient governments, thus reducing the confusion that now exists as a result of so many separate aid programs; (2) that certain administrative economies could be gained as a result of fewer meetings and less staff travel; and (3) that a single organ of management and policy control would ensure fuller consistency as between the two programs.

Some details leading up to the merger are discussed in the following pages in connection with the field administration of UN technical assistance programs, but the main issue provoked by these proposals has turned over the extent to which the "interagency" character of EPTA should be diminished by downgrading the status of the interagency committee that replaced TAB. The specialized agencies insisted that the new interagency board should have not merely "advisory" but "managerial" functions, while the UN Headquarters generally favored the more centralized pattern of management established by the Special Fund.

Another issue was the appointment of a single Administrator for the consolidated program, or an Administrator and Co-Administrator, which ACC and others favored, emphasizing the desirability of retaining the special characteristics of each of the two programs. Some of the underdeveloped countries and the Soviet bloc feared that either EPTA would be completely absorbed into the Special Fund type of project programming or that consolidation might impede the eventual transformation of the Special Fund into a capital development fund.

So far as governmental attitudes were concerned, a good deal of apathy hung about the whole idea of program merger, with a majority of the underdeveloped countries apparently inclined to prefer many *separate* agencies and *separate* programs on the dubious assumption that they would get more aid that way, and this was doubtless one reason why there has been a considerable clamor for the creation of new agencies: for industrial development, for science and technology, for housing, building and planning, and for trade.

In proportion as the major operational programs achieve unity of central direction, coordination of their operations at the regional and country level should be facilitated. It makes little sense to maintain a multiple-management program alongside a similar one under centralized management. In the consolidated UNDP, the specialized agencies will still have a significant role to play, not only as "executing agents" for approved projects but also as sources of ideas for new projects.

Conclusions

On balance, the notion of "coordination" in the evolution of the UN system of economic and social activities has shifted from an essentially negative, policeman-type of operation directed against "overlaps" to the much more intricate problem of how to allocate the inadequate resources of the UN family so as to produce maximum long-range developmental impacts. In the former sense, coordination tended to become a cliché, evoking exaggerated hopes from the coordinators and stubborn resistances from the coordinated. This stage is largely over, whether officially admitted or not. Now the administrative problem is how to strengthen the instrumentalities for program building and appraisal, a task involving the major functional agencies fully as much as the UN itself. Additional "coordinative" machinery is not required in any formal sense; existing arrangements and procedures, including in particular ECOSOC and ACC and their committee structures should be rationalized and strengthened to meet the formidable tasks that loom ahead as the UN moves into the space age.

The pace at which the UN system creates constructive plans for handling these new tasks will ultimately depend upon how successfully member governments, Eastern as well as Western, underdeveloped and advanced, manage to achieve an action consensus. Unless they can integrate their own economic and social policies as they impinge upon the international domain, there is comparatively little the UN system itself can do by way of internal manipulation: with more generous budgetary support it might of course attract better equipped professional personnel and thus potentially provide more enlightened program leadership. This would appear to offer the greatest hope for progress toward maximization of long-range impact.

But the over-all framework will and should remain a rather dispersed and pluralistic one. The values of such pluralism ought not to be sacrificed for some tidy organizational symmetry that is probably illusory in any case. The wise warning of H. G. Nicholas is worth noting in conclusion: "Excessive coordination may be purchased at the cost of curtailing initiative and liveliness of the units concerned. The only perfect coordinator is death." [57] What should be sought, observed Dag Hammarskjöld a few years ago, "is the optimum balance between a system with a large number of autonomous bodies and a system with a strong concentration of tasks within a lesser number of organizations. The way will have to be found by trial and error." [58]

Equally important to the future of a strengthened UN sys-

[57] H. G. Nicholas, *United Nations as a Political Institution*, p. 130.
[58] In an address at the University of Chicago Law School, May 1960.

tem designed to cope with world-wide problems of economic and social development is the field administration, including the special roles of the UN Resident Representative and the regional commissions, which must complement the resolutions and recommendations of both ECOSOC and the General Assembly.

By Gerard J. Mangone

FIELD ADMINISTRATION:

THE UNITED NATIONS

RESIDENT REPRESENTATIVE

In the winter of 1965 the General Assembly of the United Nations approved a resolution that called for the merger of the Expanded Programme of Technical Assistance and the Special Fund into a new United Nations Development Programme.[1] This action culminated several years of studies and reports that had persistently aimed at an improvement in the administration of UN assistance to the economically underdeveloped states of the world. Whatever changes may eventually take place in the reorganization of these two voluntary aid-giving agencies within the new UNDP, the role of the individual, now designated as Resident Representative of the UNDP, who had been designated as Resident Representative of the Technical Assistance Board of the EPTA and Director of Special Fund Programs in some sixty-seven[2] countries seems bound to continue its fascinating evolution in UN field administration.

EPTA, which had been in existence since 1949,[3] and the Special Fund, which was established in 1958,[4] have both depended

[1] GA Resolution 2029 (XX), 22 November 1965.
[2] Included in this number are seven regional representatives serving more than the one country in which they are stationed. E/TAC/153, 10 May 1965, pp. 59–60.
[3] ECOSOC Resolution 222 (IX), 15 August 1949.
[4] GA Resolution 1240 (XIII), 14 October 1958.

upon the donations of states that in 1965 ran to something over $50 million for EPTA and about $85 million for the Special Fund. Although couched in different mandates, both have been basically technical assistance programs: EPTA generally has provided individual experts to countries seeking advice for economic development or local training, and it has granted fellowships to enable the nationals of underdeveloped countries to study abroad, as well as establishing regional centers or seminars for the improvement of skills; the Special Fund has stressed preinvestment projects, larger in scope than EPTA, such as resource surveys and training or research centers, and it has provided small capital equipment as well as individuals or teams of experts, and fellowships.

The governing body of EPTA, however, had been TAC, composed of all the member states of ECOSOC plus twelve other states elected by the Council. Actual operations of EPTA were coordinated by TAB, consisting of an Executive Chairman, and the executive heads of ten agencies related to the UN [5] plus the UN's BTAO, all of which shared in the implementation of technical assistance programs under EPTA and are referred to as "participating organizations."

The Governing Council of the Special Fund, on the other hand, had consisted of twenty-four states elected by ECOSOC, half of which had been chosen from the developed world and the other half from the underdeveloped world. Actual operations depended upon a single Managing Director with a Consultative Board consisting of the Secretary-General of the UN, the President of IBRD, and the Executive Chairman of TAB.

Under the new UNDP there is one Governing Council of thirty-seven states for both merged programs with the Managing Director of the Special Fund taking the title of Adminis-

[5] FAO, ICAO, ILO, ITU, UNESCO, WHO, WMO, IAEA, UPU, and IMCO.

trator and the Executive Chairman of TAB assuming the title of Co-Administrator.

For their field administration, however, both EPTA and the Special Fund have used the same office of the UN Resident Representative although the Resident Representative has had different responsibilities for each program. The remarkable development of this administrative institution which, without premeditation, has grown into an articulate field network of the United Nations around the world not only indicates the way in which the UN is moving forward to achieve its high purposes of international economic and social development but also one of the frontiers of world order.

Early History of the United Nations
Resident Representative

The origins of the UN Resident Representative, a short and appropriate institutional title, antedate EPTA. As early as December 1946 the General Assembly had discussed a "regular" program of technical assistance to underdeveloped countries. Three months later ECOSOC requested the Secretary-General to establish machinery within the Secretariat to render assistance to member governments that might seek the advice of experts for the solution of economic and social problems.[6] In December 1948 the General Assembly approved its first major resolution on this subject with a list of principles for the provision of technical assistance and an appropriation of funds.[7] Meanwhile, a visiting UN mission to Haiti had made a number of recommendations for aid to that country to be supplied by different specialized agencies of the UN. At the end of 1949 the UN decided to appoint under their regular technical assistance program a "Representative of the Secretary-General" to aid in the implementation of these recommendations under in-

[6] ECOSOC Resolution 51 (IV), 29 March 1947.
[7] GA Resolution 200 (III), 4 December 1948.

structions to help the Haitian government define its needs "with sufficient precision to enable the Secretariat of the United Nations and the specialized agencies to respond as promptly as possible with the services of properly qualified technicians." [8] In May 1950, therefore, little noted and hardly more than an administrative appointee with vague terms of reference, the first UN representative for technical assistance programs within a country, John Wakefield, actually began his duties.

Only two months later the Secretary-General, with great prescience, noted that UN representatives might be useful to underdeveloped countries that still lacked coordinating machinery in viewing their requests for technical assistance within their over-all needs for economic development. He also suggested that the appointment of UN representatives in underdeveloped countries would help to avoid the confusion bound to arise from a flow of technical assistance through several channels, and, with tact, if not resolution, he indicated that the services of such UN representatives would be available to organizations engaged in technical assistance programs "to the fullest extent to which the agencies wish to use them." [9]

The technical assistance activities of the UN began to increase rapidly in 1950 soon after the approval of EPTA, and the advantage of having a single UN country representative became evident. The basic ECOSOC resolution[10] on EPTA had requested the Secretary-General to invite ACC [11] to set up a board, consisting of the executive heads (or their representatives) of the UN and of the specialized agencies that were participating in the program, to help coordinate it. The Secretary-General was made *ex-officio* Chairman of TAB, but generally

[8] E/1576, 28 December 1949.
[9] E/1700, 21 July 1950.
[10] ECOSOC Resolution 222 (IX), 15 August 1949. For an anniversary review of EPTA after fifteen years of operations, see E/TAC/153, 10 May 1965.
[11] As indicated earlier, a standing committee, dating from 1946, of the executive heads of the specialized agencies. The Secretary-General of the UN is chairman.

the Assistant Secretary-General for Economic Affairs, David Owen, represented him at its meetings. The Chairman was also authorized, after consultation with other participating organizations, to designate an Executive Secretary.

In 1950 the Secretary-General, in consultation with ILO and FAO, appointed a "Joint Representative," Thomas Hebben, Jr., to Pakistan. Some of the organizations participating in EPTA began making analogous arrangements, appointing joint representatives within a country. These officials, while administratively dependent upon one of the participating organizations (for example, FAO, UNESCO, ILO) also served any other participating organization that wished to use them. It soon became customary for general reports of such joint representatives to be sent to the Executive Secretary of TAB, Manuel Perez-Guerrero, who, in turn, circulated them to all the participating organizations of EPTA. At the end of 1950 the Secretary-General as the nominal Chairman of TAB appointed a "Liaison Officer," Marcel DeBaer, in Iran, the first field official to represent all EPTA participating organizations. Early the next year Raymond Etchats was appointed as the first TAB "Resident Representative" and assigned to Colombia in April 1951.

In reviewing this novel institutional development for the field work of EPTA, TAC in 1951 expressed ambivalent views. While welcoming the possibility of an improved coordination of technical assistance within a country, TAC stressed that the device of the Resident Representative should not be automatic everywhere but "only where particular circumstances warrant it." [12] The particular circumstances were not spelled out further, but the implication that the interests of the participating organizations in each country ought not to be disturbed by a Resident Representative could not be escaped.

In May 1951, nevertheless, TAB decided, after a review of the field establishment of EPTA, to approve the appointment

[12] E/1920, 28 February 1951.

of three more resident representatives with the understanding that they would report to TAB on general matters and to the individual participating organizations on technical matters that concerned them.

No mention at all had been made of a Resident Representative or any field staff for TAB in the basic resolution of ECOSOC that had established EPTA. Except for guiding principles that had been laid down in Annex I, suggesting that requests for assistance within the sphere of two or more organizations should be handled jointly by the organizations concerned and that there should be coordination among them at the planning level before making commitments to governments, no single official had been envisaged as having a canalizing and mediatory role. The spontaneous way in which joint representatives, liaison officers, and resident representatives had sporadically been selected, appointed, and charged with mixed responsibilities in 1950 and 1951, therefore, precipitated a decision by TAB in January 1952 that all resident representatives should have the same status and terms of reference and that all of them should be responsible to TAB through its Executive Secretary. By the summer of 1952 there were fifteen "representatives" for TAB in the field. TAB itself was then reorganized.

Ever since the inception of EPTA, the specialized agencies, some of which had engaged in technical assistance for many years prior to the founding of the UN, had been wary of any imposition of UN controls on their share of the program. The UN itself had become a member of TAB, participating in EPTA through its TAA,[13] which received requests for aid outside the interests of the specialized agencies, such as mining, power, water transport, and so forth. The specialized agencies

[13] In 1958 TAA was amalgamated within the UN Department of Economic and Social Affairs and technical assistance operations, as distinct from economic-social research and planning, were assigned to BTAO in the Department. As a participating organization of EPTA, however, the technical assistance work of the Bureau is identified as UNTA.

also had to deal with the direct power of the Secretary-General of the UN, for as *ex officio* Chairman of the Board, he had the power to appoint resident representatives. A limited reorganization of TAB, therefore, was favored by the specialized agencies in 1952, since they wished to moderate the UN power over EPTA by having the permanent chairman of TAB one step removed from the Secretary-General and more responsible to the whole Board.

Following a report of ACC on the organization of TAB, TAC itself reviewed the work of the Board and recommended to ECOSOC the creation of a full-time Executive Chairman. TAC suggested that one of the functions of the Executive Chairman should be the appointment of the "TAB Resident Representatives" and the establishment of their terms of reference. ECOSOC resolution 433 A (XIV) of 11 June 1952 provided for the appointment of an Executive Chairman of TAB by the Secretary-General, after consultation with the executive heads of the participating organizations. He was given a precise set of functions in the areas of programming, financing, earmarking of funds, and administrative management in general, and he was further empowered to appoint, in agreement with the Board, "Resident Technical Assistance Representatives." The Executive Chairman of TAB was authorized to determine the terms of reference for resident representatives, supervise their activities, and establish an effective system of reporting between them and the Executive Chairman. This resolution was the first "legislative" reference to the UN Resident Representative in UN history and the action of ECOSOC was noted "with satisfaction" by the General Assembly later that year.

After 1 January 1953 all technical assistance resident representatives were members of the TAB secretariat. A Resident Representative appointed by the Executive Chairman of TAB under EPTA's reorganization seemed less formidable to the specialized agencies than a direct representative of the Secretary-General, while they earnestly believed he would gain their cooperation better in the field by leaving to them the full operational authority they desired. The members of TAC, moreover, had no desire to move precipitately in establishing a strong field official, and they respected the experience of the specialized agencies in technical assistance. Thus the administrative mandate of the Resident Representative was couched in broad and vague terms in May 1952 by TAC: namely that the Resident Representative ought to

cooperate with and assist the government of the country concerned in making arrangements designed to facilitate the development of plans and projects and be available in the development of such plans [and] . . . coordinate and integrate the expanded technical assistance activities of the participating agencies within a country, relying on representatives of the participating agencies for judgments on technical matters and provide administrative support as required.[14]

But how the Resident Representative was to work in practice had to be left to negotiation and the accumulation of experience. All TAC could lamely say at the time was that there was a need for the "closest contact" between the experts and the resident representatives and that it was "the responsibility of both the officers of the participating organizations and the resident representatives to assure an active relationship."[15]

The first resident representatives of the UN faced uncharted assignments as they moved into host countries. They had to meet the suspicion and sometimes the antagonism of the specialized agencies in the field as well as attempt to win the confidence of local governments for their weak and uncertain role. But in one respect they proved immediately useful. "I had hardly been in Belgrade more than a few hours," reported one of the pioneer resident representatives, Myer Cohen, "when

[14] E/2238, 29 May 1952.
[15] *Ibid.*

an expert in the technical assistance program knocked at my hotel door. He complained that his room had no bath and asked me to intervene with the hotel manager to get him better accommodations."

In Yugoslavia, Colombia, Iran, and elsewhere the new resident representatives soon found themselves on safe grounds in rendering administrative services to incoming experts or missions—greeting them at the airport, helping them through customs formalities, reserving rooms, changing money into local currency, receiving and forwarding mail, supplying information about housing, transport, maid service, and so forth. Some of the early resident representatives indicated that they spent nearly all their time in the first year on such administrative arrangements, plus exchanging barrages of paper reports and correspondence with the headquarters at New York. In subsequent years they found too little time or opportunity for program development, including planning and coordination, or evaluation, partly owing to the burden of their administrative chores, partly owing to the inability of the host government itself to plan and initiate properly requests for technical assistance, and partly owing to the "share" system that had been fastened upon EPTA.

Agency Share System under the Expanded Program of Technical Assistance

Under the agency share system that existed in EPTA from 1950 to 1956, each of the participating organizations automatically received a percentage of the total funds pledged for technical assistance by the contributing states. In the first fiscal year, for example, 85 percent of the $20 million pledged was to be divided among the agencies as follows: FAO received 29 percent, the UN 23 percent, WHO 22 percent, UNESCO 14 percent, ILO 11 percent, and ICAO 1 percent. The remaining 15 percent of the total, plus any amount pledged in excess of

$20 million, was to be alloted to TAB for subsequent alloca-
tion. This "scientific" division of EPTA funds was reached after
a tendentious squabble with lobbying by both the specialized
agencies and the UN in ECOSOC. When no agreement could
be reached on the percentages of the fund that each participating
organization should receive, each member of ECOSOC was asked
to write on a piece of paper the share for each agency he believed ought to prevail. These figures were then averaged—and
the percentages cited above eventually resulted.[16]

Governments then negotiated directly with representatives
of the organizations participating in the EPTA technical assistance, and it was essentially up to these organizations to decide
how much assistance they would give to any country within
their total allocation from the EPTA fund. Moreover, the percentage of EPTA's funds that was reserved for TAB as an en-
tity also labored under an apportionment system, neither rigid
nor automatic, but inescapable in view of the fact that TAB
itself was nothing more than the participating organizations with
an Executive Chairman. Under these circumstances the capacity
of a Resident Representative to shape a country technical assistance program was negligible, and his powers of coordination,
without any budgetary tools for transferring resources, depended upon sheer personal magnetism—a weak reed in the
quicksands of bureaucratic struggle. In some countries, the
Resident Representative became the mission chief for one or
more of the specialized agencies, because the agencies had no
other representative there. In these instances he had somewhat
better access to the headquarters planning and operations of
the participating organizations, but he still exercised very little
control over the framework of their technical assistance programs.

[16] In 1952 and 1953 the participating organizations automatically received
50 percent of the total EPTA funds rather than 85 percent; but in 1954 and
1955 their initial share was raised again to 75 percent, reflecting the tug of
war between centralization and decentralization.

The early years of the Resident Representative institution, in sum, were hardly auspicious: in the United States the foreign policy of the United States was under vicious attack by Senator Joseph McCarthy and to some extremists the UN epitomized world government and international communism, with such people suspicious of the appointment of any international civil servant as a threat to the American way of life. At the same time the specialized agencies resented any intrusion by the UN into their field work. ACC aptly described the fragile role of the Resident Representative by stating: "He would work in close collaboration with agency representatives and experts, but he would not interfere in any way in the normal relationship between agencies and local government departments." [17]

The main attack, however, upon the Resident Representative came from the budget-conscious General Assembly, for the position was still so weak and so suspect that it became an easy target for the platitudes of cost-cutting in the UN. In August 1953 the Soviet Union and Poland, speaking in TAC, doubted the advisability of appointing any resident representatives and felt that mounting expenses could be trimmed by eliminating the posts.[18] A few months later the delegate from India to the Second Committee of the General Assembly protested against the high administrative costs of the technical assistance program, alleging that the use of resident representatives imposed a heavy financial burden upon technical assistance and suggesting that there be fewer resident representatives by appointing them on a regional basis rather than to individual countries.[19]

Economy measures, as well as recruitment problems, in fact, forced some retrenchment in the TAB field establishment during 1953 and 1954, as the pledges to EPTA fell far short of the technical assistance requested by the economically underde-

[17] E/2450, 28 May 1953.
[18] *Yearbook of the United Nations*, 1953, p. 308.
[19] *Ibid.*, p. 310.

veloped nations. Program levels had to be lowered and some activities curtailed, while cutbacks were made in the number and quality of resident representatives: senior resident representatives in Turkey, India, Indonesia, and the Philippines, for example, were replaced by temporary officers; in some areas two or more countries were placed under the jurisdiction of a single representative, and the number of internationally recruited field staff was reduced from eighty-seven to fifty-three, mostly by replacing them with local personnel.[20]

Country Programming

As experience with EPTA increased, it became evident to the UN that the countries receiving technical assistance had little incentive for planning and setting priorities under the prevailing share system among the participating organizations. Each participating organization under that system naturally attempted to negotiate agreements with the relevant ministries within a government that would spend the full amount allotted to the agency for that year, since the funds had to be earmarked for use in the same year that they were received. Strong pressures to utilize the money immediately available to the participating organizations were put upon financially weak governments, and all too often a recipient country would be tempted to use its scarce resources to support projects that were outside its own priorities for national development.

The French delegate to ECOSOC proposed that the burden of establishing priorities for technical assistance be shifted to the countries receiving aid under EPTA by eliminating the share system among the participating organizations and substituting "country targets," allocations of a maximum sum to a country rather than a percentage to each of the specialized agencies and UNTA. Each country could then determine its own priorities for technical assistance within the country target.

[20] E/2714, 4 April 1955.

In June 1954 the French proposals, with some modifications, were adopted,[21] and full-scale programming under the new system began in 1955 for 1956. Immediately the participating organizations complained that unless they had some idea beforehand of the percentage of EPTA funds that they might be asked to administer in a coming year, their own planning of personnel and budgeting of funds would be stymied. To quiet these fears TAB began to divide the total amount pledged annually into unofficial "agency planning shares," which the participating organizations could then use as guides. Ironically enough, these shares were almost identical to the percentage of the total funds that each participating organization had administered in the previous year. Moreover, TAB was confronted with the vexing problem of establishing some rationale for the country target figures. Each of the participating organizations, therefore, was asked to send to TAB its estimated subtotal of technical assistance expenditures for each country based upon the agency's previous share of EPTA funds in that country and the agency's forecast of continuing projects. These subtotals then formed the basis for the total country target, and they were also transmitted to recipient governments as "guides," not binding but presumably helpful for planning. As a final safeguard for the participating organizations, the resolution that introduced country programming stipulated that no agency should receive less than 85 percent of the total EPTA funds allotted to it in the current year.

Coupled to the idea that country planning would force more responsibility for setting priorities with the recipient government was the belief of its sponsors that the role of the Resident Representative would increase in importance through consultation and coordination. As phrased by the ECOSOC resolution, programs were to be

[21] ECOSOC Resolution 542 B (XVIII), 29 July 1954.

drawn up at the country level by the requesting governments, in consultation with the resident representatives or such representatives of TAB as may be especially assigned for the purpose, due regard being paid to continuing commitments. . . . The responsibility for co-ordinating consultations between Governments and participating organizations shall rest with the resident representatives. . . . The country programmes shall be forwarded by requesting Governments, with an indication of priorities established by them, to TAB through the resident representatives.[22]

This was the first time that the resident representatives were actually given a mandate by a formal UN resolution, enlarging and reinforcing the previous guides of TAB. Nevertheless, consultation and coordination put few teeth into the administrative authority of the resident representatives. EPTA provided them with no line authority over the participating organization, either by budget or personnel control, and no resources through which they might distinctly influence the decisions of host governments.

As Walter R. Sharp noted in his distinguished study of field administration in the United Nations system,[23] only UNTA among the participating organizations of EPTA welcomed a wider role for the resident representatives in country planning. "Most of the major specialized agencies then looked upon the new arrangements with a cold eye, certain of them evincing a disinclination to cooperate." Some WHO officials regarded the Resident Representative as an agent of TAB imperialism and sincerely argued that governments ought to do their own planning and coordination directly with the UN and the specialized agencies. In addition, some FAO and ILO officials opposed the new country programming arrangements on the grounds that rivalries between the ministries of a government would be exacerbated and that "weaker" ministries might not get a fair share

[22] *Ibid.*
[23] Walter R. Sharp, *Field Administration in the United Nations System; The Conduct of International Economic and Social Programs* (New York, Frederick A. Praeger, 1961), p. 379.

of the technical assistance available if forced to conform by some coordinating unit in order to meet a country target figure. UNESCO's reaction to the new system of allocating technical assistance was somewhat more sympathetic, chiefly because it had no general field structure of entrenched interests and the agency decided to make substantial use of the Resident Representative at that time rather than establish an expensive field organization of its own. In any case, the responsibilities of the Resident Representative had been phrased in such an equivocal way by ECOSOC that conflicting interpretations of his role were bound to be made by the recipient governments, by the participating organizations, and by the resident representatives themselves.

The underlying assumption of country programming, of course, was that each country would develop a strong, competent planning unit that would set technical assistance priorities among its own ministries and then deal directly with the Resident Representative who, according to TAC, "should always be treated as the principal channel of communications between TAB and the recipient countries on general programming matters." [24] The existence of such efficient planning units in underdeveloped countries in 1956 was more wish than reality. Most of the countries covered by EPTA at that time lacked well-conceived national development plans. Although thirty countries had established some kind of coordinating agency for external technical assistance, the units varied considerably in form, power, and effectiveness. Some of them were interministerial committees with comprehensive functions for planning and coordinating all foreign economic assistance; others dealt only with external technical assistance; and two were restricted to aid from EPTA only. Five countries had an *ad hoc* committee, under the Ministry of Foreign Affairs, mainly for preparing the annual program requests formally submitted by the Ministry.

[24] E/TAC/48, 12 April 1956.

In one country the coordinating unit for all external assistance was lodged in the Ministry of the Treasury and in another in the Minister of the Economy.[25] The mere establishment of a coordinating unit in a country, moreover, generally by administrative fiat, proved no guarantee to action: staff was frequently inadequate both by number and training, the turnover of personnel was exorbitant, and financial support for the intensive work required was lacking.

Some of the participating organizations ignored the "subtotals" informally apportioned to them for country planning by TAB and brazenly snubbed the coordination function assigned to the Resident Representative. When country programming began in 1956, specialized agencies like FAO, WHO, or ILO did not hesitate to encourage some of the ministries with which they dealt to request EPTA help far beyond their tentative allocations and to disregard the resident representatives in such negotiations. The specialized agencies obviously feared that a portion of their EPTA funds might be reduced under country planning, but they also acted earnestly upon a belief in the urgency of their own technical work for sound national development. The specialized agencies also suspected that the Resident Representative, being the official country representative of UNTA might favor the activities of the UN over other participating organizations. Given no real power for programming, in the sense of setting priorities and reallocating resources under EPTA, resident representatives in the field had little to depend upon except personal influence and the respect they could earn in assisting governments, agencies, and experts.

A new formal statement of the responsibilities of the Resident Representative had been developed for the text of the "Standard Agreement to Cover Appointment of Resident Representatives or other TAB Field Officers" in 1955[26] by TAB. Later

[25] E/2965, May 1957, pp. 68–70.
[26] Cited in E/AC.49/3, 9 January 1962, pp. 6–7.

that year, however, TAC approved a draft resolution suggesting a further delineation of the Resident Representative's role, urging TAB in selecting resident representatives to give emphasis to qualifications and experience in over-all economic planning and financial administration as well as ability to "appreciate local circumstances." [27]

TAB responded to TAC's suggestion in its annual report of 1956 by outlining eight points on the role of the Resident Representative, which were the fullest exposition of his duties that had been attempted up to that time.[28] (1) TAB stressed the fact that the Resident Representative related to the participating organizations only through EPTA and that he had nothing to do with the regular programs of technical assistance carried on by the specialized agencies under their own budgets. (2) The Resident Representative was called upon to exercise "objective judgment" in assisting governments to draw up their annual programs, giving due weight to the views of each of the participating organizations. (3) The Resident Representative was advised to consult with the government's coordinating authority in drawing up the country programs and to coordinate consultations between governments and participating organizations, but the participating organizations would remain responsible for advising and assisting the appropriate government authorities in the technical planning of individual projects. (4) The Resident Representative was expected to hold joint meetings with field representatives of the participating organizations before final program consultations and also to ask a field representative of the participating organization to join him in any high-level discussions with a technical department of the government. (5) The Resident Representative was required not only to help the government in planning its program, but in its evaluation, which

[27] E/2923, 8 August 1956.
[28] E/2965, May 1957.

would be done by keeping himself generally informed about the work of the experts, visiting projects, and receiving reports to the governments from the participating organizations or the experts themselves. Since all this depended upon the cooperation of the participating organizations, they, in turn, were asked to inform the Resident Representative of their activities relating to the technical assistance programs, including notice of visits of officials of the participating organizations to the country. (6) The Resident Representative was expected to take responsibility for maintaining cooperative arrangements with other programs of technical assistance within the country, and, (7) to take the additional responsibility of providing administrative support services, such as transport and secretarial assistance, "at the request of the participating organizations," while making arrangements for paying local living costs and other payments to experts, "at the request of the employing organization." (8) The Resident Representative was instructed to maintain a central file on all the nationals awarded fellowships and scholarships, and, "when requested," assist in any process connected to these awards.

The caution in defining the role of the Resident Representative is only too apparent in the guidelines to his performance enumerated above, with deference being paid in virtually every paragraph to the independence of the participating organizations in EPTA. Consultation and coordination, once again, were the key words, with TAB calling upon the participating organizations to make use of the resident representatives for better programming and more efficient administration, while warning the Resident Representative to respect the autonomy of each of the participating organizations and their special relationship with host governments.

Despite the high hopes for a more rational and flexible use of technical assistance in national development under country programming, the shares of the participating organizations in the funds of EPTA were, in fact, adjusted very slightly, as indicated in Table IV.

TABLE IV

PERCENTAGE EXPENDITURES FROM THE EXPANDED
PROGRAMME OF TECHNICAL ASSISTANCE BY
PARTICIPATING ORGANIZATIONS, 1955–1959*

Participating Organization	1955	1956	1957	1958	1959
UNTAO	21	24	22	22	22
ILO	11	11	11	11	11
FAO	31	28	29	26	26
UNESCO	13	13	14	17	16
ICAO	4	4	4	4	4
WHO	18	18	18	18	17
ITU	1	1	1	1	1
WMO	1	1	1	1	2
IAEA	0	0	0	0	1
Total	100	100	100	100	100

* E/3226, May 1959, p. 17, and E/3337, May 1960, p. 10.

The powers of the Resident Representative in program planning or coordination, moreover, increased very little under the new system. Indeed, the machinations of the participating organizations accounted only in part for the weakness of the Resident Representative, for he had to live with (*a*) a program of technical assistance that had been entrusted to functional agencies and organized on committee principles; (*b*) the necessary continuation of old technical assistance projects and the shortage of new funds that limited any important reallocation of resources in programming by TAB; (*c*) the lack of any power in the field to transfer funds from one agency to another; and, finally, (*d*) the failure of many recipient governments to put their own house in order by creating a sound development plan[29] and a strong national coordinating unit, thus allowing,

[29] According to TAB's Report to TAC for 1957 only nine out of thirty-eight countries surveyed had full-fledged development plans in operation; in 1958 only nine out of forty-four still met this standard, while twenty-five had some "sectional" development plans. The ten other countries either were preparing a plan or had no plan at all. A/3080, May 1958.

by default, independent arrangements between the specialized agencies and the respective ministries for the total country program.

Yet the institution of the Resident Representative survived —and increasingly both governments and participating organizations and experts recognized its utility whether as a mere mailbox and paymaster or a valuable repository of diplomatic and technical assistance experience. When the UN Special Fund was initiated, therefore, the Resident Representative was immediately available for the field administration of this new program, and he acquired both greater responsibilities and a higher status.

The Special Fund

On 14 December 1957 the General Assembly adopted resolution 1219 (XII), finally deciding that

there shall be established as an expansion of the existing technical assistance and development activities of the United Nations and the Specialized Agencies a separate Special Fund which would provide systematic and sustained assistance in fields essential to the integrated technical, economic, and social development of the less developed countries.

The resolution climaxed a debate of nine years in the councils of the UN in which the member states, both developed and underdeveloped, agreed in principle with providing economic assistance through the UN but differed widely on how much aid should be channeled through the UN, especially whether a large-scale capital aid program in addition to technical assistance ought to be funneled through that multilateral organization.

Although the debate was not stilled, a preparatory committee of sixteen countries proceeded under resolution 1219 (XII) to draft detailed rules governing the proposed organization and the result was General Assembly resolution 1240 (XIII) on 14 October 1958 which established the Special Fund.

The creation of the Special Fund added a new and important dimension to the UN's efforts to provide technical assistance to the underdeveloped world. Although the Special Fund was conceived as distinct from EPTA, both in its organization and its objectives, the two programs were expected to work in coordination with each other as a common UN enterprise to assist national economic and social progress. The Special Fund was designed to undertake pre-investment surveys of natural resources, with investigations of the feasibility of exploiting such resources to achieve national development goals, and to establish or strengthen technical training as well as educational and applied research that might hasten economic and social progress. Moreover, in contrast to EPTA, the Fund was expected "to concentrate, as far as practicable, on relatively large projects and avoid allocation of its resources over a great number of small projects." [30]

For the field organization of the Special Fund, the Resident Representative was a natural locus of consultative and administrative services. By its resolution establishing the Special Fund, the General Assembly had called upon the Managing Director to "enter into an agreement with the Executive Chairman of the Technical Assistance Board concerning the role of the resident representative in the work of the Fund," [31] and it was soon agreed that the Resident Representative

should normally serve as the channel of communication between the government concerned and the Special Fund. He assists the governments with the submission of requests, through the explanation of Special Fund objectives and criteria, and . . . on the forms of presentation. He briefs and provides administrative support to the Special Fund and Executing Agency personnel concerned with technical consultations regarding plans of operations. He assists the Special Fund and Agencies in the negotiation of plans of operations. He has the main responsibility for the collection of government

[30] GA Resolution 1240 (XIII), 14 October 1958.
[31] *Ibid.*, Section IV, 30.

payments toward the local operating costs of Special Fund proj-ects.[32]

Following the assignment of these new responsibilities the Resident Representative of TAB assumed in 1961 the additional title of Director of Special Fund Programmes.

Unlike EPTA, requests for Special Fund assistance have been submitted at any time by governments: there were no country targets or agency subtotals, and all applications have been chan-neled through the Resident Representative to the Managing Di-rector of the Special Fund. Under EPTA, the participating or-ganizations and the ministries of the government have had a close and often exclusive relationship, with proposals for tech-nical assistance being worked out between them for submission to the coordinating unit of the government, then to TAB, with the advice of the Resident Representative. Under the Special Fund, however, the Resident Representative (as Director of Special Fund Programmes) has had to be consulted and has had to assist in the preparation of the actual request of a govern-ment while it is obtaining the technical counsel of a participating organization.

The Resident Representative's advice on the policies, criteria, and procedures of the Special Fund, moreover, went far be-yond ceremony, for he forwarded all proposals, with his com-ment, directly to the Managing Director. The Managing Di-rector used his Consultative Board of the Secretary-General, the President of IBRD, and the Executive Chairman of TAB, as well as any of the participating organizations he invited, for project deliberations, but his decision to submit a Special Fund project to the Governing Council was final. The Governing Council, moreover, meeting twice a year, invariably approved such recommendations while reserving to itself broad questions of policy.

[32] E/3337, May 1960, p. 49.

Since the Special Fund was based upon a "projects first, funds second" procedure, there was no need for a country to use up an allocation of funds, as it did under the EPTA country target figure, by supporting projects of questionable value. There was little room for the participating organizations to oversell their services, although they obviously encouraged projects in which they would become the executing agency. Governments recognized that the Resident Representative was central to the preparation of Special Fund requests and that his advice on priorities could be crucial to a favorable reception of their proposals in New York.

Under EPTA, except when he was acting for BTAO or as a chief of mission for a specialized agency, the Resident Representative had been principally a "coordinator" of negotiations; in all Special Fund proposals from a country he became a vital participant. Thus, the advent of the Special Fund not only added new planning, programming, administrative, and evaluating responsibilities to the UN Resident Representative but also gave him prerogatives that he had not hitherto enjoyed. Nevertheless, it would be an error to suppose that the expansion of the work of the Resident Representative stemmed only from the inception of the Special Fund; EPTA and the Special Fund formed two interrelated parts of the total UN assistance program to the economically underdeveloped countries of the world.

*Growth of the Expanded Program
and Special Fund Activities*

The regular programs of technical assistance offered by the UN and the Specialized Agencies, EPTA and the Special Fund have had a rapid growth, reflecting an ever-increasing commitment by the nations of the world to an ever-increasing demand by the underdeveloped countries for assistance through public international organizations. Especially since 1960, with the formation of many new African states, which are severely limited in their economic resources yet proud of their political independence, new requests for international assistance have been adding to a rising number of proposals from the Latin American and Asian states. This phenomenon has markedly influenced the field organization of TAB in general and the Resident Representative in particular.

Since 1952 EPTA has steadily increased its resources and gradually altered its procedures. In 1952 sixty-five countries pledged only $18,797,232 to support EPTA. But over the next several years the number of participating countries and their contributions grew slowly and steadily. After a small setback in 1959, the pledged amounts increased again, as indicated in Table V.

TABLE V

PLEDGES BY COUNTRIES TO THE
EXPANDED PROGRAMME OF
TECHNICAL ASSISTANCE,
1959–1965

Year	Pledged to EPTA (in dollars)	No. of Countries
1959	29,420,000	83
1960	34,023,400	85
1961	42,408,500	91
1962	45,438,600	92
1963	50,149,700	105
1964	51,596,000	108
1965	54,015,373	119

SOURCE: *Technical Assistance Newsletter*, II, No. 24 (July 1964), p. 4, and E/TAC/RET/292, 23 November 1965.

When EPTA was established in 1950, moreover, there had only been six participating organizations: FAO, WHO, ILO, UNESCO, ICAO, and UNTA. Their field organizations were limited and the Resident Representative was frequently designated as their official country representative. In 1952 WMO and ITU became participating organizations, making special use of the Resident Representative's services, for their small programs did not generally require an official country representative. In 1958 IAEA also became a participating organization, designating the Resident Representative as their country agent where they carried out projects under EPTA. By 1959 fourteen out of thirty-four resident representatives were acting as mission chiefs for FAO; twenty for UNESCO; eleven for ICAO; and twelve for IAEA. All the resident representatives, of course, were technical assistance mission chiefs for the projects carried on by the UN itself under EPTA.

Biennial and Project Programming

As early as 1959 TAB had recognized the limitations of the country programming procedures initiated in 1956. Annual programming of technical assistance for a country sometimes resulted in the acceptance of inadequately investigated projects, without assurance of local support or the existence of the best technical conditions for success; it was difficult to recruit the highest qualified expert owing to stringent time limits; finally, the necessity of planning and negotiating projects every year was time-consuming and, in the case of continuing projects, repetitive. In a report containing proposals for biennial rather than annual programming, the Board cogently summarized a key failing of EPTA:

for the Government of an underdeveloped country the planning procedures of EPTA are more involved and time-consuming in relation to the amount of assistance received than those of most other aid programs.[33]

Essentially the recommendations of TAB were accepted by TAC in the summer of 1959, retaining annual pledges and annual budgeting for EPTA, but establishing a two-year programming cycle. Moreover, balances held by participating organiza-

[33] E/TAC/84, 13 May 1959.

tions at the end of the first year could be retained by them for the succeeding year's program. ECOSOC adopted TAC's recommendations without a change and authorized the first biennial programming for 1961–62.[34]

At the same time TAB began considering "project programming" by which projects intended to continue for more than two years would be planned for their entire duration, so that recipient countries would have to prepare their requests in much greater depth, thinking through their long-range objectives, their priorities in the national development plan, their own local costs, and their commitment to supply counterpart personnel for the EPTA experts.

Elimination of Agency Planning Shares

In the summer of 1960 TAC considered the recommendation of TAB for project programming. During these discussions the United States representative to the Committee called for a comprehensive review of the administration of EPTA, alleging that "much of the structure, machinery, and procedures of the Expanded Program of Technical Assistance was the consequence of the superimposition of one solution to one problem, on a second solution to a second problem, and so on." He went on to say that project programming might improve the country programming process, but it would also tend to freeze a large percentage of EPTA resources each year and that country programming under EPTA basically suffered from the strait jacket of agency subtotals within a country target and agency planning shares from which the subtotals were derived. Although the subtotals were not binding, he noted that, if a recipient country tried to shift assistance from one field to another, there was a real possibility that its total aid would be reduced. The United States then advocated

[34] ECOSOC Resolution 785 (XXX), 3 August 1960.

the elimination of the practice of allocating to the Participating Organizations planning shares [in order to] increase the latitude enjoyed by benefitting countries in making use of the opportunities offered by EPTA.[35]

TAC, therefore, prepared a resolution for ECOSOC that approved in principle the TAB proposals for project programming and asked TAB to submit to TAC in the following year "specific recommendations for simplification and improvements . . . in particular, by project planning, the elimination of agency subtotals from country targets, and the elimination of the . . . system of agency planning shares." [36]

In 1961, however, TAB failed to mention in its report to TAC the elimination of agency planning shares and country subtotals. When pressed, the Executive Chairman explained that the Board had assumed as a result of the 1960 ECOSOC resolution that these devices would not be used in preparing the program scheduled to begin in 1963. Nevertheless, the TAB report emphasized that the aggregate of the continuing commitments by each participating organization in each country would "set the floor below which the target of that country would not be allowed to fall" and that such commitments would be treated as the most important element in fixing individual country targets. Furthermore, TAB assumed that the clause limiting the reduction of any participating agency's share to 85 percent of its allocation in the current program year, as approved by ECOSOC resolution 542 B (XVIII) on 29 July 1954, would not be affected by any amendments in country programming procedures.[37]

Here TAC balked. It prepared a resolution for ECOSOC that authorized project programming for all EPTA projects from 1963 onward, called for a continuation of the biennial pro-

---

[35] E/TAC/SR.218, 15 July 1960, pp. 14–15.
[36] ECOSOC Resolution 786 (XXX), 3 August 1960.
[37] E/TAC/105, 18 April 1961.

gramming cycle on an experimental basis, provided for TAC approval of long-term projects for four years (thus assuring the participating organizations of some continuity in the amount of EPTA funds they administered from year to year), but specifically abolished country subtotals and agency planning shares as well as revoking the 85 percent clause of the ECOSOC resolution of 29 July 1954.[38]

The introduction of project programming, with its emphasis upon more substantive and longer projects and with its elimination of agency planning shares and country subtotals was intended to strengthen the planning, coordination, and implementation of technical assistance in recipient countries and therefore the role of the Resident Representative. The TAB and the ACC reports during these years had usually noted the growing accommodation and cooperation between the resident representatives and the participating organizations in the field, indicating that their positions in programming both with the government and the specialized agencies was improving. Several of the members of TAC, however, were still not convinced that the relations of the Resident Representative were as harmonious as depicted nor as useful as they might be to achieve the goals of UN technical assistance within a country. Through project planning, some members of TAC hoped to bring the role of the Resident Representative in EPTA a little closer to the powers he exercised as Director of Special Fund Programmes within a country.

Growth of the Special Fund

The dramatic increase of Special Fund activities after 1960 made a tremendous impact upon the responsibilities of the UN Resident Representative and the entire field organization of TAB. The pledges of governments to the Special Fund rose very rapidly, as indicated in Table VI. By May 1965, moreover,

---

[38] Approved by ECOSOC Resolution 854 (XXXII), 4 August 1961.

the Fund had earmarked a cumulative total of about $441 million for some 485 projects in the underdeveloped world. Another $645 million was being contributed locally to those projects by the recipient countries.

TABLE VI

ANNUAL PLEDGES TO THE
UNITED NATIONS SPECIAL
FUND, 1959–1965

Year	Pledges (in millions of dollars)
1959	25.8
1960	38.7
1961	48.1
1962	60.3
1963	73.5
1964	80.8
1965	91.6

SOURCE: SF/L.98, 14 January 1964, p. 13,
and SF/L.115/Rev.8, 23 November 1965.

FAO has been designated as the executing agency for about 40 percent of the Special Fund projects. The UN itself has handled about 20 percent of the projects, UNESCO about 15 percent, and ILO about 11 percent. IBRD, ITU, ICAO, WHO, and IAEA have also been executing agencies for Special Fund projects. The Special Fund has remained, as intended, "a pre-investment development assistance" agency, not a capital development fund, and essentially a technical assistance organization. About 51 percent of the Special Fund's money to the program has been going to international experts, 19 percent toward contractual services, 25 percent toward imported equipment and 5 percent toward fellowships, while under EPTA in 1963 about 80 percent went toward expert missions, 14 percent toward fellowships and 5 percent toward equipment and supplies.[39]

[39] *Impact—United Nations Special Fund Report,* April 1964, p. 16, and E/3871, 6 May 1964, p. 20.

The Special Fund and Field Administration

The introduction of Special Fund activities in 1960 to the TAB field organization, therefore, added new responsibilities for planning, programming, and administration to the offices and called for a rapid expansion of staff and facilities. In 1960, to illustrate, there had been 60 professional and general service international staff manning a total of 44 TAB field offices; by 1964 there were budgetary provisions for 201 professional and 75 general service international staff for a total of 83 field offices. Many of the new offices were created in African countries that had recently gained their independence while others were established in countries that had previously been served by a regional office. In 1960, moreover, the budget had provided for 39 resident representatives (including regional representatives); by 1965 the number had been increased to 65.[40]

This extraordinary expansion was largely financed by annual subventions from the Special Fund, since the Special Fund accounted for most of the increasing duties imposed on the Resident Representative as Director of the Special Fund Programmes. At first the subvention amounted to only 9 percent of the TAB field costs paid by the UN, but in 1965 the Special Fund probably covered about 51 percent of field expenditures, as indicated in Table VII.

In addition to the TAB field organization costs paid by EPTA and the Special Fund, the recipient governments contributed, either by payments or by direct furnishing, an office for the local headquarters, equipment, supplies, local secretaries, translators, transportation, communications, and so forth, according to the agreements between the Executive Chairman of TAB and the host governments. In 1960 local costs amounted to $650,950, or 28.5 percent of the total estimated field costs, and in 1964

---

[40] The 78 offices existing in 1965 included 65 resident and regional representatives and 99 deputy or assistant resident representatives. See E/4021, 30 April 1965, p. 207.

TABLE VII

SPECIAL FUND SUBVENTIONS OF THE TECHNICAL
ASSISTANCE BOARD FIELD ORGANIZATION, 1960–1964

Year	Subvention (in dollars)	Percent of TAB Field Office Costs
1960	150,000	9
1961	410,000	17
1962	771,200	22
1963	1,504,100	33
1964	2,814,000	47
1965	3,662,400	51

SOURCE: E/4021, 30 April 1965, p. 213.

they were estimated at $1,824,800, or 22.6 percent of the total.

One of the pioneering resident representatives has recalled that on his first mission in 1952: "I had to fight like a tiger to get a secretary. The headquarters in New York doubted that I needed one." In consequence of the expansion of activities in the field offices of TAB, the Resident Representative, once a mere liaison officer, found himself, in addition to his other responsibilities, the chief administrator of a large staff, both internationally and locally recruited, with all the problems of personnel administration indigenous to any public organization. As the head of the TAB/Special Fund office, the Resident Representative has directly supervised anywhere from a half-dozen to a hundred people, and he has participated in interagency reviews of local salary scales, adjustments in allowances, or the revision of exchange rates. Indeed the Resident Representative has been considered to be the "head of a mission" by host governments, and they usually have extended diplomatic status with appropriate immunities from local jurisdiction to him.

Additional Responsibilities of the Resident Representative for Other Programs

Apart from the capital assistance of IBRD and its affiliates, UN organizations have been spending roughly $350 million a year on economic-social assistance to member countries. About

$40 million of that total has been spent in a single year in the regular technical assistance programs of the UN and specialized agencies and close to another $40 million has passed through UNICEF; while WFP has received a three-year pledge (1963–65) of $90 million for its activities. Each of these programs has left a mark upon the institution of the UN Resident Representative.

Regular Programs

The regular program of UN technical assistance has been financed out of the regular budget of the UN from revenues assessed by the General Assembly upon members of the UN under Article 17 of the UN Charter, and they have been administered through BTAO in the Department of Economic and Social Affairs. About two thirds of the roughly $6.5 million designated in both 1963 and 1964 for UN regular program technical assistance went to economic development and social welfare projects, while the balance was divided among human rights, public administration, and the narcotics control program.

In many instances there are no substantive differences between the technical assistance furnished through regular programs and through EPTA, although special activities have been devised to meet special situations. OPEX, for example, since 1961 has been a service of the UN under its regular budget, later supported by EPTA, by which senior officials are recruited and seconded to a requesting government. In 1963 there were seventy-eight OPEX appointments made at a cost of $789,200, while in 1964 about eighty-three appointments were made at a cost of $848,200. These expert officials have occupied executive and managerial jobs within national governments, supplying a scarce resource vital to the development of a country until they can train a national replacement.

The UN, of course, has also acted as a participating organization (UNTA) of EPTA and an executing agency for the

Special Fund, receiving allocations from those accounts for such undertakings that go beyond its regular program, while it has had a special relationship with UNICEF, with responsibility for technical advice in the implementation of projects.

Several of the specialized agencies have also carried on technical assistance work financed from their own budgets, some of them antedating the constitution of the UN and the establishment of EPTA. But the expenditure of the specialized agencies for technical assistance out of their own budgets has varied widely, with a few of the agencies almost entirely dependent upon EPTA and the Special Fund for their technical assistance activities. By far the largest regular program of the specialized agencies has been that of WHO, accounting for almost 75 percent of all regular program expenditures, an amount three times greater than the EPTA allocation to WHO. By contrast the regular program of FAO has been only a small fraction of its EPTA funds. In any case all the UN and specialized agency regular programs together have amounted to less than one third of the resources available to EPTA and the Special Fund, and, if WHO were excluded, no more than 10 percent.[41]

Although some basic responsibilities have been assigned to the Resident Representative under EPTA and the Special Fund in the field, each participating organization has been able to decide for itself which, if any, administrative functions it will request from him and his office. The pattern of such services utilized by the specialized agencies varies from country to country—or even from program to program. Thus, in one country a Resident Representative may be requested by one agency to pay travel subsistence allowances for all of its experts, while another agency within the same country may request such services for its EPTA experts only, and a third agency may decide to handle this administrative service for its experts without any reference to the Resident Representative at all. No generalization is pos-

[41] E/3851, 31 January 1964.

sible, except one: the Resident Representative has been the chief of mission for all UNTA projects and therefore has handled all the details associated with these operations. In recent years, this has become an increasing responsibility, for the UN regular program of technical assistance has tripled since 1960, as indicated in Table VIII.

TABLE VIII

BUDGETARY APPROPRIATIONS FOR THE
UNITED NATIONS REGULAR PROGRAMS
OF TECHNICAL ASSISTANCE, 1960–1966

Year	Appropriations (in millions of dollars)
1960	2.4
1961	3.4
1962	5.8
1963	6.7
1964	6.4
1965[a]	6.4
1966[a]	6.4

SOURCE: E/3471, May 1961; E/3757, 13 May 1963; E/3870/Add. 1, 10 June 1964; E/4016/Add. 1, 10 May 1965.
[a] Budgeted.

The United Nations Children's Fund and the World Food Program

UNICEF was created long before the institution of the Resident Representative. First organized as an "emergency" fund by the General Assembly in 1946 to assist the children of war devastated areas, UNICEF became a permanent agency in 1953 and gradually expanded its activities from direct aid to children to maternal care, disease control, nutrition, and so forth. The money for UNICEF comes from the voluntary contributions of governments and individuals, but its Board is responsible to the General Assembly through ECOSOC, its Executive Director is appointed by the Secretary-General, and its personnel are members of the Secretariat of the UN.

The UN Resident Representative in the field often provides assistance to UNICEF programs: he may disseminate information about the program, assist UNICEF officers on inspection visits, help in the customs clearance of UNICEF supplies, and provide other administrative support. In at least one instance the Resident Representative has been the country representative of UNICEF. Moreover, he frequently facilitates coordination between UNICEF projects and related undertakings by WHO, FAO, UNESCO, or other participating organizations of EPTA.

In 1963 the Resident Representative received still another responsibility: Agent of the WFP in the host country. Following an ECOSOC resolution in the summer of 1961 and the proclamation of the General Assembly on the Development Decade,[42] thirty governments pledged contributions to a new WFP in September 1962. Additional governmental pledges raised the total resources for an experimental three-year program (1963–65) to $90 million in cash commodities and services. WFP is operated jointly by the UN and FAO through a twenty-member intergovernmental committee, an Executive Director, and a small secretariat with headquarters in the FAO building in Rome. Essentially food is provided partly for aid in emergencies, partly for preschool and school feeding, but mostly for implementing pilot projects for economic and social development, such as land settlement and development, price stabilization, community development, and so forth. The Resident Representative helps to formulate requests for WFP aid by host countries and helps to coordinate such requests with other UN programs in the country.

UNHCR has also received minor assistance from the Resident Representative and the TAB offices in investigating the circumstances of refugees in his country or assisting with visits of UNHCR officials.

[42] GA Resolution 1710, 19 December 1961.

Directors of United Nations Information Centers

No one could have envisaged in 1950 that the UN Resident Representative for Technical Assistance would, among other things, be entrusted with responsibility for the UN Information Center within a country. In 1960, however, David Blickenstaff, the UN Resident Representative in India, was appointed in a dual capacity as Director of the Information Center in New Delhi under the Office of Public Information in the UN.

One of the reasons for this appointment was the desire to conserve professional posts while opening new information centers around the world, and, in fact, about twenty new information centers of the UN were established between 1960 and 1964. The policy of dual appointments also attempted to meet the recommendations of ACABQ that so far as possible there should be close coordination in the field offices of the UN family. Thirteen resident representatives were serving as directors of UN Information Centers in 1964.

The increased burden, however, turned out to be too much of a load for one executive officer. Recently the Office of Public Information has been appointing full-time professional information officers to centers where in the past there was a combined representation. But in these instances the UN Resident Representative has been designated Head of the UN Offices in the country with the Director of Information, for representational purposes, serving under him.[43] Thus, by administrative change, the UN information centers may eventually become more closely linked to the Resident Representative with an information officer responsible to the Office of Public Information in New York for his technical functions but implementing country policy in consultation with the UN Resident Representative.

[43] Letter from William C. Powell, Acting Director, External Relations Division, UN Office of Public Information, 22 July 1964.

The Career of the United Nations Resident Representative

Until 1966 resident representatives were appointed by the Executive Chairman of TAB in agreement with the Board after consultations with (*a*) the TAB Appointment and Promotion Board, including a representative of the Director of the UN Office of Personnel, (*b*) representatives of participating organizations, (*c*) the Managing Director of the Special Fund, and (*d*) the host government. Resident representatives were hired into the TAB field organization either by outside recruitment, normally on a fixed-term contract that could later be converted into a permanent TAB appointment, or else by transfer or secondment from one of the participating organizations.

In 1965, out of seventy resident representatives, six had been seconded from specialized agencies, usually with a fixed-term appointment of two years with TAB and a permanent or indefinite appointment from their parent organization; thirty-seven had fixed-term appointments; and twenty-seven had permanent TAB appointments, which confer no tenure in the UN system outside TAB.[44]

About half of the resident representatives were already on the staff of an international organization when they took up their duties with TAB, and almost all the rest have had some service with their national governments in administrative, technical, or diplomatic functions prior to their appointments to the TAB field organization. Resident representatives have been appointed at any age, some quite young and others with a long career of public service behind them. The median age of resident representatives in 1965 lay in the middle or late forties. Almost half of them held graduate degrees.

In a tabulation of 46 regional and country resident representatives in 1964, it appeared that 26 of them had served more

[44] Letter from C. L. Law, Executive Officer, TAB, 16 December 1965.

than ten years with the UN system and 17 had served as Resident Representative for more than four years. By nationality, 20 of the 46 resident representatives tabulated came from Europe, including 2 from Poland, 2 from Yugoslavia, and 1 from the USSR; 11 resident representatives were nationals of the United States, Canada, and New Zealand; 7 came from Latin America, 6 from Asia, and 2 were nationals of African states. Put another way, 31 resident representatives were nationals of developed countries while 15 were nationals of underdeveloped countries.

In the budget estimates for 1965 TAB proposed 76 resident representatives for the field organization, 64 deputy resident representatives, 39 assistant resident representatives for program, and 56 assistant representatives for administration, as well as liaison officers, program officers, correspondents, international office assistants, and local staff, such as chauffeurs and messengers, totaling an organization of 1,364 employees. In 1965 appointments as Resident Representative were budgeted in levels from P-4 ($13,900–$18,630 gross salary per annum) to D-2 ($24,050–$26,000 gross salary per annum) plus dependence and educational allowances as well as small post adjustments where the cost of living is higher than the base (Geneva in 1956 less 10 percent). Representation allowances in the 1965 budget estimates averaged out to little more than $1,000 per year per resident representative.

New Terms of Reference for the United Nations Resident Representative?

The growing complexity and cost of EPTA, Special Fund activities, and the UN regular program of technical assistance, as well as the burgeoning activities of other UN aid agencies in the underdeveloped world, was bound to call for a reexamination of the relationships among these organizations and the role of the Resident Representative.[45] New hopes for strengthening his position had been precipitated by the introduction of project programming to EPTA, for it was expected that, without the restriction of agency subtotals, the Resident Representative would have a greater influence over the shape of the final country program and some members of TAC had believed that the emphasis upon well-conceived long-term projects would require both governments and the participating organizations to seek his advice and counsel in order to gain approval under EPTA. The Venezuelan representative to TAC went even further in the summer of 1961, foreseeing the Resident Representative as a "superminister" over the government's own ministers:

The final approval of projects would depend on him; he would have a say in all matters affecting their selection, preparation, and implementation; he would assess their value for the country's general development; and he would even be able to influence the composition of the national planning and coordinating units.[46]

The United States also presented a statement that called attention to the need for an increased role for the Resident Representative in the program process, emphasizing the importance of determining the highest priorities in national development planning and concentrating the very limited resources of the UN upon them. According to the American statement, each of the participating organizations working in particular fields had only a part in the over-all development scheme, and the resident representatives were not yet concentrating upon planning advice as one of their principal tasks:

Both . . . difficulties could be overcome if the country representatives of the United Nations and its agencies formed a more tightly

[45] On 22 December 1960, ECOSOC adopted Resolution 806 (XXX), which stated that, when referred to collectively, EPTA and the regular programs of the UN, IAEA, and the specialized agencies would be known as UN Programs of Technical Co-operation. When referred to separately, the individual programs retain their original names.
[46] E/TAC/SR.240, 5 July 1961, p. 4.

co-ordinated group, of which the resident representative would logically be the chairman, and which would help to focus the attention of the various branches of the host government on the need for central direction of development planning.[47]

These views were generally shared by the Sudanese representative to TAC, who indicated that the Resident Representative had been extraordinarily helpful to many African countries in finding their way through the complications of UN technical assistance machinery and who deplored the proliferation of separate specialized agency country representatives.[48] Along somewhat similar lines, the New Zealand representative suggested that the creation of a large number of newly independent states ought to enable the UN to capitalize upon the strategic position of the Resident Representative, who could either give or arrange technical advice in drawing up development priorities and who should be able to discourage the inclusion of relatively unimportant projects in the program.[49]

Not all the representatives to TAC agreed. The USSR admitted that the Resident Representative performed a useful function before an underdeveloped country established a strong and effective coordinating agency for technical assistance in its own government, but, once such machinery had been established, the Resident Representative became a mere intermediary who hampered direct contacts between governments and the responsible authorities in the UN and the specialized agencies. He advocated, first, the appointment of the nationals of the recipient countries as deputy resident representatives; second, their gradual promotion to the posts of resident representatives as they acquired experience in the coordination of technical assistance; and, finally, the transfer of the functions of the Resident Representative to the national coordinating agency itself.[50]

[47] E/TAC/SR.232, 27 June 1961.
[48] E/TAC/SR.236, 30 June 1961, p. 5.
[49] *Ibid.*, p. 10.
[50] E/TAC/SR.234, 29 June 1961, p. 8.

In consequence of these discussions in the summer of 1961 TAC drafted two resolutions which ECOSOC approved.[51] The first authorized the establishment of an *ad hoc* committee of eight (later increased to ten) member states appointed by the President of ECOSOC to study ways and means of bringing about a closer relationship within the UN system of agencies, "giving special attention to the potential role of the resident representatives," so as to provide more concerted advice on the technical preparation and implementation of country programs, as well as on the technical aspects of parts of the program, to those countries that request such assistance. The second resolution requested ACC to draw up proposals "by which resident representatives may, for purposes of coordination, be kept informed about, and, as appropriate, associated with inquiries and negotiations" not only involving EPTA and the Special Fund but also other programs of technical cooperation undertaken by the UN, the specialized agencies, IAEA, or UNICEF, "whether financed from voluntary funds . . . or from the regular budgets of their organizations."

These were strong resolutions, not only designed to carry the potential of the Resident Representative a few steps beyond his previous interests and responsibilities but also to put him eventually in a pivotal position for all technical assistance flowing through the channels of the UN system.

The Ten "Principles" of the Administrative
Committee on Coordination

In October 1961 ACC approved ten principles for field coordination between the resident representatives and the participating organizations. Essentially they were designed to increase the Resident Representative's access to information in order to facilitate his coordination of UN technical assistance.

ACC agreed that programming negotiations between officials

[51] ECOSOC Resolution 851 (XXXII), 4 August 1961.

of the participating organizations and officials of the ministries were to be held with the "advance" knowledge of the Resident Representative and that no changes in the approved EPTA program were to be made without informing him; that a Resident Representative should also be informed promptly about the appointment of new agency mission chiefs in the new country and that he ought to introduce new arrivals to the appropriate officials of the host government; that the Resident Representative should be informed at all stages of development and operation of "comparable" technical assistance programs carried out by the participating organizations, or of any regional projects in which their country might participate. Finally, ACC approved the principle that the Resident Representative should be given "advance notice" of all visits by headquarters officials to the field and should be kept "fully informed" about the purposes and the results of discussions between such officials and the host government.

Inadvertently, perhaps, these principles advertised the weakness of the Resident Representative within the EPTA programming process. The very laboring of the norms that were actually supposed to prevail in the relationships between the Resident Representative and the participating organizations was in answer to current criticisms that appeals to "coordination" were meaningless unless, above all, the participating organizations felt it their duty to keep the Resident Representative fully informed on all UN technical assistance activities within a country.

The Mandate of the Ad Hoc Committee

The mandate of the *ad hoc* Committee given by ECOSOC resolution 851 (XXXII) of 4 August 1961 had gone beyond an analysis of the potential role of the Resident Representative. The Committee was also directed to study the steps needed (*a*) to organize the technical cooperation activities of the UN, the specialized agencies, IAEA, and the Special Fund to provide greater aid in the preparation of their country development programs; (*b*) to bring about closer coordination among these UN technical cooperation activities; and (*c*) to assist member states by providing technical cooperation services most conducive to their national development—it being understood that the actual preparation of country development programs, their coordination, and their implementation remained the prerogative of the recipient governments.

Although the Committee did not have specific instructions to study a merger of EPTA and the Special Fund, as the United States had suggested in the 1961 summer meeting of TAC,[52] it began to give attention to this idea as soon as it started to function in January 1962. In order to be fully acquainted with the problems of coordinating the UN technical cooperation programs, the Committee addressed a list of some fifty questions to the UN, UNICEF, the Managing Director of the Special Fund, the specialized agencies, and the Executive Chairman of TAB.

*Views of the Executive Chairman of the
Technical Assistance Board*

The Executive Chairman pointed out that, in programming, the Resident Representative called to the attention of recipient governments the desirability of a national development plan and a national coordinating authority for economic and technical assistance and that the Resident Representative tried to facilitate the work of the coordinating authority by explaining the procedures of EPTA as well as the terms of reference and

[52] The U.S. Assistant Secretary of State for International Organization Affairs established his own Advisory Committee on International Organizations, which transmitted to him on 28 June 1963 "A Report on the Technical Cooperation Programs of the United Nations System of Organizations." Among other things, it recommended that a merger of EPTA and the Special Fund be sought and that the Resident Representative be assigned new and clearly defined functions that would leave no doubt about his central role as coordinator of UN technical cooperation activities and spokesman for the UN system.

fields of competence of the participating organizations. He also attempted to ensure that the obligations that the recipient government assumed under the technical assistance program were clearly understood and that the government observed its own planning priorities.

In executing the projects the Resident Representative, according to the Executive Chairman of TAB, normally reviewed projects by discussions with mission chiefs, meetings with experts, and so forth, and, to some degree, varying from country to country, his office provided administrative assistance, including briefing of experts on arrival, introducing them to local officials, arranging for clerical aid, transport, and sometimes housing facilities. He often paid the local currency entitlements to the experts, sometimes provided secretarial assistance, and occasionally was asked to make representation to the recipient government to ensure the necessary local conditions for the expert to pursue his work effectively. The Executive Chairman of TAB noted that the Resident Representative also assisted in the execution of fellowship programs, sometimes participating in the selection of fellows but generally arranging for medical and language examinations, international transportation, and so forth.

With respect to coordination the Executive Chairman of TAB indicated that the Resident Representative, with the close cooperation of government, saw all requests for assistance and copies of related correspondence whether the projects fell under EPTA, regular technical assistance programs, OPEX, or the Special Fund; that he maintained, "as appropriate," continuing contacts of other foreign aid programs in the country and exchanged with them information concerning projects planned or in execution; and, finally, that he promoted in all possible ways a cooperative approach by the participating organizations in the provision of technical assistance, keeping in mind the need for governmental support of both the technical and interministerial levels.

The replies of the Executive Chairman of TAB to the *ad hoc* Committee, although discreetly couched, intimated some problems. He made it perfectly clear that the Resident Representative had no "authority" with respect to the development of country plans or programs, that his duty was to encourage sound planning and programs, and "to be available to advise" the government. In a survey of forty-four recipient countries, moreover, he observed that eight or nine of them did not have any national coordinating machinery and the resident representatives considered about one third of the existing coordinating agencies to be "relatively ineffective." Moreover, "experience has shown that the respective functions of the Resident Representative and of the agency representatives have not always been fully understood" and that, in fact, "technical consultations," within the province of the participating organizations of EPTA, and "coordination" by the Resident Representative required a "hand-in-glove" relationship, with a continuous and full flow of information between the participating organizations and the Resident Representative. The Executive Chairman cited one case where the requests or instructions of national coordinating units had little weight upon either its own ministries or the international organizations. Indeed, nine different offices had been established by international organizations in the country, some prior to the TAB office, and each dealt with some aspect of technical assistance. The implication was that in this case the "hand-in-glove" relationship had been a very loose fit. Finally, the Executive Chairman remarked that very few countries have established committees on which representatives of the various bilateral and multilateral aid programs are formally represented:

Only in 15 per cent of the countries surveyed does such formal representation exist, and then it is usually effected by inviting representatives of the aid-giving organizations to sit at some or all meetings of the Government's own coordinating committee. It must be noted that, in some cases, the Governments have very specifically stated that they did not consider such participation as either desirable or necessary, and have discouraged even informal meetings between the aid-giving organizations, preferring to deal directly and independently with each one.[53]

Views of the Specialized Agencies

From the specialized agencies the *ad hoc* Committee also received replies to its questionnaire on possible improvements in the coordination and administration of UN technical cooperation programs. The agencies generally took a dim view about an immediate merger of EPTA and the Special Fund or any change in the terms of reference of the Resident Representative. Somewhat typical was the comment of ILO:

As regards the advantages or disadvantages of merging the Expanded Program and the Special Fund, the ILO is not convinced that any immediate unification of this kind would be desirable [and] . . . the desirable relationship between Resident Representatives and agency representatives is one of close cooperation based on their respective functions and responsibilities. These are defined in the ACC statement of October 1961. . . . No further elaboration seems to be necessary at this stage.

While recognizing that the new programming procedures of EPTA were bringing it closer to the Special Fund and that an integrated program for all long-term and large-scale projects might be more economical and less confusing to recipient countries, ILO believed that it would be necessary to retain the inter-agency coordinating machinery "which exists at present under EPTA." Small and short-term projects, in the view of ILO, could be handled separately, either through the existing machinery of EPTA or an expanded regular budget program. "Meanwhile, it would appear wise not to precipitate action in this matter but to await the results of further experience." [54]

[53] E/AC.49/R.2/Add. 6, 4 April 1962, p. 17.
[54] E/AC.49/R.2/Add. 3, 28 March 1962, pp. 7, 19.

Ad Hoc *Committee's Progress Report of 1962*

On the basis of the replies to its inquiries the *ad hoc* Committee, after further discussion, issued a progress report in May 1962.[55] Several recommendations were made for the improvement of coordination of the UN technical cooperation programs at headquarters, the regional level, and in the field. With respect to the Resident Representative, the emphasis of the report fell once again upon increasing his access to information: governments were again urged to establish national coordinating machinery, and, at the government's request, the Resident Representative "might" give assistance to this endeavor; periodic meetings of those concerned with various UN programs might be held under the chairmanship of the "appropriate" government minister for review of technical assistance within the context of the national development plan; and seminars "might" be organized to acquaint government officials with the procedures and activities of the UN programs.

Furthermore, the *ad hoc* Committee recommended that, "whenever possible," the visits of agency representatives to recipient countries for program planning should be made simultaneously, so that they might harmonize their technical assistance recommendations, eliminate overlapping, and assist the governments in coordination; copies of correspondence involving UN technical assistance programs should "normally" be sent to the resident representatives, and resident representatives should "normally" be consulted on the administrative needs of experts, such as housing, visas, and transport. The Resident Representative, "wherever feasible," should be informed of visitors from participating organizations.

The Committee also stressed the desirability of different UN programs sharing common premises in the field, thus bringing under one roof as many UN services as possible, and it endorsed

[55] E/3639, 21 May 1962.

the ACC principle that informal meetings of the agency representatives should be convened periodically under the chairmanship of the Resident Representative to consider matters of coordination—"without in any way interfering in the constitutional relationships of the agency field representatives with their
headquarters."

The *ad hoc* Committee's recommendations were greeted in
the 1962 TAC meetings with a mixed reaction. Generally a
favorable but a "wait-and-see" attitude prevailed. The representatives of the specialized agencies, however, appearing before
TAC regretted that ECOSOC would even consider the *ad hoc*
Committee report before ACC had an opportunity to pass judgment on the recommendations, and they took specific issue with
any requirement that the Resident Representative be involved in
technical negotiations between the participating organizations
and the recipient governments, that he be sent copies of correspondence, that he be consulted about visitors from the headquarters, or that he necessarily be involved in the administrative
backstopping of technical experts. Some of these views were
later reflected in ACC's observations on the *ad hoc* Committee's
recommendations.[56]

New Zealand and France in TAC emphasized the inherent
conflict between technicians and administrators in organizations
and stated that, in the last resort, coordination did not depend
so much upon structures or formulas but upon men. In the
words of the French representative, future studies on coordination should attempt to "define a philosophy of coordination and
to propose methods likely to promote the desired coordination
without which the most ingenious organic measures might remain a dead letter." [57]

TAC then drafted a resolution, later approved by ECOSOC,
requesting ACC to consider the report and implement those

[56] E/3695, 10 October 1962.
[57] E/TAC/SR.275, 20 December 1962, p. 5.

recommendations which, in its view, could be implemented, requesting the Committee to continue its work for two more years and increasing the Committee's membership from eight to ten.[58] At the same time it requested the Secretary-General to make a study of the possible advantages or disadvantages of merging some or all of the technical assistance programs of the UN. The resolution also stressed the importance of appropriate cooperation between the resident representatives and the executive secretaries of the regional economic commissions, noting that the first of a series of meetings between resident representatives and the staffs of the commissions had been held in Santiago, Bangkok, Addis Ababa, and Geneva.

Ad Hoc *Committee and the Technical Assistance Committee Meetings in 1963*

The *ad hoc* Committee resumed its meetings in March 1963 and heard statements from the Deputy Under-Secretary for Economic and Social Affairs, the Managing Director of the Special Fund, the Acting Commissioner for Technical Assistance, and representatives of the specialized agencies on steps taken to implement previous recommendations on technical assistance activities. The Committee then continued its discussions on coordination at the headquarters, including a possible merger of EPTA, the Special Fund, and/or regular programs of technical assistance, coordination at the regional level, including a possible strengthening of the regional economic commissions, and coordination in the field.

With respect to resident representatives, the United States urged that

(1) they should have a central role in coordinating technical assistance; (2) they should be the main channel of contact between

---

[58] ECOSOC Resolution 900 (XXXIV), 2 August 1962. The original members of the *ad hoc* Committee were Brazil, Ethiopia, France, Japan, the USSR, the United Arab Republic, the United Kingdom, and the United States. Added later were Jordan and Indonesia.

Government and Headquarters; (3) their comments and recommendations should be required on all voluntary programs, and they should be free to comment on the regular programs of the United Nations and of the specialized agencies, the World Food Programme, and the programs of UNICEF.[59]

France and Jordan, in some respects, went further: the former declared that the Resident Representative should be "the exclusive link between recipient governments, TAB, the Special Fund and the specialized agencies," while the latter felt that the resident representatives should be the "sole representatives of all programmes and the only channel of correspondence." The Brazilian representative thought the Resident Representative "the cornerstone of field coordination." Japan not only urged strengthening the powers of the Resident Representative, but proposed that the meetings between the officials of the recipient governments and the participating organizations, as recommended by the *ad hoc* Committee, should also be attended by those responsible for carrying out bilateral assistance programs, a view supported by the United States and the United Kingdom but strongly opposed by the USSR and France.

The old position of the USSR, moreover, that resident representatives should be nationals of the recipient countries was advanced again by the United Arab Republic, only to be opposed by Jordan, Japan, Brazil, and the United Kingdom, while the United States had some "misgivings" about it. France gave two cogent reasons against the use of a national as a Resident Representative within a country: first, a constructive exchange of views to relate UN technical cooperation programs to a developing country's needs would hardly be fruitful between two nationals of the same country, and, second, the few people equipped with Resident Representative's skills in the developing countries could render more valuable services if they were as-

[59] E/AC.49/SR.23, 14 May 1963, p. 11. Other commentaries on the role of the resident representatives in these meetings have been drawn from E/AC.49/SR.22, 13 May 1963, and E/AC.49/SR.24, 13 May 1963.

signed to another country. Finally, some members on the *ad hoc* Committee suggested that the institution of the UN Resident Representative should "ultimately" be abolished. Even the United States agreed that the institution was a temporary one but cautioned that "it should not be abolished while its services were still needed."

The *ad hoc* Committee of Ten had requested ACC to report in 1963 on how well the recommended principles for UN field coordination were working in practice. Based on still limited experience, ACC answered that "the general level of coordination in the field is now good" and that there was no need to add to or revise the principles enumerated, although "continuous efforts are needed on all sides to maintain and improve on the present practice." [60]

TAC discussed the *ad hoc* Committee's interim report[61] in the summer of 1963 that touched the problems of technical assistance coordination at all levels. Insofar as the field organization was concerned, some members were not convinced by the bland statements on "coordination" by ACC. Yugoslavia noted a tendency for participating organizations to by-pass both the national coordination agency and the resident representatives. Greece vigorously confirmed this view, and Nigeria stated that the enthusiasm of certain specialized agencies in forging ahead with a specific project had been such that "they had left the Resident Representative completely in the dark." Australia also contested the ACC's conclusions by stating that the flow of information needed by the Resident Representative from the participating organizations to discharge his important function was inadequate.

Poland, however, consistent with the position of the USSR, did not object to the ACC report itself but was disturbed by the possibility that a strengthened Resident Representative might

[60] E/3765, 6 May 1963.
[61] E/3750, 18 April 1963.

exercise an undesirable pressure on recipient governments and interfere in their domestic affairs. The Polish representative deplored the trend to regard resident representatives "as ambassadors plenipotentiary of the United Nations Technical Assistance Administration and the specialized agencies," and he urged that the functions of the Resident Representative be transferred in the near future to the recipient governments themselves.[62]

A draft resolution, later adopted by ECOSOC,[63] noted "with appreciation" the work done by the *ad hoc* Committee and requested the Secretary-General to transmit the interim report to the member governments of the UN, of the specialized agencies, and of IAEA and then to prepare an analysis of their views for consideration by the *ad hoc* Committee early in 1964.

Further Steps toward Coordination in the Field

In November 1963 TAC pressed further upon TAB to consider administrative improvements and economies that might result from a fuller use of the facilities of the Resident Representative's office by the participating organizations of EPTA. The Executive Chairman reported back to TAC in October 1964, observing that there was a genuine need for a senior technical adviser being designated as mission chief by a participating organization in countries which had substantial programs of assistance and that host governments might find such a senior adviser or agency country representative useful, even when development plans were formative. Such appointees could render extraordinary advisory assistance to a ministry including the development of sectoral plans, the allocation of priorities, and the best use of various sources of aid.[64] The increase in agency programs, moreover, within countries required on-the-spot coordination of the work of the experts in one technical

[62] E/3783/Add.1, 29 June 1963, pp. 7–36.
[63] ECOSOC Resolution 954 (XXXVI), 5 July 1963.
[64] E/TAC/148, 13 October 1964.

field. A country representative of a participating organization could evaluate the progress of the projects for which the agency was responsible and bring to the Resident Representative full information about programs within his technical competence, thereby assisting the Resident Representative as a technical adviser and improving the ability of the Resident Representative to advise the central planning machinery of the government on the capacity of the UN family of organizations to meet the needs of the country.

The Executive Chairman of TAB suggested that the Resident Representative would continue to provide administrative-house-keeping services, still at the option of the participating organization but, to be hoped, more widely used and not duplicated by the participating organization in the country, thus freeing the agency country representative for his professional duties. In sum, the Resident Representative would have a general representational responsibility for all activities under EPTA, Special Fund, and WFP, while the agency country representative would have full functional responsibilities for the participating organization's activities. The Executive Chairman regarded the roles of Resident Representative and agency country representative as complementary, stating that they do not conflict or overlap nor are they interchangeable. TAB now felt that the time had come, where agency programs had reached a "substantial" level, for participating organizations to designate their mission chiefs and that it was no longer feasible to ask the Resident Representative to assume the duties of an agency country representative except on a temporary basis.

Slowly but surely, by pragmatism and promise, the role of the Resident Representative was being developed, brought into place within the UN family of aid-giving agencies, specialized, and stabilized, so that with time his functions would become indispensable to both the UN system and the recipient governments.

Merger of the Expanded Program and the Special Fund:
United Nations Development Program

In March 1964 the *ad hoc* Committee resumed its meetings. It had in hand the two reports by the Secretary-General on the desirability of merging some or all of the technical assistance programs that had been prepared in response to the ECOSOC request for a study in the summer of 1962, as well as some of the reactions of governments[65] to the *ad hoc* Committee's interim report of 1963. In his first report the Secretary-General recommended a merger of EPTA and the Special Fund at the intergovernmental, interagency, and management levels, giving it the name of the United Nations Development Programme (UNDP), and outlining its structure. In his second report the Secretary-General felt that the merger of the regular programs of technical assistance with either EPTA, the Special Fund, or a combination of them under the proposed UNDP "would raise more problems than it would resolve and the disadvantages would outweigh any possible advantages." [66]

The *ad hoc* Committee then concentrated almost solely on the merger of EPTA and the Special Fund. After a great deal of debate the Committee drafted a resolution[67] for consideration by TAC and ECOSOC in their summer 1964 sessions. Essentially the draft resolution proposed (1) the combination of EPTA and the Special Fund in a program to be known as the United Nations Development Programme, but with the specification that the "special characteristics and operations of the two programmes as well as two separate funds will be maintained"; (2) the provision of a single Governing Council, elected by ECOSOC with an equal number of representatives from the developed and underdeveloped nations, that would perform the

[65] E/AC/49/8, 15 January 1964, and the documents cited in footnote 66 for mixed comments on technical assistance program coordination.
[66] E/3850, 9 January 1964, and E/3851, 31 January 1964.
[67] For text of resolution see E/3862, 10 March 1964.

functions previously exercised by TAC for EPTA and by the Governing Council for the Special Fund; (3) the establishment, in place of TAB for EPTA and the Consultative Board of the Special Fund, one Inter-Agency Consultative Board.

The Inter-Agency Consultative Board would be an "advisory committee" composed of the Secretary-General, the executive heads of the specialized agencies and IAEA, and the executive directors of UNICEF and the WFP. It would "advise the management" on the programs and projects submitted by governments, through the Resident Representative, to the Governing Council for approval; "be consulted" in the selection of agencies for the execution of projects; and "be consulted" on the appointment of resident representatives and "review" annual reports submitted by them.

The resolution was approved by a vote of 6 to 3, with 1 abstention.[68] Although the United Kingdom and France voted for the draft resolution, they doubted that the merger would have all the advantages claimed for it; however, they believed that it might be a satisfactory form of organization to preserve the separateness of the two programs under the supervision of a combined governing body. Brazil voted against the draft resolution because it feared that a decision on any institutional change affecting the Special Fund might prejudice the consideration of transferring that Fund into a capital development fund, as the underdeveloped countries had always wished, and, in any case, Brazil did not share the view that a reorganization was imperative in order to provide a more solid basis for the future growth of the UN assistance programs financed by voluntary contributions. The USSR voted against the draft resolution on the grounds that (a) it was merely a subterfuge to impose the procedures and principles of the Special Fund upon EPTA; (b) it ran counter to the views expressed on the merger by a

[68] *For:* France, Indonesia, Japan, Jordan, United Kingdom, and United States; *against:* Brazil, USSR, and United Arab Republic; *abstained:* Ethiopia.

number of governments; and (c) the vote of the *ad hoc* Committee was premature, lacking a full analysis by the Secretary-General of the advantages and disadvantages of the merger along with the comments of all interested governments. Ethiopia abstained, hoping that the UN would not lose sight of the importance of creating a capital development fund and because it seemed that the draft resolution did not take full account of the need for a more effective and efficient use of funds.[69]

Meetings of the Technical Assistance Committee and the Economic and Social Council in 1964

At the 1964 summer session of TAC support for a merger of EPTA and the Special Fund was expressed by several spokesmen for the specialized agencies, as well as by the Executive Chairman of TAB, the Associate Managing Director of the Special Fund, the Under-Secretary for Economic and Social Affairs, and the Secretary-General of the UN—all of whom appeared before the Committee.[70]

A considerable majority of the members of TAC expressed their support of, or concurrence in, the *ad hoc* Committee's proposal, but they generally made it clear that they believed the separate identity and characteristics of EPTA and the Special Fund should be preserved within UNDP. Various reservations on specific aspects of the proposed merger, moreover, were voiced, with some TAC members wishing to see further details discussed before any commitments. A main point at issue was the desirability of unification of the programs at the management level, and the underdeveloped countries again emphasized that the proposed reorganization should not prejudice any action that aimed at establishing a UN capital development fund. Several TAC members repeated the view that the role of the Resident Representative should be strengthened and that

[69] E/3862, 10 March 1964.
[70] E/3933, 8 July 1964, p. 30.

relations between the regional economic commissions and the organs and staff of the proposed UNDP should be as close as possible.

Arguments in TAC flatly against the merger included objections on the grounds that (*a*) not enough developing countries had been heard on the subject, that (*b*) the Secretary-General had not "sufficiently explored" the advantages and *disadvantages* of the merger, that (*c*) such a merger would have little justification unless it were combined with practical steps for the international financing of development, and that (*d*) it would lead in fact to the absorption of EPTA into the Special Fund.

No resolutions were passed at the TAC meeting, but in the summer of 1964 ECOSOC approved a resolution that was essentially the draft resolution calling for a merger of EPTA and the Special Fund that had been approved by the *ad hoc* Committee in March. The nineteenth General Assembly, which met in December, 1964, failed to consider the ECOSOC resolution, owing to the crisis over the payment of UN peace-keeping expenses that led to the Assembly's adjournment, but in November 1965 after debate in the Second Committee of the twentieth General Assembly, largely over the composition of the single Governing Council for the two programs, the merger of EPTA and the Special Fund into UNDP was approved.

Conclusions

Anyone who pursues the multilateral negotiations, resolutions, and decisions of the UN with its affiliated agencies must be appalled by the interminable discussions that so often lead to no action. So much seems to be said about so little. Yet such procrastination is inevitable, for sovereign states, divided by ministries and parties, are hardly single-minded, and, in concert with a hundred or more nations, the achievement of a specific agreement, rather than a pompous declaration of principles, comes close to being miraculous.

Only a strong stomach and a strong back can bring negotiators to read reams of mimeographed paper, listen to hours of droning debate, and sit politely through a multitude of receptions, parleys, committees, and councils, all in the interest of a multilateral accord. As Adlai Stevenson once said, the social life of a diplomat is "protocol, alcohol, and Geritol." The wonder is that the form and function of international organizations change as much as they do, that an institution like the UN Resident Representative can be administratively created and gradually woven into the context of active programs, and that, with expanding responsibilities, the office may in its own small way keep the UN moving forward toward the major principles of the Charter.

The Resident Representative and
Programming Technical Assistance

As Director of Special Fund Programmes the Resident Representative has been central to all negotiations and approval of projects supported by the UN Special Fund within a country. But despite all the principles enunciated and the suggestions made about the positive role of the UN Resident Representative, his influence, except in a few nations, was quite marginal, if not negligible, in programming under EPTA. Whereas it is easy to blame the entrenched interests of the specialized agencies for this impotence, the main difficulties of EPTA appear to have lain in, first, the inability of most governments in the underdeveloped countries to make a coherent allocation of resources, owing to specious national planning and the incapacity of the chief executive to lead, coordinate, or control his own ministries; and, second, the paucity of resources that must be divided among the participating organizations by their own recommendations and then allocated to 121 underdeveloped countries and territories receiving assistance.

The point of leverage for the UN Resident Representative

for advice on technical assistance programming has been—
and ought to be—the national coordinating unit. Indeed, if the
national coordinating unit has both economic wisdom through
a sound planning agency and political strength, it may not require the Resident Representative's advice on programming at
all once it has ascertained its EPTA country target figure. In
the vast majority of cases, however, the national coordinating
unit, if any, has merely reflected interministerial compromises
on a division of the EPTA country resources after the ministries themselves have reached "agreements" with the participating organizations that catered to their own technical interests.
Sometimes the Resident Representative has been advised of, or
participated in, these negotiations and understandings between
the ministries and the participating organizations—and sometimes he has not. In any case he had no legal power to allocate
or transfer funds from one participating organization to another
or to deny the distribution of the projects requested by the recipient government. He had to rely upon suggestion and persuasion in his meetings with representatives of the specialized agencies or the national ministries or the national coordinating unit
—if he was asked for advice. Sometimes he was, and sometimes
he was not. Furthermore, one must assume that, if the Resident
Representative is to guide the programming of EPTA within a
country along rational lines, he must understand the asserted
national priorities, including the use of capital funds, so that he
can point out inconsistencies to the recipient government.
Otherwise, one must assume that the Resident Representative
has a better plan for the distribution of the limited EPTA
resources than actually emerges from competitive interagency
and interministerial negotiations. Either of these assumptions
is open to question.

Each of the participating organizations of EPTA has a fair
claim to make some contribution to economic development,

whether in health, education, food cultivation, labor productivity, civil aviation, or other specialized activities. To suggest priorities on a clean slate in a well-governed and well-administered country would be a formidable undertaking for a Resident Representative. But in EPTA the specialized agencies themselves have had programs and agents with established connections in technical ministries within a country, and they had also sat on the very board that recommended the magnitude of the program, suggested the geographical distribution of the funds, and submitted an evaluation of technical assistance activity. Regardless of project planning the percentage of expenditures for each participating organization remained relatively stable over the years, as is shown in Table IX.

About 15 percent of the total EPTA fund has gone to regional projects, over which the country Resident Representative had little or no say. And the EPTA resources to be programmed in each country have been quite limited. Only three countries (India, Pakistan, and Iran) received $1 million or more in EPTA assistance for more than two years between 1950 and 1964. In most countries the figures have ranged between $100,-000 and $500,000 per year. Most of the EPTA projects, moreover, have tended to be continuing projects.

Broad economic and social problems requiring technical assistance cannot be dented, let alone solved, by one expert in one or two years. Projects are likely to be repeated and experts to be duplicated, not because of vested interests and bad planning but because of the obvious need of making an impact upon the problem by siege rather than disjointed attack. Faced with such continuing commitments and having received from TAB a country target figure lower than the previous biennium, one Resident Representative in 1964 simply called the participating organizations together and asked them to scale down proportionately their shares of the country program. "A percentage allo-

TABLE IX

EXPENDITURES ON THE FIELD PROGRAM AND THE SHARES OF PARTICIPATING ORGANIZATIONS, 1959–1963

(In Thousands of U.S. Dollars)

	1959		1960		1961		1962		1963	
	Amount	Percent	Amount	Percent	Amount	Percent	Amount	Percent	Amount	Percent
UNTA	5,850	22.0	6,212	22.3	6,160	19.7	8,824	19.8	8,168	20.7
ILO	2,869	10.8	2,745	9.0	3,121	10.0	4,403	9.9	3,770	9.5
FAO	6,821	25.7	7,129	25.5	7,961	25.4	10,543	23.6	10,442	26.4
UNESCO	4,334	16.3	4,361	15.6	5,672	18.1	8,935	20.0	5,953	15.1
ICAO	1,206	4.5	1,287	4.6	1,415	4.5	1,651	3.7	1,623	4.1
WHO	4,443	16.8	4,819	17.3	5,596	17.9	7,335	16.4	7,063	17.9
WMO	428	1.6	443	1.6	457	1.5	842	1.9	917	2.3
ITU	308	1.2	325	1.2	452	1.5	957	2.1	791	2.0
IAEA	276	1.1	592	2.1	450	1.4	1,146	2.6	667	1.7
UPU									104	0.3
Total	26,535	100.0	27,913	100.0	31,284	100.0	44,636	100.0	39,498	100.0

SOURCE: E/3871, 6 May 1964, p. 11.

cation was the fairest and easiest, given the limited funds and the endless struggle if I had to suggest a greater reduction in one agency than in another."

If EPTA resources continue to be small and dispersed among a few thousand projects, the merger of EPTA and the Special Fund into UNDP will add very little authority to the Resident Representative unless there are accompanying changes in program planning. He can hardly be expected to make fine discriminations between an expert in rice culture and an expert in fundamental education without reference to larger project and sector planning. In any case, he must still respond to the decisions of the national coordinating unit and the pressures of their technical ministries in the country, while he still needs the counsel and assistance of the local representatives of the specialized agencies. The Resident Representative will undoubtedly be better informed and more involved in EPTA negotiations, particularly if they should complement Special Fund projects, and his prestige will be increased with both the specialized agencies and the recipient government. The change will, it is hoped, intimate a somewhat more rational approach to the whole UN technical assistance program in the field, although specific and immediate advantages might seem slight.

The Resident Representative as Coordinator and Evaluator

To the extent that the Resident Representative will be more fully informed about all technical assistance negotiations within a country, he may be able to "coordinate" such activities better. But the word has been used in several senses: coordination can mean the elimination of duplication; it can also mean the reinforcement of related technical activities either within a multilateral program or between multilateral and bilateral programs to achieve the planned objective.

Coordination has most frequently been sought in the UN and

bilateral programs in order to eliminate overlapping with a view
toward cutting costs. The same problems that have weakened
the Resident Representative in program planning in EPTA
apply to his role as a coordinator where (*a*) he has an uncertain
relationship with the national coordinating unit and the participating organization, with (*b*) no power to withhold, transfer, or add funds and (*c*) little or no influence upon the establishment of regional programs. Moreover, it makes little sense to
speak about the coordination of technical assistance as a reinforcement of economic plans without reference to bilateral
technical assistance, capital development resources, and trade
policy. In some governments one agency may consider and
correlate all foreign aid, but in others technical assistance may
be handled by a separate bureau or department.

If the Resident Representative has had problems in coordinating UN programs, he has been faced with tremendous difficulty in keeping abreast of the complementary or competitive
efforts of other technical assistance programs, both public and
private. In 1963 Chile, for example, was receiving technical
assistance from eleven bilateral programs, four foundations and
intergovernmental agencies, six programs of UN agencies, and
three regional programs. As one Resident Representative said:
"The problem is not the number of technical assistance activities
being carried out by various organizations in any one country—
it resides in the adequate coordination of these programs and
the correct use of the help that is given."

In some countries the UN technical assistance programs are
small by comparison with other multilateral and bilateral economic and technical assistance, whereas in others they not only
bulk larger than all other programs combined but have a long-
range impact on domestic and foreign investment within a
country. All that the Resident Representative has been able to
do is keep himself informed as fully as possible about all economic assistance activities within a country, so that for Special

Fund projects, where he has played a decisive role, or for EPTA activities, where he has played an advisory role, he could act with intelligence.

With regard to the UN programs, the Resident Representative is certainly better informed than he was a few years ago, but contacts with bilateral programs vary from country to country. Sometimes, where the United States AID program bulks large, the American Mission cannot take the UN technical assistance programs very seriously; sometimes the donor agencies meet together with the recipient government; sometimes they meet without the recipient government; but most frequently they do not formally meet at all, confining a random exchange of information to telephone calls, intimate lunches, or *ad hoc* arrangements.

One Resident Representative stated in 1964 that the host country disapproved of any formal meetings of the donor agencies; another said it took him eighteen months to win the approval of the host country for such meetings; and a third reported that, although the host government wanted such meetings, he disapproved, because the participating officials would be at too high a level and thus would merely seek to make a show place of the meetings rather than to arrive at any real coordination.

This last observation points up another difficulty of coordination: the willingness of high level officials from different agencies to cooperate does not guarantee that the same understanding will be reached by technical experts of different programs, who by lack of proximity, weakness of communication, or the demands of their parochial projects have little contact with each other.

The implementation and evaluation of both Special Fund and EPTA projects have taken up a large portion of the Resident Representative's time. Among other things he must frequently contend with (*a*) delays in the recruitment and arrival of experts, (*b*) misunderstandings between the executing agencies of

Special Fund projects and the recipient government, (*c*) changes in the local government, including the dismissal or transfer of ministers interested in particular projects, (*d*) an absence of counterpart personnel by reason of resignation, removal, or nonappointment, (*e*) the failure of governments to supply local costs in accordance with the basic technical assistance agreement, (*f*) other delays and misunderstandings due to a modification of the original project, ineptness of either UN technical assistance or government personnel, interagency and intergovernmental administrative conflicts, and so forth.

Such problems keep a Resident Representative hopping between technical assistance agencies, project sites, and government ministries while he tries to maintain his own office as a neutral place for cooperation, information, and administration. By visits to project sites and sometimes by monthly meetings with experts and other gatherings of specialized mission chiefs, he endeavors to keep in touch with the operating projects of EPTA and the Special Fund. But it should be recognized that his evaluation reports, which ought to be keys to programming decisions, have been of limited use.

In the first place, judgment about the efficiency of an expert or a project ought to come from the government. Yet governments, meaning the institute, commission, board, or some ministerial agency receiving technical assistance, have naturally been reluctant to criticize their own projects and rarely complain about the foreign experts supplied by the UN. In cases of language cripples or abominable personalities, of course, action has been taken by the responsible UN agency after complaint by the government, but the initiative lies with the government. So far as evaluations of EPTA are concerned, the Resident Representative has been wary, partly because technical judgments have been involved, but also because, as one Resident Representative put it,

since most of the projects are continuing and I have no discretion
in the reallocations of sums, unfavorable comments would hardly
change anything. Besides, copies of the evaluation report are sent
to the Headquarters of the Specialized Agency, which are themselves members of the TAB, so that any Resident Representative
would hesitate to criticise their activities. As a result the reports
tend to be vapid and innocuous.

In any case the evaluation of technical assistance under EPTA
has posed problems. The economic and social effect may be so
slow and indistinct that only in retrospect could the UN have
been able to distinguish good projects from bad. Some comparative criteria might be established, such as the rate of progress,
the ability of experts, and the support of projects by government. Whether the Resident Representative under UNDP,
moreover, should be an evaluator either of the EPTA projects
or the Special Fund projects to which he has already contributed a favorable judgment of feasibility is open to study. The
donor nations in the future organization of technical assistance
might well require a more disinterested and substantive appraisal
of voluntary technical assistance programs through another UN
agency, and in 1965 a special evaluation of technical assistance
in five countries was begun by a team appointed by the Secretary-General.

The Resident Representative as Administrator

The institution of the Resident Representative originally responded to the field administration needs of the UN technical
assistance programs. None of those requirements has been reduced, while additional responsibilities have been added to the
office. First, the Resident Representative has provided a full
scale of administrative services for UNTA and the technical
assistance activities of one or more of the specialized agencies
when he is acting as their chief of mission; next, he has provided

the essential administrative services for Special Fund projects when they are being proposed, investigated, and brought to the plan of operations signed by the Special Fund, the executing agency, and the recipient government, with continued responsibilities, at the option of the executing agency after the plan of operations has been signed; finally, he has been asked to provide few or many or all administrative services by any of the participating organizations of EPTA or by UNICEF, WFP, UNHCR, and possibly other UN agencies.

Today a constant stream of officials from New York, Montreal, Geneva, Paris, Rome, and Washington and experts from almost anywhere arrive and depart at the airports of countries receiving UN technical assistance. The Resident Representative, or one of his staff, is expected to meet, greet, and orient very many of these visitors, providing them not only with minor services of customs clearance or hotel accommodations but with major time in arranging interviews with host government officials. Important dignitaries must be met—often by the Resident Representative in person—at distant air terminals with frequently delayed planes; and the arrangement of appointments with ministers or a chief executive—often requiring the personal presence of the Resident Representative—chews up the limited working hours in underdeveloped countries.

Paperwork, moreover, in UN headquarters-field relationships has tended to pile up badly. There has been widespread complaint in the field against the numerous and detailed reports demanded by the UN at its head offices as well as the slowness of correspondence in which replies to inquiries seem to drag at turtlelike pace from desk to desk, making the rounds from the field to specialized agency headquarters to New York and back again, sometimes never emerging from the bureaucratic morass.

Program adjustments have also been a constant administrative burden. A project-by-project examination of the approved EPTA programs in the field has revealed scores of changed, transferred, or aborted items because of faults on the part of the recipient government or the failure to recruit the right experts: all these rearrangements, not really involving large sums of money—or, for that matter, crucial problems of economic development—have caused constant administrative headaches for the office of the Resident Representative. Special Fund projects, too, have been drawn-out affairs, first requiring presentation through the Managing Director and approval by the Governing Council of their general purpose and organization, then funding, and then requiring the development of a plan of operations between the executing agency and the recipient government. There have been delays of one or two years between approval by the Governing Council of a Special Fund project and the arrival of the first expert. Put another way, there could be a delay of two and one-half to three years between the time that a ministry of a government or the national planning unit is enthusiastic about a Special Fund proposal and the time that the project goes into action.

The Resident Representative, moreover, was occasionally in the unpleasant and paradoxical role of suggesting or encouraging technical assistance projects while acting as a bill collector. He sometimes has had to urge governments to pay their pledges to EPTA or the Special Fund in New York and to fulfill their promise to provide local costs for projects within the country. The accounting for local costs is far from scientific, with the quoted value of offices, transportation, communications, supplies, and so forth, doubtful. Some ministries have delayed in providing or paying anything, and some treasuries have refused to recognize commitments by their own ministries. The Resident Representative has had to spend too many hours on this thankless task of bill collecting.

As the manager of a growing establishment, which in some countries runs to dozens of office employees, the Resident Representative has delegated to his Deputy and/or Assistant responsibilities for programming and administration. There has been a natural tendency for him to be more personally engaged in Special Fund activities than in EPTA activities, though he assumes equal responsibility for supervision of the work in his office for both programs. But delegation is one of the hardest things for any manager to learn, and not all resident representatives have been skillful administrators. Even delegation brings no escape from responsibility, which, due to the development of international organization, continues to weigh more heavily each year upon the Resident Representative and which must be matched by an expanding and efficient field organization.

The Resident Representative as a Diplomat

Even though the Resident Representative has played a marginal role in programming EPTA, a central role in Special Fund projects, and a most useful role in administrative services, the key to his success and his future may lie in his role as a diplomat. His function in programming is not to set priorities but to encourage the recipient governments to do so, not to allocate resources according to his ideas but to remind governments of their own rationale, not to decide among competing technical agencies but to bring them, by all the arts of diplomacy, into a cooperative relationship that will best achieve the economic and social needs prescribed by the government.

Philip M. Glick pointed out in 1957[71] that the Resident Representative gives technical assistance on technical assistance to a government: how to request it, how to use it, how to get more of it, and how to guide and control it. None of this can be done in sensitive underdeveloped countries without tact, circumspection, and a keen regard for protocol. And the same manners must be evident before the specialized agencies, which, at times, seem to have all the attributes of sovereign nations. As one

[71] Philip M. Glick, *The Administration of Technical Assistance* (Chicago, The University of Chicago Press, 1957).

expert in Latin America mischievously murmured: "Ah! The World Health Organization, it's a separate country with its own flag." A good Resident Representative, therefore, must obtain respect through his knowledge of the host country, and he obtains leadership only when the participating organizations of EPTA and the executing agencies of the Special Fund recognize that he serves their interest best by his patient mediation among them, headquarters, and the host government.

Whatever the diversity of the UN system in an underdeveloped country, however, the Resident Representative has been commonly regarded as the "UN man." Although his diplomatic immunities and privileges scarcely have raised him above the level of the expert of the EPTA projects or the manager of a Special Fund project, he has been the invited guest to the innumerable receptions, public addresses, and other ceremonial occasions that clog the calendar of every diplomat abroad. And he has felt the need to reciprocate, like other diplomats, not from social affability but from the necessity of using such occasions for gaining information and starting negotiations. Entirely dependent upon the voluntary contributions of states and legally representing only a small part of UN interests in the world, the Resident Representative nevertheless has found himself regarded as a UN "presence," if not an "ambassador," with inadequate allowances for representation, and small confusions by all who deal with him over his rights and responsibilities.

Needless to say that when the host government has been nonplussed over any UN economic and social matter, it has more often than not telephoned the Resident Representative, whether the question involved an abstract technical assistance program problem or a specific police report about the death or madness of an expert. Like a diplomat, the UN Resident Representative must be prepared to cope with anything in a calm and precise way with the least possible offense to everyone. In the hustle of economic development plans, national coordinating units, EPTA and Special Fund organization, and programming, the distinctive diplomatic ability required for resident representatives within the operations of the UN system should be stressed as the primary criterion in their selection and recruitment, with a knowledge of economic development and a fitness for administration in an important second place. Indeed, as the institution of the UN Resident Representative grows and is strengthened, as it will be in the coming years through UNDP, more emphasis will need to be placed upon the qualities of the Resident Representative for negotiation, mediation, and analytical reporting at high levels of interagency and intergovernmental activities.

The Future of the United Nations Resident Representative

Despite the several intimations in the committees and councils of the UN that the office of the Resident Representative will eventually wither away, on the presumption that national coordinating units can take over entirely their own planning and administration of multilateral economic assistance, all evidence seems to point to a proliferation of the responsibilities of the Resident Representative. In line with the peaceful development of international organization, reaching further into the security, the economic and social development, and the legal norms of nations, an increase in regional, field, and country offices for multilateral agencies can be expected. These will perceptibly alter the patterns of UN activities over the next decades, for they will shift from temporary, sporadic, and voluntary programs to permanent, continuous, and regular operations, not only in economic and social affairs but in legal and political matters.

Even assuming that in the near future all the underdeveloped countries were able to establish strong, purposeful, and competent national coordinating units for technical assistance, it seems unlikely that they could or would want to deal directly with several headquarters for several UN programs; it seems less likely that the UN itself and the specialized or affiliated agencies would be satisfied with transient officials or a proliferation of uncoordinated offices within a country for the efficient programming, administration, and evaluation of their assistance programs. The suggestion, moreover, that the UN Resident Representative ought to be a national of the country, as a bridge to the extinction of the office, opens grave questions about the conflict of interests between an international civil servant with individual responsibility for UN programs and a resident national dealing continuously with his own governmental officers.

Furthermore, the UN assistance programs have demonstrated a capacity to grow, to take on new approaches to economic and social development, whether by different forms of support of their projects or by emphasizing different functions. Without the waste of war, substantially increased resources will be available in the future to multilateral agencies and imaginative plans will endeavor to reorient or integrate UN assistance efforts. Certainly the connection between capital development and technical assistance will grow stronger and multilateral economic aid will have to take greater cognizance of national fiscal policy and trade patterns. Not only the specialized agencies, but other departments and bureaus of the United Nations will have need for a UN country office that can be an impartial source of information and can negotiate agreements, administer operations, and evaluate programs.

The trend to house all UN activities in one UN building in a host country should be encouraged and, as UN public information gradually becomes a staff function of the office of the Resident Representative, so may the country representatives of the specialized agencies be regarded eventually as technical advisers to the Resident Representative, assisting him in planning, coordinating, and implementing every economic and social program of the UN. Despite the complaint of the expert hobbled in some way by the administrator and diplomat or the lamentations of parochialism in international organization, the trend toward a political and administrative consolidation of the work of multilateral agencies will continue. Men have hardly begun to plan and organize in global terms, despite the tedious platitudes about the interconnectedness of world society.

In a large and noble vision of the future, the UN will require a permanent UN presence in every state of the world. Technical assistance merely opens the door to mutual cooperation and benefits among states through international organization. But almost imperceptibly new channels of direct and local communication between states and the world-wide organization of the UN for revenue-raising, law-making, and peace-keeping will have to be created if the planet is eventually to be governed by the common interest of mankind.

Whether the institution of the UN Resident Representative will begin to play a vital role in this development cannot be predicted. Yet fifteen years ago, a mere wink in the eye of history, no one could have surmised the number and status of the present resident representatives. Survival and growth are the tests of political institutions, for they must match and respond to public needs. To those accustomed to view organizations in terms of hierarchy and command, the UN Resident Representative seems a weak reed for building world order; but, to those inclined to view organizations through purpose, motivation, and vitality, the UN Resident Representative may be a lively prologue to the plot for international peace and prosperity.

By Robert W. Gregg

PROGRAM DECENTRALIZATION

THROUGH THE

REGIONAL ECONOMIC COMMISSIONS

The United Nations, more in the spirit of hope and exhortation than of prophecy, has labeled the 1960s the Development Decade. Although other major issues, such as the cold war and the liquidation of colonialism, still occupy prominent positions on the agenda, economic development has rapidly become a major preoccupation of the UN. The underdeveloped states have naturally sought to strengthen their representation in ECOSOC and the Secretariat while concentrating as much authority as possible in the hands of the UN organs or agencies in which they enjoy a preponderant numerical strength. Of special interest to the underdeveloped countries, therefore, have been the three UN regional economic commissions that serve Africa, Asia and the Far East, and Latin America (ECA, ECAFE, and ECLA).

The regional economic commissions, which have been established by ECOSOC and whose secretariats are parts of the UN Department of Economic and Social Affairs, are not a new phenomenon nor is the demand that they be given greater authority with respect to the UN's economic and social activities of recent vintage. However, there has been since 1960 a pronounced increase in interest in decentralizing responsibility for the UN's technical assistance programs to the regional commissions. This advocacy of decentralization is part of the pattern of confrontation by developed and developing states, that is also indicated by UNCTAD and the still inconclusive battle for a UN capital development fund. In essence, the underdeveloped world seeks both a redistribution of the world's wealth *and* a larger measure of control over those UN programs that assist such a redistribution. Decentralization of economic and technical assistance to the UN regional commissions would, in the opinion of many governments of underdeveloped states, contribute to that larger measure of control.

Decentralization is not a precisely defined concept; it tends to be employed interchangeably with "deconcentration" and "devolution" in reference to UN administrative decision-making.[1] In effect, decentralization is a generic term that embraces both administrative delegation without a final transfer of authority (deconcentration), and the transfer of power to make final decisions (devolution).[2] The broader term is the one used in debates and in resolutions adopted by UN organs, although it seems obvious that in some instances deconcentration has been intended and in others devolution. In the final analysis, however, one must agree with Walter R. Sharp that "the real test of decentralization lies not so much in the work-load of an agency's field offices as in the frequency with which they decide matters themselves and how important such matters are."[3]

Decentralization in the United Nations

Although the UN, according to the letter and spirit of the Charter, is a centralized organization both at the intergovern-

---

[1] See Walter R. Sharp, *Field Administration in the United Nations System: The Conduct of International Economic and Social Programs* (New York, Frederick A. Praeger, 1961), p. 5.

[2] *A Handbook of Public Administration* (United Nations, 1961 [ST/TAO/M/16]), p. 64.

[3] Sharp, p. 507.

mental level and in the Secretariat, there has been a discernible trend toward decentralization. This trend has not been dramatic. Nevertheless, a review of the history of UN economic and social activities reveals a persistent and unrelenting pressure for decentralization that has borne more fruit with the passage of time and has recently become a major "minor issue" in UN circles. A veteran UN official has observed that the scales seem to be tipping in favor of decentralization in the perennial contest between the forces for centralization and decentralization in the administration of UN economic and social programs.[4]

Every international agency, of course, has experienced both "centripetal and centrifugal pulls in program-making and administration."[5] In WHO, for example, decentralization is much more comprehensive and highly developed than in the UN.[6] Decentralization within the UN, however, is of more importance than similar developments within the specialized agencies because the UN and its regional commissions can command considerably more political attention and potentially more resources in the areas which they serve than do the regional units of the other agencies.

The history of decentralization within the UN itself may be divided conveniently into two periods. At first the regional commissions had almost no responsibility for technical assistance, in considerable part because TAA and the UN Department of Economic and Social Affairs, in which the commission secretariats are located, were two distinct entities. In 1959, however, TAA and the Department of Economic and Social Affairs were merged—BTAO replaced TAA. Almost simultaneously, a regional economic commission for Africa was created in 1958, and

---

[4] W. R. Malinowski, "Centralization and Decentralization in the United Nations Economic and Social Activities," *International Organization*, XVI, No. 3 (Summer 1962), p. 521.

[5] Sharp, p. 507.

[6] See Robert Berkov, *The World Health Organization: A Study in International Decentralized Administration* (Geneva, Droz, 1957).

sixteen African states were admitted to membership in the
United Nations in 1960. The subsequent years have been characterized by an increasing demand that the operational economic-social responsibilities of the UN devolve upon the regional economic commissions. In the first of these two periods,
according to one observer, decentralization was essentially a
slogan; in the second it began to become a reality.[7]

The Creation and Growth of the Regional Commissions

The view that regional organizations should be the building
blocks of the UN was rejected at San Francisco in 1945. Those
"massive pillars upon which the world organization would be
founded in majesty and calm"[8] were the subject of several
articles[9] in the Charter. But the result, applying only to security
questions, was a far cry from the Churchillian vision.

In the economic and social field, moreover, there is no echo
of the regional approach to international organization to be
found anywhere in the Charter. The UN Conference at San
Francisco briefly considered, but did not pursue that possibility.[10] While Article 68 provided for setting up commissions
under the aegis of ECOSOC, it suggested functional rather than
regional criteria, and the Charter conveyed no intention to par-
cel out to regional subdivisions the limited power and authority
of the principal UN organs.

At an early date, however, the UN embarked upon a limited
regional approach to economic problems. The decision to create
regional economic commissions, neither invited nor precluded
by the Charter, was an important step. Although the UN has

[7] Malinowski, p. 541.
[8] Winston Churchill, quoted in Inis Claude, Jr., *Swords into Plowshares,* 3d
ed. rev. (New York, Random House, 1964), p. 106.
[9] Articles 51–54.
[10] See Leland Goodrich and Edvard Hambro, *Charter of the United Nations:
Commentary and Documents,* 2d ed. rev. (Boston, World Peace Foundation,
1949), p. 311.

subsequently expanded its operations in the field to an extent undreamed of either by its Geneva-bound predecessor or by its own founding fathers, the regional economic commissions with their secretariats remain "the only important example of geographic decentralization within the UN proper." [11] The road to the modest decentralization of the UN began, therefore, in June 1946, when ECOSOC created its Temporary Sub-Commission on the Economic Reconstruction of Devastated Areas,[12] an action which led to the establishment of the regional commissions.

The decision of the Sub-Commission's Working Group for Europe to recommend the creation of an economic commission for Europe had the effect of setting in motion a chain reaction that produced both ECE and ECAFE in 1947, ECLA in 1948, and, after the lapse of ten more years, ECA in 1958.[13] The dichotomy of views between developed and developing states that was to characterize the debate on decentralization in the 1960s was already in evidence during the debate on the establishment of regional commissions in 1946 and 1947. ECOSOC, largely guided by the developed states, rejected the idea of regional commissions, only to be reversed by the General Assembly, which, even then, was dominated by the underdeveloped states. The division was also apparent in the disinclination of North American and Western European members to establish commissions other than the one for Europe. In the Second Committee of the General Assembly one of the first UN coalitions among the underdeveloped, non-Western countries emerged to support both an Asian commission and a Latin American commission. This exercise in international log-rolling undermined the argument that reconstruction was to be the rationalization

[11] Sharp, p. 53.
[12] ECOSOC Resolution 2/6, 21 June 1946.
[13] The establishment of an Economic Commission for the Middle East has been considered but has been rendered impossible by the enduring schism between the Arab States and Israel.

for new economic commissions and guaranteed that the claims of the major regions would be partly channeled into their own regional commissions.[14]

The regional economic commissions have been authorized, among other things, (1) to initiate measures for facilitating regional economic and social development; (2) to study regional economic and technological problems; (3) to render advisory services to countries within the region; (4) to assist ECOSOC in discharging its responsibilities, including those in the field of technical assistance; and (5) to help formulate policies as a basis for practical action in promoting country and regional development. In each of these areas of responsibility the commission must act within the framework of UN policies and under the general supervision of ECOSOC, but these limitations are deceptive. In practice the commissions have more discretionary authority than their terms of reference would suggest. Subordinate to ECOSOC and hence ultimately to the General Assembly, on paper, the commissions enjoy a broad measure of *de facto* freedom. They simply are not overruled by ECOSOC, which periodically takes note of their annual reports and endorses their work programs but otherwise permits them to go their several ways.

An explanation for this *de facto* strength has been offered by a former Chief of the Regional Commissions Section at Headquarters, W. R. Malinowski. He has noted that the commissions' strength derives

from the almost completely inclusive character of their membership within their respective regions; from their tendency to act by agreement rather than by voting . . . from a varying but marked degree of regional consciousness, solidarity, or "regional nationalism"; and . . . from the self-imposed discipline which leads members of the UN regional commissions to behave in a way expected of UN

[14] These debates are described in David Wightman, *Toward Economic Cooperation in Asia: The United Nations Economic Commission for Asia and the Far East* (New Haven, Yale University Press, 1963), Chap. 2.

members; i.e., in accordance with the principles of the UN Charter and the decisions of the General Assembly and ECOSOC. The strength of the regional commissions is also due to the practical nature of their activities.[15]

It might be added that the growth in importance of the commissions, both within the UN system and within their respective regions, is a facet of the recent surge of interest in economic regionalism and a reflection of the disappointment of developing states with the composition and performance of intergovernmental and secretariat units at UN Headquarters.[16]

What each commission has done with its rather considerable independence has depended upon a variety of considerations, including the stage of development and sophistication of the region, the homogeneity of states within the region, and the quality of leadership supplied by the Executive Secretary. Each commission has developed its own distinctive style; each has carved out its own area of emphasis and specialization.

ECLA, for example, has not had the elaborate committee structure that characterizes the other commissions, nor has it met annually as do ECE, ECAFE, and ECA. It does, however, possess "a cohesive personality which evokes loyalty from the staff, and a set of distinctive beliefs, principles and attitudes . . . which is highly influential among Latin American intellectuals and policy-makers." [17] ECLA has been a pioneer among the commissions, rewriting economic development theory under the stimulating leadership of its former Executive Secretary, Dr. Raoul Prebisch, whom an observer credited with the feat of making ECLA into a kind of responsible political opposition in

[15] Malinowski, pp. 523–24.

[16] See Robert W. Gregg, "The Political Role of International Economic Organizations: The United Nations Regional Economic Commissions," paper presented at Grenoble Round Table Meeting of the International Political Science Association, September 17–18, 1965.

[17] Albert O. Hirschman, "Ideologies of Economic Development in Latin America," in Hirschman, ed., *Latin American Issues: Essays and Comments* (New York, The Twentieth Century Fund, 1961), p. 13.

Latin America.[18] Its economic doctrines have been partially institutionalized in the Central American Economic Integration Program and in the Latin American Free Trade Association; UNCTAD has its doctrinal roots in research conducted by ECLA. Although there are those who question its sense of direction and disparage its common market schemes, ECLA has been characterized both by *élan* and ability and paid the compliment of attention.

ECAFE, on the other hand, has been a more conservative organization, slow to embrace new ideas, generally satisfied to perform routine tasks efficiently. The human resources have been available in Bangkok, but the *élan* has been missing. Stretching from Japan to Iran and from Nepal to New Zealand, the region served by ECAFE is less homogeneous than Latin America, a potpourri of languages, cultures, and economic, social, and political systems. Moreover, the commission has been handicapped by the influence of its non-Asian members, while many members have found it difficult to plan, organize and implement programs with the Indians and Japanese, whose technological expertise makes them today's leaders of ECAFE. Some observers argue that ECAFE's major task is to instill the habit of consultation and cooperation in Asia, and such projects as the Asian Highway, Mekong Basin development, and the Asian Development Bank are modest steps in that direction. In 1965 some UN observers began to detect a new sense of vitality in ECAFE and some loss of that quality in ECLA; but over a period of many years, the latter has been the more stimulating and creative commission.

The third regional commission in the developing world, ECA, is suffering from its newness, from serious staffing problems in a region where the talent pool is still shallow and from the fact that many African countries are not yet able to assimilate the

[18] Andrew Schonfield, *The Attack on World Poverty* (New York, Random House, 1960), p. 49.

kinds of advice and services that ECLA and ECAFE make available. ECA has been a kind of catalyst and educator, helping African states to know what they need, which is a first step in the direction of economic and social development. In 1965, therefore, there seemed to be considerable ardor in Addis Ababa, but a lack of human resources in Africa to accomplish the high aims of ECA.

Unlike the other commissions, ECE serves a region that is comparatively developed. Indeed, the major function of ECE has been to serve as a bridge between East and West Europe. Otherwise it has been concerned with relatively specific problems, almost all of which have been significantly different from the broad-gauged projects that preoccupy ECLA, ECAFE, and ECA. Some of these problems, such as the transport of dangerous goods, have been completely decentralized, with all responsibilities resting in Geneva.

The growth of technical assistance programs affects all of the commissions, but especially those serving the developing areas of the world, and this increasing flow of aid has stirred a controversy over the amount of discretion which the commissions and, more importantly, their secretariats should have vis-à-vis UN Headquarters in New York.

The Commissions and the Evolution of the Decentralization Controversy

During the 1950s a dialogue unfolded between those who wished the commissions to have more of a role in the operational activities of the UN within the several regions and those who preferred to retain centralized control over such programs in New York; the evolution of this centralization-decentralization controversy has been closely intertwined with questions of Headquarters organization.

As early as 1949, the Secretary-General had told ECAFE that it was his policy "that the secretariats of the regional economic commissions shall play a full and active role in the development of the [technical assistance] programme and should have an important part in stimulating and developing its implementation." [19] Statements of this kind became almost ritualistic during the next decade, but very little was done at the UN to make decentralization a reality, for the global approach to economic questions was favored by many Secretariat officials.

Gradually, however, the political climate within the UN became more hospitable to decentralization. The pronounced increase in the number of underdeveloped states within the UN; the evolution to paramountcy of the economic tasks on the UN's long agenda; the emergence of a crude UN party system, which is, to a very considerable extent, a multiregional system; the resultant increase in bargaining among the UN's "parties"; the decision of the USSR to shift tactics and play an active role in UN economic affairs and to pursue policies which would enhance its standing with the developing world; the disenchantment of the numerous and vocal developing states with ECOSOC and the Department of Economic and Social Affairs, both of which seemed to be too Western in composition and too remote from the grass-roots problems of economic and social development: all of these factors contributed to the ripening of the decentralization issue.

Meanwhile, structural changes and experiments affecting the formulation of UN technical assistance programs and the relationship of the regional commissions to those programs were taking place. After EPTA had been launched, TAA was set up within the UN Secretariat to administer the UN's share of the program. The Department of Economic Affairs, of which the regional secretariats were an integral part, did not, therefore, have responsibility for the new program. Cooperation between TAA and the substantive departments of the Secretariat, more-

[19] E/1576, 28 December 1949, quoted in Malinowski, p. 530.

over, was frequently disappointing. A Survey Group appointed by the Secretary-General in 1954 to make recommendations with respect to the organization of the Secretariat called attention to the need for rationalizing the use of the various components of the Secretariat in order to maximize the effectiveness of the UN's technical assistance programs.[20] The Secretary-General, endorsing the recommendations of the Survey Group, noted that they involved "a change from a centralized type of operation to a partly decentralized one." [21] Under the prevailing circumstances, however, decentralization had to wait upon the integration of TAA and the Department of Economic and Social Affairs,[22] which did not take place until February 1959.

THE TAA OUTPOSTING EXPERIMENT. One of the most important developments of the 1950s with respect to the decentralization of technical assistance was the experiment in outposting of TAA officers to Latin America from 1956 through 1958. Technically, no "outposted" official or unit can be classified as a true instance of decentralization, for outposting, by definition, means that the authority continues to reside at headquarters. Nonetheless, the experiment was conducted within the context of the debate on decentralization, was repeatedly referred to as decentralization, and shed some light on that phenomenon.

The decision to outpost several officers from TAA's Program Division was an outgrowth of recommendations made by the Survey Group. Shortly after that report had been received, the Secretary-General proposed that staff units be assigned to the ECAFE and ECLA secretariats. The resistance to this proposal that was encountered in ACABQ, the Fifth Committee of the General Assembly, and TAA itself resulted in the dilution of the

[20] "Organization of the Secretariat—Report of the Secretary General's Survey Group," 15 November 1955, No. 55-27697, cited in Malinowski, pp. 531–32.
[21] A/3041, 23 November 1955.
[22] The Departments of Economic Affairs and Social Affairs were merged in 1955.

authorization given to the Secretary-General; TAA officers were to be outposted only to Latin America and only on a trial basis.[23]

During the debate in the Fifth Committee the Secretary-General remarked that the proposal was not "connected with the philosophy of decentralization." [24] The decision to outpost TAA officers, however, was clearly a step in that direction. "Creeping decentralization" is a term that some elements in the American press might have employed had they been interested in such matters. Some observers were convinced that the experiment was undertaken for the express purpose of avoiding the amalgamation of TAA and the Department of Economic and Social Affairs, and they later declared that the experiment was terminated when the merger at headquarters deprived "outposting" of its *raison d'être*. In any event the announced reason for the action was to serve the underdeveloped regions better by bringing the program operations of TAA closer to the recipient states and the substantive divisions of the regional commissions.

The actual "decentralization" experiment was quite modest, involving only four people in Santiago and two at ECLA's subregional office in Mexico City. It should be emphasized that these men were not attached to ECLA but simply located physically in its two principal centers in order that they might enjoy the benefits of whatever substantive backstopping the ECLA staff could supply. The experiment was widely regarded as a failure,[25] although TAA officials who were outposted dissented from this verdict. Probably the experiment proved very little because TAA never gave its field officers an opportunity to exercise the kind of discretion in the field that would reveal the virtues and vices of decentralization. Decentralization, it has been suggested, rests upon a tripod, the three legs of which are

[23] See Sharp, pp. 188–89, and documents cited therein.
[24] GA *Official Records*, Tenth Session, Fifth Committee, 524th Meeting, 6 December 1955.
[25] For comment, see Sharp, pp. 277–80.

direct assistance to governments, the preservation of a unified UN policy, and a measure of autonomy;[26] but the third leg was missing. Without any autonomy the outposted units at times were a bottleneck, adding steps and stops to the processing of requests and reports to and from headquarters.[27]

Although the Latin American states generally approved establishment of the technical assistance units in Santiago and Mexico City and although ECLA urged their continuation,[28] the relationship between these units and the ECLA secretariat, while cordial, was never entirely satisfactory.

TRANSITION TO THE DEVELOPMENT DECADE. Although the decentralization process had no single point of origin, pressure for a more important role for the regional commissions in the field of technical assistance gradually grew with the numerical strength of the underdeveloped states in the UN, and the merger of TAA with the Department of Economic and Social Affairs in 1959 kindled new hopes for decentralization. Many UN observers hoped that this merger would lead speedily to a genuine decentralization of technical assistance activities from the Department to its regional units, but the pace has been slow and the results piecemeal.

In the transition period following the merger of TAA and the Department of Economic and Social Affairs, the operational role of the regional secretariats was enlarged by the sporadic and pragmatic assignment to the several commissions of responsibility for specific projects, not by any self-conscious attempt to realize decentralization. By the time the Development Decade opened, it was too late to argue that the commissions should be passive, research-oriented bodies.

When the Secretary-General took stock of the situation in 1961, he noted that the merger between the traditional research

[26] Malinowski, p. 532.
[27] See Sharp, pp. 277–80.
[28] ECOSOC Resolution 125 (VII), May 27, 1957.

and the more recent advisory and operational activities of the Secretariat at the regional level had lagged behind progress at Headquarters; but he also saw evidence of the beginning of a greater operational role for the commissions.[29] Several projects were singled out for special comment by the Secretary-General,[30] including development of the Mekong River as an outstanding example of a project "conceived in a regional commission" and supported by the research work and advisory services of the regional secretariat. ECAFE had served and advised the Committee for Coordination of Investigations in the lower Mekong Basin development project, while the Executive Agent worked in the regional headquarters with ECAFE's secretariat. Another illustration of the growing strength of a regional commission in the operational field was the development by ECA of a long-range program in statistics, combining research, training, and advisory services. ECLA, which has had a larger operational role than ECAFE or ECA, was also cited by the Secretary-General for its regional training center in economic development, an example of a project closely integrated with the commission's regular research activities and advisory services to governments. ECLA had also assumed full responsibility for all substantive aspects of several joint ECLA/BTAO projects during the 1950s and for the substantive management of economic advisory groups, organized by the Commission and BTAO for the first time in 1959 at the request of certain governments to assist them in creating economic policy-making machinery.

In effect, all three of the regional commissions were in the process of acquiring a new role when the decentralization controversy in the UN came to a head in 1961.

The critical round of consultations, reports, and action began with the adoption of resolution 793 (XXX) by ECOSOC on 4

[29] A/4911, 14 October 1961, para. 13.
[30] The projects identified in these paragraphs are surveyed in *ibid.*, paras. 19–22, E/CN.14/103 [n.d.], Annex; and the annual reports of the regional commissions to ECOSOC.

August 1960. ECOSOC expressed the view that the operational role of the commissions should be enlarged and that the Secretary-General should take steps to achieve that objective. In its resolution 1518 (XV) of 15 December 1960, the General Assembly directed the Secretary-General to report to both the Council and the Assembly during 1961 on the specific steps taken "in implementation of Council Resolution 793 (XXX) regarding the decentralization of activities and operations and the increased utilization of the services of the regional economic commissions."

The Secretary-General's *Report to the Sixteenth General Assembly*[31] is an important document, a canvas on which he attempted to sketch the outlines of the existing division of labor between Headquarters and commissions and to suggest the principles and practices that might be adhered to in its subsequent evolution. This report did not dispose of the issue of decentralization; it was followed during the sixteenth General Assembly session by an extensive debate in the Second Committee. Numerous resolutions were subsequently adopted by both the Council and the General Assembly, of which General Assembly resolution 1709 (XVI) of 4 January 1962 was the most important, culminating the debate in the sixteenth session. Without specifying exactly what steps were to be taken, the resolution made it clear that decentralization was an official policy and asked for an accounting by the Secretary-General of the steps that he was taking to achieve that end.

In the operative paragraphs of the resolution, the General Assembly urged

[31] A/4911, 14 October 1961. The *Report* was issued subsequent to the report of the Secretary-General's Committee of Experts on the Activities and Organization of the Secretariat, A/4776, 14 June 1961, and following consultation with the regional commissions and the specialized agencies. The commissions had expressed predictably pro-decentralization sentiments and the agencies were cautious if not negative; but the Committee of Experts was so outspoken in its advocacy of decentralization that the Secretary-General felt obliged to take issue with some of its views. See A/4794, 30 June 1961.

the strengthening, without delay, of the secretariats of the regional economic commissions as executive arms of the Organization in the economic and social fields, including technical assistance operations, by means of an increasing delegation to the regional secretariats of substantive and operational functions and responsibilities and the provision of the requisite resources, including personnel, while maintaining the central substantive functions, including policy guidance and coordination, and without affecting the provision of assistance to countries that are not members of any regional economic commission; [and further requested] . . . the Secretary-General to take immediate steps toward the full implementation of the policy of decentralization through appropriate administrative arrangements to be decided upon in consultation with the Advisory Committee on Administrative and Budgetary Questions and, when necessary, the Technical Assistance Committee, taking into account the recommendations made by the Committee of Experts in Part V of its report and the Secretary-General's comments thereon; [and again urged] . . . that the decentralization of the economic and social activities of the United Nations should among other things, aim at achieving simplicity of procedure and of administrative methods for technical cooperation.

Although the Assembly insisted upon preserving a balance between Headquarters and the field and insisted that there are still some functions better performed centrally, the main thrust of this resolution and of all those adopted subsequently by inter-governmental organs of the UN has been prompt and substantial decentralization.

In the brief period of time that has elapsed since the Assembly directed that the policy of decentralization be implemented, the Secretary-General has made a number of progress reports[32] while both ECOSOC and the General Assembly have reiterated their requests for official action.[33] In effect, the "legislative"

---

[32] See especially E/3643, 13 June 1962; A/5196, 2 October 1962; E/3786, 10 June 1963.
[33] See ECOSOC Resolution 879 (XXXIV), 6 July 1962; GA Resolution 1823 (XVII), 18 December 1962; ECOSOC Resolution 955 (XXXVI), 5 July 1963; GA Resolution 1941 (XVIII), 11 December 1963.

phase ended and both ECOSOC and the General Assembly continued to assess the progress of decentralization.

Implementation of Decentralization

According to the Committee of Experts,[34]

the vital question is the translation of the policy of decentralization into terms of practical administration. To do this there must first be a clear definition in specific and positive terms of what is meant by decentralization. It can mean full devolution of administrative, executive and financial authority within defined limits or spheres. On the other hand, it can mean increased consultation with, and participation of, the regional body in activities for which Headquarters retains ultimate responsibility, both administrative and financial.

The Secretary-General was charged with the task of implementation through "appropriate administrative arrangements." His mandate was couched in general terms. There were clearly two distinct schools of thought, however, although the Assembly ultimately adopted resolution 1709 (XVI) without formal opposition. One school was represented by the Ghanaian delegate who concluded that "a large range of tasks and responsibilities should be transferred or delegated to the regional secretariats," [35] and the other by a Belgian who stressed that decentralization "should be carried out prudently and without undermining the directing functions of Headquarters." [36] An extreme version of the former position was adopted by the Committee of Experts, which asserted that "one of the benefits of decentralization would be that the United Nations would divest itself of all operational tasks at Headquarters with perhaps some minor exceptions." [37] The developing states, supported by the Commu-

[34] A/4776, 14 June 1961, para. 109.
[35] GA *Official Records*, Sixteenth Session, Second Committee, 753d Meeting, p. 217.
[36] *Ibid.*, 758th Meeting, p. 241.
[37] A/4776, 14 June 1961.

nist bloc, tended to subscribe to this viewpoint. The Western states preferred to talk of "increased participation" of the regional commissions in the UN's economic and social projects, a much more modest departure from past practices than the "full devolution" urged by the Committee. In effect, the two schools could be labeled the "regionalists" and the "centralists" although in the prevailing political climate of 1961 they became regionalists with enthusiasm and regionalists with misgivings.

In practice the implementation of decentralization in the UN has progressed along lines suggested by a delegate from the Netherlands to the sixteenth General Assembly session, who urged the following Golden Rule: "Do not decentralize that which can be better done at the center, and do not centralize operations which the regional organs are better equipped to carry out." [38] It is difficult to disagree with this rule; like the platform of an American political party, it is broad enough for almost everyone to stand on. But the rule, presumably pragmatic instead of dogmatic, really does not solve the problem of implementation for the simple reason that there is considerable disagreement over which tasks can be better handled centrally and which regionally. Nonetheless, there has been a tendency for the Secretary-General to justify the pace of implementation in terms not unlike those employed by the delegate from the Netherlands. Thus in his report to ECOSOC's thirty-sixth session, he spoke of "the pragmatic approach followed in implementing the policy of decentralization." [39]

In the case of projects for which the regional secretariats generally possess the required expertise and experience, a large delegation of authority is taking place; in the case of projects requiring primarily the mobilization of resources from outside the region immediately concerned, major responsibility belongs to Headquarters, combined with as much consultation with the regional secretariats as is possible.

[38] GA *Official Records*, Second Committee, 756th Meeting, p. 231.
[39] E/3786, 10 June 1963, p. 3.

Although no dramatic steps have been taken to implement Council or Assembly resolutions, there have been some changes of a tangible nature in the administration of UN technical assistance programs "designed to take full advantage of the closeness of the regional secretariats to the problem of economic and social development at a time when the Organization is expected to play a greater part in the solution of those problems." [40]

The Growth of Regional Projects

The most conspicuous evidence of decentralization lies in the area of regional technical assistance projects, which have been increasing each year and for which the commission secretariats have assumed greater responsibilities. Country projects, of course, have been the backbone of UN technical assistance efforts, but a small percentage of the funds available under EPTA has been used for regional projects. This percentage, however, was gradually increased from 10 percent in 1957 to 15 percent for the 1963–64 biennium,[41] and the regular UN program funds, which are not so restricted, have been used to an ever greater extent for regional projects; 37.5 percent of the regular program for 1965 was allocated to regional projects, an increase of 7 percent over 1964.[42] The significant percentage increase in both the number of regional projects and the amount of UN funds being spent on them reflects the shift of the UN's operational center of gravity in the direction of the regional commissions.[43]

Although there is today a large and growing number of regional projects in the areas served by ECA, ECAFE, and ECLA, as Table X indicates, the inherent limitations of the regional approach to technical assistance restrict these projects

[40] *Ibid.*, p. 2.
[41] E/3871, 6 May 1964, p. 52.
[42] Adapted from data compiled by UN Administrative Management Service.
[43] For a critique of regional projects by UN resident representatives, see E/4021, 30 April 1965, p. 261.

TABLE X

GROWTH OF THE UNITED NATIONS REGIONAL PROJECTS
BY REGION, 1961–1966
(*In Millions of U.S. Dollars*)

Regular Programs	1961	1962	1963	1964	1965	1966
Africa	.45	.86	.94	1.03	1.03	.99
Asia and the Far East	.19	.28	.39	.31	.58	.60
Europe	.05	.05	.03	.06	.03	.06
Latin America	.31	.38	.44	.52	.54	.52
Middle East		.03	.03	.04	.05	.14
Total	1.00	1.60	1.83	1.96	2.28	2.31
Expanded Program						
Africa	.15	.21	.43	.62	.49	.48
Asia and the Far East	1.9	.27	.38	.41	.43	.37
Europe	.02		.01		.03	
Latin America	.31	.36	.35	.48	.46	.46
Middle East	.04	.02	.03	.05	.04	.04
Total	.71	.87	1.20	1.56	1.45	1.35

SOURCE: E/4075, 14 June 1965, Annex, p. 24.

to two main categories: (1) regional advisers, essentially a
mobile staff of experts who are viewed by many as the most
important kind of regional project; and (2) seminars, the
workshops, study tours, and training courses. Projects in regional development or cooperation, such as the Mekong River
development, financed in large part by the Special Fund, must
be placed in another category.[44] Furthermore, there are regional
institutes that complement the work of the regional commissions and in some cases take over operational responsibilities
from the commissions' secretariats, such as the Institute for
Economic and Social Planning in Santiago and the institutes for
economic development and planning in Bangkok and Dakar.
The Latin American Institute for Economic and Social Planning is a joint project of ECLA, the Organization of American
States, and the Inter-American Development Bank, financed by

[44] For a listing, with costs, of all regional projects under EPTA and the
regular program for 1963, see E/3786, 10 June 1963, Annex II.

the Special Fund and by Latin American governments through IBRD. This Institute has assumed the responsibility for the direct administration of economic advisory groups, intensive development planning courses, and research with respect to planning, while in Asia a similar body has taken over ECAFE's in-service training program.[45]

The UN strategy with respect to regional projects has been to use, where possible, the regular program of technical assistance for impact projects and to shift the established projects to EPTA, while at attempt is often made to transfer the financing of successful regional projects to the Special Fund. The strategy of the Secretariat may be viewed as an effort to free the larger resources of the UN regular program of technical assistance for new projects in areas such as industrialization, planning and programming, and housing.[46] However, regardless of whether the project is part of the UN regular program, EPTA, or a Special Fund project, responsibility for its execution may devolve upon the regional secretariat. The decision to decentralize a project is not related to the source of support nor to the duration of the project.

Most regional technical assistance projects have been decentralized,[47] but a few have not; some projects, such as the training program for African economists or the foreign service officers training program have found UN Headquarters the logical source of support; others have not been wanted by the regional commissions, such as the Railway Training Center at Lahore, Pakistan, an old and not conspicuously successful project, for which ECAFE sought no responsibility. Other projects

[45] For information on the three institutes, see ECOSOC Official Records, Thirty-sixth Session, Supplement No. 4 (E/3766/Rev.3), 13 June 1963, pp. 51-52; Thirty-seventh Session, Supplement No. 4 (E/3857/Rev.2), May 1964, p. 62; Supplement No. 2 (E/3786/Rev.1), May 1963, p. 33; Supplement No. 10, (E/3864/Rev.), May 1964, p. 4.

[46] E/3786, 10 June 1963, p. 10.

[47] In 1963, 42 of 45 regional projects were decentralized to ECA, 25 of 32 to ECAFE, and 30 of 33 to ECLA. *Ibid.*, p. 5.

involved Headquarters and the commission secretariats jointly because the projects were developed cooperatively at their beginning.

With these exceptions, it seems virtually axiomatic that a regional project will be decentralized. The crucial question for a regional commission, therefore, is not whether a project should be decentralized, but how many and what kinds of regional projects it should be willing to undertake. Unfortunately, certain kinds of regional technical assistance projects are of questionable value, such as the short training course or seminar, which too frequently attracts civil servants of limited ability who attend courses of a few weeks' duration, then return to busy desks and hurriedly dash off brief reports that are duly noted and then forgotten by their superiors. Within a matter of weeks there is often no visible residue of benefit from such courses.[48] Another kind of regional project that the regional commissions are probably well advised to eschew is the premature experiment in regional integration or cooperation.

The most satisfactory regional projects have probably been the long-term training programs. TAB has singled out for mention as particularly successful such dissimilar projects as the statistical training centers in Africa and the basic training courses conducted by the Latin American Institute for Economic and Social Planning.[49] These courses were of sufficient length (nine months and eight months, respectively) to make possible the development of a sophisticated curriculum, tailored to the needs of the fellowship holders.

Operational Procedures for Regional Projects

Regional technical assistance projects are developed by the regional secretariats and approved by the regional commis-

[48] Some of the problems of these training courses, including the critical problem of communication, are identified in the *Annual Report of the Technical Assistance Board to the Technical Assistance Committee* for 1963. See E/3871, 6 May 1964, esp. pp. 76, 88–89.

[49] *Ibid.*, pp. 106–8.

sions.[50] In the case of ECAFE, for example, the Commission made 50 percent of the project proposals for the 1961–62 biennium, 70 percent for 1963–64, and some 90 percent of the proposals for the 1965–66 period.[51] Whatever the apparent source of a regional project proposal, such as a continuing project held over from previous years, an outgrowth of the commission's work program, or the result of recommendations made by the commission itself, one of its committees, or a working group, the point of origin of the project in most cases has been the regional secretariat.

Technically the final decision on the approval of a project was made in New York by TAC, but the actual negotiation took place in the regional centers, not between the commissions and UN Headquarters officials but among the various heads of a commission's substantive divisions and the Executive Secretary, whose decisions with respect to priorities were, for all practical purposes, final.

If the projects now reflect the regional commissions' preferences and consist of projects suggested and carefully nurtured by the regional secretariats, it is equally true that the commissions have not been free to ignore legislative requirements in drafting their projects. For example, the commission may not submit a request for approval of an abstract research project that properly belongs within the regular work program and not under technical assistance; the requirement of practicality must be met. Furthermore, project descriptions must indicate, among other things, the documents and/or resolutions embodying the request, the states expressing interest in the project, the proposed date, the name of the host country, the nature of the project, the number and costs of experts or fellowships or participants, the available counterpart contributions, and any relationship to country projects.[52] Moreover, the target figures within which

[50] UN Interoffice Memorandum No. 187, Rev. 1, *Operational Procedures for Regional Projects*, 31 December 1963, p. 2.
[51] Percentages supplied by the Office of the Executive Secretary, ECAFE.
[52] UN Interoffice Memorandum No. 187, Rev. 1, pp. 1–2.

the regional secretariats must draft their requests have been set centrally, not regionally. Except for these conditions, however, planning and programming are decentralized.

The decision to decentralize implementation of a project is the product of consultation between the UN Commissioner of Technical Assistance, the ranking official in the Department of Economic and Social Affairs with responsibility for technical assistance operations, and the Executive Secretary of the Regional Commission.

The task of implementing a project may be divided into two categories: substantive backstopping and administrative management. Substantive backstopping, which includes the writing of technical studies and the preparation of an agenda for conferences, the actual conduct of in-service training or seminars, and the preparation of final reports, is usually the unchallenged responsibility of the commission. There is, moreover, a continuing responsibility of the substantive divisions of the regional secretariats for regional projects, as illustrated by the designation of someone from the division most closely associated with the project to follow it through; for example, the Chief of the Statistical Development Section of ECA was chosen as the Project Officer for the statistical training centers in Addis Ababa, Achimota, and Yaounde.[53]

The administrative management aspects of regional technical assistance projects were suggested by the Secretary-General when he spoke of "the efforts made to decentralize completely if possible the responsibilities for implementing regional projects, *subject to the requirements of central financial control and of personnel policies for a world-wide recruitment of experts.*"[54] The extent to which the regional secretariat enjoys discretion within these important limits are indicated by some

---

[53] See ECA, Technical Assistance "Project Data Sheets," 30 September 1963 (File Ref. No.: TA/210/2 [420–22, 420–23, and 420–24]).

[54] E/3786, 10 June 1963, p. 5 (italics added).

of the procedures that are involved in implementing a technical assistance project.

If a project has been approved for decentralization, financial authority to execute the project is delegated to the regional secretariat. The responsibility vested in the regional secretariat is considerable. It becomes responsible for preparing job descriptions and formally appointing project personnel, for awarding fellowships and sending invitations to conference participants, and for administering experts and fellowships. Of special importance are the authority to engage technical assistance experts (up to level 5) for a period of twelve months' duration or less and to transfer funds from one item to another within the budget for a given project, both without the necessity of securing the approval of headquarters.[55] Prior to decentralization, all of these tasks were performed centrally or necessitated central clearance.

In spite of this impressive evidence of decentralization, the regional secretariat does not have complete freedom in the implementation of projects. The most significant restrictions concern upward revision in a project component, such as an increase in the number of experts, even if the change can be accommodated within the total project budget. Likewise, appointments of project personnel for more than twelve months, extensions bringing service to more than twelve months, and appointments at level 6 and level 7 (equivalent to D-1 and D-2) require Headquarters' approval, while recruitment outside the region is handled by TARS in New York or Geneva.

What the regional secretariats desire, of course, is flexibility. As the Executive Secretary of ECLA has said:

The essence of successful decentralization is that the secretariat of the regional commissions must have sufficient authority to take immediate operational decisions, combined with sufficient means to implement them. This must be done in agreement with the governments concerned, and based on authority for alteration of the pro-

[55] UN Interoffice Memorandum No. 187, Rev. 1, pp. 3–4.

gram, financial amendments or emergency recruitment as may be
required acting within the basic rules and regulations established
by appropriate bodies responsible for over-all direction of the technical assistance programs.[56]

Recent steps to decentralize administrative aspects of regional
projects have gone a considerable distance toward meeting this
criterion, although the currently applicable procedures for
regional projects do not give the regional secretariats a free
hand. Although the regional secretariats might prefer to control
the day-to-day administration of regional projects to a greater
extent and might, in particular, desire greater authority to juggle
project components, it should be noted that the wishes of the
regional secretariat have been rarely overruled, with the result
that the principle of central administrative control has been preserved inviolate, while the preferences of regional officials have
been honored.

Technical Assistance Coordinating Units

Two other important developments in the implementation of
the policy decision to decentralize have been the establishment
in the regional commissions' secretariats of technical assistance
coordinating units and the appointment of a rapidly growing
number of regional advisers.

The technical assistance coordinating units are new, although
they are in a sense lineal descendants of the units outposted to
ECLA several years ago. The technical assistance coordinating
officer in each of the commissions is, in the first place, a physical
token of the reality of decentralization of technical assistance.
For the first time, there is an office within each of the regional
secretariats of which the *raison d'être* is technical assistance
activities. This does not, of course, imply that the substantive
divisions of the commissions have not been concerned with
technical assistance. In fact, the Secretary-General has stressed

[56] E/CN.12/669, March 1963, p. 5.

the nonseparability of the two kinds of activity. But the establishment of such a unit in the Office of the Executive Secretary has had the effect of calling attention to the importance of the commission's operational activities.

In no case is the technical assistance coordinating officer outposted from Headquarters; he is an integral part of the regional secretariat, responsible to the Executive Secretary.[57] However, like the Chief of the Division of Administration and the personnel and finance officers in the regional secretariats, who are the choice of Headquarters, the technical assistance coordinating officers are selected by BTAO, and they have a responsibility for maintaining UN standards in the regional context. It might be said that these units were created as much for keeping decentralization on the tracks laid down by Headquarters as for giving the regional commissions a larger role in technical assistance activities. More than one technical assistance coordinating officer has reported a feeling of alienation upon assuming his post in the region, for he has invariably served previously with BTAO in New York and generally will serve in the regional commission for only a few years before being replaced by another person designated by BTAO. Inevitably, these officials have approached their new assignments as BTAO people, not regional experts. One coordinating officer observed that upon transfer from Headquarters to the regional commission he was immediately besieged with requests from officials in the substantive divisions who had obviously assumed that new ground rules were now in force, and he was forced to explain that, although decentralization had taken place, the rules for technical assistance had not changed.

There are now technical assistance coordinating officers in each of the four commissions. The units have not been created simultaneously and ECLA, with two such officers in Santiago

[57] For a description of these units, see GA *Official Records,* Seventeenth Session, Supplement No. 5, A/5205, February 1963, p. 30.

and one in Mexico City, had in 1965 more of a "technical assistance staff" than the other commissions in the developing world.
However, the coordinating units perform the same services in
each commission, subject to variations in the sophistication of
the commission secretariat and the style of the coordinating
officer. His role is essentially one that was previously performed
at Headquarters.[58]

In the planning of technical assistance programs, the coordinating officer's job is not to quarrel with the need for a proposed
project but rather to see to it that the project conforms with
the requirements of UN technical assistance legislation. He plays
no role, therefore, in substantive planning, a task left to the
substantive divisions. But he does measure each project against
principles laid down by the responsible organs in New York.
If the project per se meets the test of acceptability, the coordinating officer seeks to insure balance within the project and
balance among regional projects. For example, a proposal calling
for twenty training personnel and only five trainees would
probably not be a "balanced" project, and to achieve a balance
among projects, the coordinating officer will try to promote a
fair distribution so that the statistics division, for instance, does
not have twice as many projects as any other single division. The
recommendations of the technical assistance coordinating unit
are not binding, but in practice they tend to be accepted by
the regional secretariat for the obvious reason that the commission is in a stronger position if its requests go to headquarters in
the most persuasive package possible.

At the implementation stage, the coordinating officer once
more assumes on-the-spot responsibility for overseeing the conformity of the project with UN regulations. He does not, on
the other hand, decide how an expert should be hired or how a

[58] The following description of duties of technical assistance coordinating
officers has been based upon conversations with men holding those posts in
ECLA, ECAFE, and ECA.

required piece of equipment should be purchased. One coordinating officer described his role in implementation as that of intermediary between substantive divisions, which want to see their projects expedited, and the administrative offices, which must enforce compliance with a multitude of UN regulations and procedures. Thus the coordinating unit becomes a clearinghouse through which are routed all requests (*a*) to personnel for recruitment; (*b*) to administrative services for purchase of equipment; and (*c*) to finance for the payment of travel allowances. In this way, the coordinating officer acquires a clear picture of the development of the several regional projects and assists the administrative officials by adding his knowledge of specific technical assistance projects to their familiarity with UN procedures.

If there are to be changes in the course of a project's implementation, and frequently there will be, the coordinating officer has to follow up such changes to guarantee conformity with UN regulations and with the resolution authorizing the particular project. At the conclusion of a project, the coordinating unit prepares the final report. In summarizing the importance of his position, a technical assistance officer noted that all the terms employed in UN resolutions and regulations governing technical assistance have a specific legal meaning and that he must see to it that they are honored if the UN is to avoid serious misunderstandings or administrative repercussions. The net effect has been that the regional commissions gained little additional discretionary authority by the establishment of the technical assistance coordinating units in their secretariats but rather acquired an expert-in-residence on the implementation of BTAO policies.

Regional Advisers

Another conspicuous development under the rubric of decentralization in the UN technical assistance field has been the increase of regional advisers, who in 1965 constituted over twenty percent of the regional technical assistance projects.[59] These advisers have been funded out of either EPTA or the UN's regular technical assistance program. A veteran of many years in a commission secretariat has called the program one of the most significant and valuable innovations in the history of UN economic regionalism. Although regional advisers are technical assistance projects themselves, they have also been a part of the effort to strengthen the regional secretariats to assume the duties attendant upon decentralization.

Although regional advisers may be recruited from within the region by the regional secretariat in accordance with rules cited above, in actual practice this delegated authority has been exercised only in a few cases. As available candidates become more numerous and as personnel sections in the regional secretariats become more proficient, this should change, but for the time being TARS handles most recruitment of regional advisers. It should be noted, however, that in all cases the regional secretariat determines requirements for advisers, establishes job descriptions, and has the final word on acceptability of the candidate.

When advisers have been appointed, the regional secretariat sends letters to governments announcing the fact and indicating the specialization and duties of each adviser. If the services of the adviser are desired, the governments communicate this fact to the commission, which works out a schedule for each adviser. The demand for the services of a regional adviser is not, of course, left entirely to the whim of individual states after the appointment. As with all technical assistance projects, the commission will have attempted to ascertain the demand prior to making the request for appointment; in fact, country requests for short-term assistance will have been a major factor in the

[59] For example, in 1960 there were 2 regional advisers stationed at the ECLA office; in 1963 the number was 20. The total number of regional adviser posts was 65 in 1963; in 1964 it was 77, and 83 were proposed for 1965. See E/3937, 11 July 1964, p. 7.

commission's decision to request the appointment. The adviser is attached to the commission and responsible to the Executive Secretary, but it is the intention of the program that he spend most of his time as a kind of roving expert, advising a number of governments upon request. In practice, the major difference between regional advisers and experts attached to country projects is that the latter usually serve in a given country longer; visits by regional advisers normally last from two weeks to two months. One of the arguments for regional advisers is that they may be employed more efficiently than individual experts serving on country projects. As one coordinating officer observed, better utilization of time and manpower is achieved because "the expert does not go fishing when the project ends—he is needed in another country."

In addition to providing expert advice directly, the advisers are also in a position to provide substantive support to some of the experts assigned to country projects. In this way the adviser may act as a long and flexible arm of the commission to which he is assigned, thereby further strengthening the bonds between the regional secretariat and country projects at a practical, working level.

Some regional advisers blend into the secretariat and perform tasks that might otherwise be neglected because of understaffing. This may happen by design, as in the case of the regional advisers in public administration who were assigned to ECA. They have constituted, in effect, a substantive division in Addis Ababa. On the other hand, a regional adviser may also spend most of his time at regional headquarters because the governments in the region have limited interest in his services. In cases of this kind, the commission may try to use the adviser to good advantage but may not report the fact of his nonutilization by governments to headquarters in New York. To report no demand for an expert's services can be compared to a failure to spend budgeted funds and may cause a reduction of experts in future years. All the commissions are agreed on the need for an increasing number of regional advisers.

Probably the number of regional advisers will continue to grow, as Table XI shows, but this institution has not been an

TABLE XI

REGIONAL ADVISERS, 1961–1965

(*Including Regional Experts and Consultants for 1961 and 1962*)

Region	1961	1962	1963	1964	1965
Africa	n.a.	n.a.	34	39	36
Americas	n.a.	n.a.	20	20	22
Asia and the Far East	n.a.	n.a.	11	18	22
Middle East	n.a.	n.a.			3
	9	27	65	77	83

SOURCE: E/4075, 14 June 1965, Annex, p. 25.

unalloyed success. TAB has noted that some governments have expressed disappointment in regional advisers to resident representatives, citing the brevity of their visits, the inadequacy of their briefing, and the insufficiency of their background information for appraising the local situation.[60] Several people associated with the regional secretariats, especially in Africa, have echoed this criticism of regional advisers, commenting upon their lack of understanding of the region to which they must adapt their advice and recommendations. Such criticism, however, is almost nonexistent in ECLA, where the overwhelming majority of advisers have been from the Latin American region. TAB, nevertheless, stresses that the expert's principal function "is not to make detailed recommendations on the spot to the government which he is visiting, but is to develop an over-all picture of the situation with respect to his specialty throughout a whole continent or some other wide grouping of nations." [61]

However his task is defined, unless the regional adviser has been intimately associated with the region for some time, he will of necessity have to spend a part, perhaps a large part, of

[60] E/3871, 6 May 1964, p. 81.
[61] *Ibid.*

his term of appointment familiarizing himself with the region. Although this may be true of many experts, the regional adviser is not only expected to help several countries directly but also to augment the resources of the regional commission. If the regional adviser is to be more than a paper asset to the commission and part of an effective decentralization of technical assistance activities, he must either know the region well to begin with or serve in an advisory capacity long enough to acquire regional competence.

Decentralization of Country Projects

Some proponents of decentralization would also like to have the authority and responsibility for country technical assistance programs located in the region rather than at headquarters. In spite of several tentative steps designed to give the regional secretariats more of a role in country projects, however, the pace of progress in this direction has been glacial.

The secretariats of the regional economic commissions have claimed to be close to the problems of individual states within their regions and familiar with the officials responsible for coping with those problems; furthermore, the regional secretariats have frequently been committed to work programs that suggest a frame of reference for technical assistance to individual countries, and they have joined in the chorus of agencies, bilateral and multilateral, that offers advice to governments. Any effort to enlarge the role of the commissions in individual countries, however, will start a reaction, for it will go against the grain of the well-established country programming.

In a progress report on decentralization in 1963, the Secretary-General listed among the steps already taken "the association of the regional secretariats with the operational activities related to country projects" and the "strengthening of relations between the regional secretariats and the Resident Representatives." [62]

[62] E/3786, 10 June 1963, pp. 5–7.

Among the further steps being taken to achieve the same end he identified "participation of the regional secretariats in the programming of the 1965/66 country projects." [63]

In practice, the regional secretariat has played an extremely modest role in country projects. The regional secretariats were given an opportunity to advise on the programming of country projects, beginning with the 1965/66 biennium, but their role was limited to (*a*) participating, with headquarters officials, in joint programming missions that worked closely with the resident representatives, and (*b*) submitting opinions on proposals for inclusion in country programs to the appropriate substantive office at headquarters, to BTAO, to the Resident Representative, and to the government. [64] The commissions, moreover, have been involved only at the preliminary stage of the programming cycle, and their role has not been remotely comparable to the one that they play with respect to regional projects.

A marginal role in programming has been matched by a relatively small role in the implementation of country projects. The Secretary-General has noted that the regional secretariats are "relied upon wherever their substantive units, together with regional advisers attached to them, are so constituted and organized as to enable them to perform the services required with their own resources." [65] In some areas, such as social affairs and statistics, substantive backstopping has been delegated to the regional secretariat, [66] but that backstopping has been limited to

[63] *Ibid.*, pp. 10–11.
[64] See E/3937, 11 July 1964, p. 8.
[65] E/3786, 10 June 1963, p. 6.
[66] The larger degree of decentralization in such fields as statistics and social affairs is a consequence of the greater experience of these regional units with technical assistance; the officers in these functional areas have frequently been detailed to the commission secretariats from headquarters. Social affairs units were for a long time outposted and staffed by the bureau in New York, with many of its senior officers having gained both headquarters and field experience. Decentralization of statistical projects is also easier to achieve because of the universally applicable standards employed by the professional fraternity of statisticians.

receiving, reviewing, and commenting upon reports from experts, and, on occasions, briefing them en route to their country assignment. Furthermore, in the case of reports from experts, Headquarters has a similar responsibility to review and comment, which suggests that duplication rather than decentralization may have been achieved. The regional secretariat also may advise on recruitment of experts, but here, too, its role is relatively modest. A more active role for the regional commissions in country projects would almost certainly lead to a deterioration in relations between the regional secretariats and the UN resident representatives, which would be contrary to the Secretary-General's assertion that one of the important features of decentralization would be a strengthening of those relations. As it is, commission secretariat personnel still tend to regard resident representatives as men of little stature who are an obstacle to their direct communication with governments, while many resident representatives are inclined to see the commissions as pleasant but unrealistic clubs in which the same old wheat gets threshed from year to year as the secretariats grow more adept at empire building.

Meetings between the executive secretaries of the commissions and the resident representatives have now become an annual event in each of the four regions.[67] But the distance between resident representatives and the commissions seems almost as great as ever; one Resident Representative alleged that one meeting of resident representatives and members of the ECAFE secretariat was brief, perfunctory, and essentially devoid of meaning, only to be followed by an ECAFE communiqué that created the illusion that new paths of cooperation had been charted. In reality the relations between resident representatives and the commissions have been very little affected yet by decentralization, which is evidence that not much

[67] ECOSOC Resolution 856 (XXXII), 4 August 1961.

decentralization has taken place with respect to country projects.

The assumption of major responsibilities for planning and allocating funds for UN country projects, moreover, would plunge the regional secretariats into a thicket where there is relatively little room for taking initiative and launching new projects. Individual country projects, while not impervious to guidance and inspiration from international officials, are simply not as easily steered by the UN, whether it be the UN in New York or the UN in Addis Ababa. It is the country itself which decides what it wants, when, and how to implement a project. The regional secretariat may, upon request, advise, but it can do little more. If the regional commissions were to move more boldly into the field of country projects, they might simply find themselves bogged down in minutiae, without contributing much to the development of the individual country or enhancing their own stature.

As for backstopping of country projects, the regional commission secretariats, if adequately staffed for the task, could be more actively involved in locating appropriate experts, could expand the present briefing of experts at their regional headquarters, and could evaluate reports in the substantive divisions of the commissions. The present situation with respect to report evaluation is clearly unsatisfactory. The commission personnel have not been excited about reading and reviewing copies of reports that also go to their counterparts at headquarters for similar handling, and many officials in the substantive divisions simply do not have a very high opinion of the individual expert as a technical assistance project. As a result, evaluative reports have tended to be perfunctory.

In ECLA, the commission best qualified in the view of almost all observers to handle decentralization, there has been very little desire to become involved in country projects, since ECLA officials maintain that support for the expert has been largely a matter of reading reports and making suggestions, which is not enough, whether it is done in New York or in Santiago. If technical assistance is to have the desired impact and is to be instrumental in rationalizing a country's development program, the vehicle for achieving this objective, according to people in ECLA, might be similar to the advisory groups, instituted officially in 1959 and now functioning under the aegis of the Latin American Institute for Economic and Social Planning. These groups integrate the recommendations of several experts with several specializations, and they would be, in the words of one ECLA division chief, better than random technical assistance for substance and better than the Resident Representative for coordination. If the regional structure for supervising country projects were modified along these lines, some of the reluctance of the regional secretariat to become involved might disappear.

The consensus of the regional secretariats seems to be that execution, which is guidance, is more important than programming, although a larger role in both may be the ultimate goal of the commissions. The main question is not shall there be decentralization, but can there be effective control at the regional level of recruitment and the work of experts.

Decentralization and the Specialized Agencies

The specialized agencies have been inclined to view with suspicion the growth of the regional commissions and their increasing involvement in technical assistance and have experienced considerable heart-burning as the word "decentralization" spread through UN circles. By some this development was regarded as a potential transfer of the jurisdictional disputes that plague the UN system from the Headquarters out to the regions.

The anxiety over decentralization was evident, for example, during the creation of the Asian Institute for Economic Development and Planning, a prospectively important organization

for which ECAFE had a special responsibility, when several
agencies sought the creation of an advisory committee in order
to play a larger role in the Institute's staffing. The Resident Representative in Bangkok had to discuss this matter at length with
ECAFE personnel, and, although ECAFE did not accede to the
wishes of the agencies, it explained that there would be no
impingement by the Institute upon areas in which the agencies
had customarily operated.

Many technical assistance projects have been joint exercises,
such as the Pulp and Paper Advisory Group for Latin America,
a joint UNTA/FAO project considered to be among the more
successful EPTA regional projects, and CREFAL.[68] Moreover,
each regional commission has contained an agricultural division,
which is jointly the responsibility of the commission and FAO.
ECA has experimented with an arrangement whereby representatives of ILO, UNESCO, WHO, and UNICEF are outposted to Addis Ababa and associated with the Social Affairs
Section in an advisory capacity.[69]

In spite of these experiments in cooperation, there continues
to be apprehension over what the decentralization of UN technical assistance will mean to the specialized agencies, which have
been inclined to view the commissions as ambitious rivals.
Several ECA officials have replied that the commission's principal job is one of salesmanship and that they are therefore
bound to come into conflict with other agencies that are also
trying to work with African governments. But as the one organization in this field that is "purely African," ECA has a
potential advantage that makes the specialized agencies particularly uneasy about decentralization and the strengthening of
the regional economic commissions. In any event, the commis-

[68] CREFAL is the Regional Fundamental Education Centre for Community
Development in Latin America, a UNESCO project in which UNTA, ILO,
FAO, WHO, and OAS participate.
[69] See ECOSOC: *Official Records*, Thirty-seventh Session, Supplement No.
10, pp. 8–9.

sions have had the problem of keeping alert to the interests of both the specialized agencies and the UN Resident Representative.

Strengthening the Middle East Office

The flurry of decentralization activity in technical assistance had the effect of calling attention to the nonexistence of a regional economic commission in the Middle East[70]—a consequence of the inability of Israel and the Arab states to work together. This impasse, however, has created an anxiety on the part of Middle Eastern states that their interests and needs may be overlooked in the UN enthusiasm for decentralization, and the General Assembly in its resolutions on decentralization specifically requested the Secretary-General to consider "the interests of states which are not members of any regional commission by taking such steps as may be necessary to insure that they receive the same benefits that they would through membership in the regional commissions." [71]

In the spirit of these instructions, an economic unit was established in Beirut in 1963 and joined to a social affairs office already in operation. The new Economic and Social Affairs Office has been characterized as a regional secretariat without a commission, but that is hardly the case. In fact, it has been a small unit, unable to give attention to many fields;[72] without an intergovernmental body the office has been merely a collection of outposted officers.

[70] Of the states in the Middle East, not all are without a regional economic commission. The United Arab Republic and such marginal cases as Libya and Sudan are members of ECA; Iran is the western anchor of ECAFE; and Turkey and Cyprus are members of ECE. This leaves Iraq, Syria, Lebanon, Jordan, Saudi Arabia, Yemen, Kuwait, and Israel without benefit of an economic commission for the Middle East. Saudi Arabia and Israel have applied for membership in ECAFE.

[71] GA Resolution 1823 (XVII), 18 December 1962.

[72] As of 15 May 1964, there were 9 professional staff and 8 general service. For purposes of comparison, note that ECA had 98 professional staff on that same date.

The Beirut office has not been a good example of decentralization, for it has been in a weak position to provide substantive or administrative backstopping and was the last regional office to acquire a technical assistance coordinating officer. As recently as 1965 there had been no regional economic projects and few regional social projects to coordinate. The Beirut office has played no significant role in country projects.

In December 1963 the General Assembly endorsed[73] ECOSOC's recommendation that the Secretary-General establist a technical assistance coordinating unit in Beirut. Some people in the UN Economic and Social Office hoped that this unit would eventually become a nucleus for an economic commission, but the act still seems far from the wish. A reconnaissance mission, headed by the Director, also toured the Middle East region in 1964 to ascertain development needs and the possible role of the Beirut office in meeting them.

Special Tasks for the Economic Commission for Europe

There is so little technical assistance supplied to the countries of Europe that ECE is a case in itself in analyzing decentralization.

Europe is primarily a donor, not a recipient, of United Nations technical assistance. This situation has suggested that decentralization is a process that only concerns ECLA, ECAFE, and ECA, but the members of the ECE secretariat are somewhat sensitive to the implication that decentralization somehow by-passes Europe, and in his reports on the implementation of decentralization the Secretary-General has repeatedly mentioned the attribution of special functions to the ECE secretariat.[74]

A special role for the ECE in the "new decentralization" has been in the process of evolving over a period of several years. On the one hand, it calls for ECE to assume a larger share of the

[73] GA Resolution 1941 (XVIII), 18 December 1963.
[74] E/3643 13 June 1962, p. 9; E/3786, 10 June 1963, pp. 7–8.

burden of helping the commissions in the developing world, and, on the other, it involves decentralization from New York to Geneva of full responsibility for some programs,[75] such as the transportation of dangerous goods. In effect, Geneva has become the UN headquarters for certain programs.

More and more ECE has been asked to perform tasks that are of direct benefit to the developing states rather than to European states. Among its most conspicuous contributions have been the secondment of ECE staff members for temporary service to other commissions, especially to ECA; cooperation in developing and supplementing the programs of the substantive divisions in the other commissions; the organization of study tours for increasingly large numbers of nationals from developing countries; the expansion of the ECE's In-Service Training Course to include fellows from the developing world who have been, in most cases, assimilated into the general work of the Research and Planning Division; and assistance to the European office of TARS in Geneva in the recruitment of the large number of UNTA experts who come from European countries.[76] The Executive Secretary of the Commission has reported that "the substantive contribution of the ECE secretariat to the total programs of the United Nations represented in 1963 some 13 percent of the total capacity of the ECE staff," [77] which does not include the work of the Geneva technical assistance office, recently transferred to ECE, with its responsibilities for arranging interregional projects, briefing experts, and otherwise supplying services of primary benefit to non-European areas.

These developments may be viewed as a form of decentralization and ECE regards them as such. But it might be more accurate to state that they signal the emergence of a New York–

[75] For a detailed description of this new role, see E/ECE/489, 15 March 1963; E/ECE/532, 2 March 1964.

[76] *Ibid.*

[77] E/ECE/532, 2 March 1964, p. 2.

Geneva axis, with ECE sharing with Headquarters some of the responsibility for providing talent, resources, backstopping, and other services to the other three commissions. The other commissions, however, while expressing their appreciation to ECE, may look upon this arrangement as a less-than-satisfactory substitute for a more direct decentralization of authority for technical assistance to all regional secretariats. ECE has, nevertheless, contributed to the strengthening of the other regional secretariats, especially ECA during its first few years of growth, and this could lay the groundwork for further decentralization of UN technical assistance.

Perspectives on Decentralization

The more developed states of the Western world generally have looked upon the decentralization of technical assistance with serious misgivings. Although they have paid lip service to it, they have warned of its dangers rather than conceded the virtues claimed for it by most developing countries.

The conflicting views of the Western states, on the one hand, and the developing countries supported by the communist powers, on the other, have been predictable in the context of contemporary international economic and political relations. The central issue has been control: which states will hold the levers of decision in the UN's technical assistance operations. The developing states have wanted to wrest control from the conservative donor states whose influence has been stronger in the Department of Economic and Social Affairs than in the field. The opponents of decentralization, however, see this trend as dangerous, for they are not willing to relinquish control to political organs and units of the UN Secretariat whose administrative skills, economic judgment, and sense of political responsibility they doubt.

Those members of the UN Secretariat whose perspective on UN problems has been informed by extensive experience at

Headquarters are generally more cautious in their approach to decentralization than those who are closely identified with a particular commission. The Under Secretary for Economic and Social Affairs has spoken revealingly of "the Headquarters view," which is still very much alive:

We were more or less dominated over a long period by a way of thinking which doubtless originated in a desire to simplify and clarify matters. According to that way of thinking the regional economic commissions were organs which should devote themselves to research and study and which should be barred from what are termed operational responsibilities.[78]

Decentralization, moreover, has been an issue about which even personnel in the regional secretariats have disagreed. Many professionals in the regional secretariats still profess to see no visible impact of decentralization upon their jobs and one Executive Secretary has labeled it as a fraud. Other persons in regional offices have reported changes in the nature of their responsibilities under decentralization that were not welcome.

The allegation that the decentralization policy is a fraud stems from a belief that the process is a slow and grudging one in which Headquarters has retained too much authority too long. As one official remarked: "Headquarters is for decentralization in theory, but doesn't really want it to work." Numerous people have cited incidents in defense of this charge. The retention at Headquarters of the files on experts who have ostensibly been "decentralized," for example, has been criticized, as has the regional officers' inability to make routine judgments with respect to entitlements or decisions about supplementary funds for a regional adviser without long and tedious referral to Headquarters. Critics in the field have also complained about the slow pace at which recruitment has been decentralized, the reluctance

[78] Statement to the Second Committee of the General Assembly, Fifteenth Session, 687th Meeting, 21 November 1960, later circulated as A/C.2/L.518, 24 November 1960, quoted in Wightman, p. 329, footnote 44.

to grant authority to make increases within components of a project and the failure to strengthen the commissions by reducing the scale of operations within the Department of Economic and Social Affairs in New York and transferring staff to the regions.

Those who believe that decentralization has not been given a fair trial by Headquarters officials tend to agree that the regional secretariats should have a larger operational role. A number of regional secretariat personnel, however, believe that an operational role for the commissions can be a nuisance that distracts it from more important business. According to one long-time UN official: "Research is the *raison d'être* of the commission, but it may be lost sight of in the anxiety to 'go operational.' Good division directors should not be forced to spend their time back-stopping technical assistance." This view was more frequently expressed within ECLA than in ECAFE or ECA. In all three commissions there has been some concern that the secretariats may be swamped with work for which they are ill-suited and/or understaffed, and the most commonly cited illustration of this problem is the obligation of the appropriate substantive division to comment upon reports of country experts. A number of regional personnel have admitted that such reports have gone to the bottom of the "in" basket or have received perfunctory review. The possibility of this happening was one of the arguments advanced against decentralization in the very beginning, and one of the reasons why General Assembly resolution 1709 (XVI) of 4 January 1962 spoke of decentralization *and* strengthening the regional economic commissions.

The various reactions to decentralization may in practice come to the same thing. No matter what the criticism of decentralization, it probably could be obviated if the regional secretariats were appreciably strengthened by the addition of more staff with more of the requisite skills for handling technical assistance activity. In this way, Headquarters might be encouraged to grant the regional secretariats greater discretion in more areas and the substantive divisions could efficiently handle technical assistance *and* research.

It should not be inferred that a policy of strengthening the regional secretariats would lead inexorably to complete decentralization. Virtually everyone agrees that there are limits to this process, and some believe that those limits have already been reached. More considerations enter the rate of decentralization than the single factor of the capacity of the regional secretariats, but the strengthening of the commissions could make it more difficult to balk decentralization.

Strengthening the Regional Commissions

Some strengthening of the regional secretariats has taken place, but there has not yet been a reduction in the size of the Department of Economic and Social Affairs in New York. The budget for the Department for 1965 called for 63 new posts, of which headquarters would receive 35, or approximately 55 percent.[79] This phenomenon, seemingly out of harmony with the announced policy of decentralization has been due to the parallel growth at Headquarters of such centers as the Industrial Development Center and the Economic Projections and Programming Center.

The staff assigned to the regional secretariats in the developing areas meanwhile has also grown, as Table XII indicates, and the growth is partly attributable to the requirements of decentralization.

The number of regional advisers has also been growing annually, as previously noted,[80] and the development institutes are

[79] This figure was conveyed to the author by the Chief of the Division of Administration in one of the regional commissions; according to this source, ECLA would receive 15 of the new posts, ECA 7, ECE 3, the Beirut office 3, and ECAFE none.

[80] See Table XI.

making possible a division of labor that may ease the burden of the substantive divisions of the commission secretariat, if not of the administrative division. Both ECE and Headquarters

TABLE XII

ECONOMIC AND SOCIAL AFFAIRS STAFF IN PROFESSIONAL
AND HIGHER LEVELS, 1956–1965
(*Established Posts Only*)

Year	Headquarters No.	AWAY FROM HEADQUARTERS[a]	
		No.	As Percent of HQ
1956[b]	245	189	77
1960[b]	250	277	111
1962[b]	268	313	117
1963[b]	288	362	126
1964[c]	335	440	131
1965[d]	352	460	141

SOURCE: A/6114, 23 November 1965, p. 8.

[a] Includes regional commission secretariats, Geneva Social Affairs Office, and Office in Beirut.

[b] Actual, as of August 31 staff listings.

[c] Authorized, as included in 1965 budget estimates, A/5805.

[d] Allocated, as included in 1966 budget estimates, A/6005.

in New York have seconded professional staff to regional secretariats.

In spite of these developments, however, it is difficult to measure the increased capacity of the regional secretariats to handle operational assignments. Qualitative as well as quantitative strength must be considered; the staff must be both knowledgeable about the region and acceptable to governments within it. Those who argue most vigorously for a larger operation role for the regional secretariats also maintain that the secretariats should be run by nationals from countries within the region served by the commission.

Although this argument is sometimes couched in circumspect language, it is a common attitude in ECLA, ECAFE, and ECA, where it is alleged that the people who should make the decisions with respect to regional matters ought to come from the region itself because they have a stake in it. To paraphrase a member of the ECA secretariat, too many experts in ECA know their field quite well but do not and cannot know Africa because they are not Africans. With a regional secretariat staffed by professionals from that region, it is argued, technical assistance can be easily and fruitfully decentralized.

The thesis that problems are better solved close to home by the people who live there has a familiar ring. So does the argument that international civil servants, no matter how talented, cannot be sufficiently altruistic or adaptable to serve dispassionately and effectively in regions remote from their home and their experience. Many experts and secretariat members undoubtedly have failed to understand the relationship between the advice they are offering and the capacity of local governments to receive that advice and put it to use. The nonavailability of good regional candidates for technical assistance assignments, especially in Africa, and the fact that those who are available tend to come from a relatively few countries within a region, make the realization of a policy of regional recruitment difficult. Moreover, a policy of regional recruitment, carried to an extreme, could destroy the concept of a truly international secretariat. Finally, if decentralization is to be pursued under central policy guidance and coordination, it would seem desirable to have more than token rotation of staff between Headquarters and the regional secretariats. But rotation of staff has not been really practiced. In 1963 and 1964, of 41 professional staff transferred from Headquarters to a regional secretariat or vice versa, 33 were administrative officers, language officers, librarians, or officers coming from or going to BTAO or the Office of Special Fund Operations. Only eight were substantive staff, and of these, six went from New York to Geneva or from Geneva to New York.[81]

Decentralization may, in fact, have the consequence of placing authority and responsibility in the commissions in the hands

[81] From monthly lists of staff moves; see A/6114, 23 November 1965, p. 14.

of a staff that is hardly international in the broad sense of the word. In May 1964, 75 percent of ECAFE's professional staff was from the Asian area and 73 percent of ECLA's professional staff was from Latin America. If the administrative offices were excluded, the percentages would be noticeably higher. Only in the case of ECA have the indigenous nationals constituted a minority of the professional staff, but the Africanization campaign in that secretariat has been pressing forward.

Other factors also affect the performance of the commissions. ECA in Addis Ababa, for example, is in the weakest position of any of the regional commissions to undertake extensive operational responsibilities because general service personnel in the commission secretariat have been relatively weak. Ethiopia has not been able to supply the kind of pool of skilled, bilingual personnel necessary to run a regional commission, and ECA, alone of the commissions, finds it necessary to recruit large numbers of general service staff outside of the local area.

Just as regionalization of the commission secretariats has been reinforced by a policy of decentralization, so may it be with another phenomenon, subregionalization. The movement to establish subregional offices has been most conspicuous in Africa, although there is some precedent for this development within ECLA, which has a major subregional office[82] in Mexico City. Long accepted because Central America is so obviously a distinct geographical area, the Mexico office of ECLA has developed a kind of relationship with Santiago that may be described as quasi-autonomous.[83] ECAFE also has a huge, diverse region to serve, but its terms of reference do not sanction the establishment of subregional offices. ECA has already created four sub-

[82] ECLA has other subregional offices, but they are not general purpose units as is the Mexico office.

[83] Not only is ECLA staffed primarily by Latin Americans, but there are extremely few South Americans on the staff in Mexico City (3 of 17) and equally few Central Americans on the staff in Santiago (7 of 52). Both figures are as of 31 May 1964.

regional offices, in Niamey, Tangiers, Lusaka, and Dakar,[84] and, in spite of skeleton staffs[85] and an official insistence that these officers would have only modest responsibilities, the first Executive Secretary of ECA spoke in terms of ten professional and six clerical staff per office within the first two years.[86] Can ECA afford such subregionalization when its own strength in Addis Ababa has been so admittedly weak?

A Balance Sheet on Decentralization

The decentralization of UN technical assistance activities seems to be the will of the majority of UN members, a response to demands that developing states play a larger role in the management of the affairs of the UN. Yet decentralization has not been a pell-mell rush to transfer authority and responsibility to the regional economic commissions, for it has been impeded by institutional roadblocks and inertia, by the absence of adequate staff resources in the regions, and by some legitimate anxiety about the wisdom of the change.

The benchmarks of decentralization, nevertheless, are conspicuous enough. Among them are: (*a*) the pronounced increase in the number of regional technical assistance projects

[84] The location of a Western African subregional office in Niamey is a story that almost defies belief. The capital of Niger was proposed on the grounds that it had no amenities and no infrastructure to support a UN office, that it was typically African, and hence a logical site if ECA wanted to share the experiences of the real, undeveloped Africa with which it was ostensibly concerned. Support for other sites melted away before this logic.

[85] In May 1964, three professional staff were located in Tangiers (two of them French, a situation which is proof of an attempt to assert postcolonial influence to some people in ECA and a coincidence to others); two officials were assigned to each of the other subregional offices. These offices were supposed to collect statistical information, organize and serve subregional meetings, carry out research of interest to area governments, provide requested advisory services, assist resident representatives to draw up country programs, organize training courses and seminars, coodinate and develop trade policies, and provide a center for consultation with and briefing of experts, regional advisers, and government officials! See ECOSOC *Official Records*, Thirty-seventh Session, Supplement No. 10, pp. 3-4.

[86] Letter of 27 July 1961, contained in E/CN.14/161, Appendix B, 18 January 1962.

and in their total cost; (*b*) the expansion of professional staff resources in the regional economic commissions; (*c*) the rapid growth in the number of regional advisers; (*d*) the creation in the regional secretariats of technical assistance coordinating units; (*e*) the adoption of a revised set of operational procedures for regional projects, which enlarge the authority of the regional secretariats in the implementation of technical assistance projects; (*f*) the inclusion of senior officials from the regional secretariats in joint programming missions to advise on the preparation of country projects.

The trend has been toward more participation by the regional commissions in more phases of more projects. One technical assistance coordinating officer has claimed that 60 percent of the time of the substantive units in the regional secretariats was being spent on technical assistance. The involvement of the commissions in operational activities, however, has been uneven, for, although they have had a major responsibility for almost all regional projects, they have had relatively little responsibility for any country projects at any stage of their life cycle.

There is disagreement among UN officials as to whether the policy of decentralization has peaked, but it is possible to identify a set of interlocking principles according to which this policy has been implemented:

1. The allocation of responsibilities and resources among headquarters and the regional secretariat is changing in favor of the latter. This is an important trend that must be recognized and turned to good advantage by the UN in the future.

2. New allocations of responsibilities to the regional secretariat should follow pragmatic criteria and decentralization should not take place until the secretariats of the commissions possess the experience and expertise required for a project. Regional technical assistance projects are appropriate subjects for decentralization; country projects are not.

3. The resources of the regional secretariats should be syste-

matically increased so that the commissions acquire the capabilities that have been identified as the prerequisite for decentralization.

4. Decentralization cannot be a one-shot proposition but a continuing process without a self-conscious beginning or predetermined ending. This theme pervades all of the reports submitted by the Secretary-General to the UN's inter-governmental organs and suggests that decentralization will be a slow process.

5. Decentralization ought not be viewed as an end in itself, but as an element in a larger and more important effort to strengthen the full panoply of UN economic and social activities, for its success or failure will be measured in terms of the usefulness of the practical results accomplished.

6. The Headquarters Secretariat and regional secretariats should develop capabilities that are complementary and mutually supporting, for decentralization does not mean that operative functions of Headquarters should wither away or that its valuable services should be quadruplicated in the field.

7. Under no circumstances should decentralization be an excuse for a compartmentalization of UN programs, nor should the concept of an international secretariat be vitiated by policies that would reduce the sense of common purpose in the UN.

8. Decentralization should achieve simplicity of procedure and of administrative methods,[87] a principle that should not override others, although greater administrative efficiency would probably be the first corollary of greater economic effectiveness. Areas without the services of a regional commission should not lack attention in technical assistance.

9. Relationships among the various agents and agencies involved in multilateral programs of technical cooperation should not be exacerbated, but improved by decentralization.

[87] ACABQ and the Secretary-General have both stressed this principle. For the comments of the former, see A/5006, 5 December 1961, and A/5584, 30 October 1963.

10. Finally, the decentralization of technical assistance activities is essentially reform, not revolution. It must be implemented within the context of existing legislation while leaving global financial arrangements and control policies intact.

The regional commissions may plan, organize, and conduct regional projects; assist government officials to prepare country projects; advise and assist in the recruitment of experts; brief experts and provide support services for them; cooperate in appraising project results; and maintain a continuous and flexible surveillance over the development of each project, all of which they are now doing.

But a number of technical assistance activities should be left to Headquarters, such as the over-all planning of field programs; the establishment of regulations governing personnel procurement, budgeting, and the management of currencies.

The UN is one organization, not a confederation of organizations. ECOSOC may hold the reins loosely, but it is the parent body to the regional commissions. The executive secretaries may be free-wheeling personalities, but they remain the Secretary-General's appointees. The regional secretariats may consist of regionally minded people who will never serve at Headquarters, but they too are subject to UN-wide appointment and its promotion machinery and procedures. The Charter, the terms of reference of the commissions, and the rules and regulations governing the day-to-day functioning of the organization all bear witness to the paramountcy of the whole over its parts. The danger lurking in the recent trend is that the commissions, becoming stronger as a result of decentralization and more parochial as a result of regionalization, may gravitate away from an identification with the UN, thus converting the UN, by a process of slow erosion, into what one international official has termed a "commonwealth of international organizations." Perhaps such fears are unwarranted, but the number of people in the regional secretariats who speak of the regional commissions and the UN as "we" and "they" has become too large. A certain amount of this feeling can be expected of any headquarters-field relationship, but a sense of common purpose has been conspicuously lacking in the regional secretariats. The feeling of "we" and "they" seems to have been institutionalized momentarily in the case of the UN Conference on Trade and Development in 1964, when the regional commissions, in effect, supplied the secretariat for the poor states.

One of the great advantages possessed by the regional commissions is that they can be informed by a universal as well as a regional outlook, for they share not only the more broadly based financial resources of the universal organization but also its greater diversity of talent, ideas, and perspectives on common and related problems. If decentralization should weaken that universal nature of the commissions, it has gone too far.

At the moment decentralization has not gone too far, and much of the energy for decentralization was transferred to UNCTAD in 1965. This does not mean that everyone is happy with the policy of decentralization: Western governments, the principal donors, worry about the loss of control over important aspects of UN programs, for they fear the transfer of authority away from Headquarters, where "reliable" people run the key offices, to the regional secretariats, where the collective ability and the judgment of the staff is questionable. Many officials in the regional secretariats are apprehensive about a workload at once larger and less familiar, and they have reservations about the utility of these new tasks and their capacity to undertake them without impairing their other duties. Some governments and some officials at both the UN headquarters and in the field foresee administrative chaos and confusion with increased costs and an increased incidence of jurisdictional squabbles within the UN family. The many advocates of more decentralization also remain dissatisfied with the measures taken thus far. But in spite of these contrary views, those measures that have been taken to implement the policy of decentralization have generally been acceptable to governments and to UN officials.

The future will undoubtedly witness a consolidation of the new distribution of responsibilities between the Headquarters and the field that has been effected in the last few years. An opportunity now exists to achieve a new balance between Headquarters and field, at once preferable to the imbalance that existed prior to the decentralization controversy and to the imbalance that some proponents of decentralization have mistakenly promoted.

There has been a considerable amount of deconcentration but very little devolution in UN technical assistance activity. If decentralization embraces both, its results have been modest. One Resident Representative some time ago expressed a conviction that there could be no half-way house in this business; either there must be decentralization on the WHO pattern or there will be none. He may have been technically correct, but he missed the point. Essentially the UN has been moving slowly toward the introduction of more flexibility into the administration of its programs in the economic and social fields by vesting more authority in the regional economic commissions. If the UN can continue to apply this policy pragmatically and prudently, a livable, even a comfortable, half-way house may yet be found.

In conclusion, a devoted and efficient Secretariat, improved programming by the General Assembly and ECOSOC, and sound field administration, centralized and decentralized, must be patiently but constantly cultivated in the UN in order to realize as fully as possible the benefits of international economic and social assistance for the entire world.

BIOGRAPHICAL NOTES

ON CONTRIBUTORS

GERARD J. MANGONE is Associate Dean of the Maxwell School of Citizenship and Public Affairs at Syracuse University and the Director of the International Relations Program. He has also served as a consultant to the United Nations and to five agencies of the United States on foreign policy and international organization affairs. Dr. Mangone has traveled abroad some time each year for seventeen consecutive years on professional assignments. He is the author or co-author of nine books on world affairs, including *The Idea and Practice of World Government* (1951); *A Short History of International Organization* (1954); and *The Elements of International Law* (1963).

LELAND M. GOODRICH, Professor of International Organization at Columbia University, has been Director of the World Peace Foundation; Member of the International Secretariat, United Nations Conference on International Organizations; member of the Board of Editors of *International Organization*. He is the author of *The United Nations and the Maintenance of the International Peace and Security* (1955); *The Charter of the United Nations* (1949); *Korea, A Study of the U.S. Policy in the United Nations* (1956); and *The United Nations* (1959).

ROBERT W. GREGG is Associate Professor of Political Science and Associate Director of the International Relations Program at the Maxwell School of Citizenship and Public Affairs at Syracuse University. He has been a Fulbright Lecturer in New Zealand and is the author of several articles in the field of international organization and relations in such publications as *International Comparative Law Quarterly*, *Western Political Quarterly*, and *International Organization*.

THEODOR MERON is a member of the Permanent Mission of Israel to the United Nations. He is a graduate of Hebrew University, Jerusalem, and received his LL.M. and S.J.D. degrees from Harvard University. Dr. Meron became a member of the Foreign Ministry of Israel in 1957 and was a counsel for Israel before the International Court of Justice. He has also represented Israel in various United Nations conferences and committees, notably as a member of the Fifth Committee of the General Assembly, and published many articles on international law and organization.

WALTER R. SHARP, Professor Emeritus of Political Science at Yale University, has been Chief, West European Section, Department of State; Chief, Organizational Planning, Food and Agriculture Organization; Senior Administrative Assistant, World Health Organization; Chief, Division of International Cooperation, UNESCO; and Co-Director, UN Public Administration Training Institute, Cairo. He is the author of *The French Civil Service* (1931); *Government of the French Republic* (1938); *International Technical Assistance* (1952); *Field Administration in the United Nations System* (1961).

INDEX